D0882881

Skills of Workplace Communication

Skills of Workplace Communication

A Handbook for T&D Specialists and Their Organizations

Richard P. Picardi

QUORUM BOOKS
Westport, Connecticut • London

Library of Congress Cataloging-in-Publication Data

Picardi, Richard P., 1941–
Skills of workplace communication : a handbook for T&D specialists and their organizations / Richard P. Picardi.
p. cm.
Includes bibliographical references and index.
ISBN 1-56720-362-0 (alk. paper)
1. Business writing. 2. Personnel management. I. Title.
HF5718.3 .P53 2001
808'.06665—dc21 2001019187

British Library Cataloguing in Publication Data is available.

Library of Congress Catalog Card Number: 2001019187
ISBN: 1-56720-362-0

First published in 2001

Quorum Books, 88 Post Road West, Westport, CT 06881
An imprint of Greenwood Publishing Group, Inc.
www.quorumbooks.com

Printed in the United States of America

The paper used in this book complies with the Permanent Paper Standard issued by the National Information Standards Organization (Z39.48-1984).

10 9 8 7 6 5 4 3 2 1

To my mother and father, the first of all the teachers for whom I am continually grateful.

Contents

Preface and Acknowledgments

One thing corporate managers, government supervisors, and English professors can all agree on is that the so-called communications revolution has yet to improve the level of communication. In fact, many people question whether there has been a communications revolution at all, or merely a great advance in the channels or technology of communicating. Even the much-trumpeted goal of a computer on every desk has proven to be another quick fix that fixes little or nothing. Machines have added to the quantity of communication, but done little or nothing to improve its quality and effectiveness.

This book is not intended to turn the clock back, but to focus on two underlying facts: not all writing is communication and not all communication is written. The writer of the most routine memo or the most complex report cannot communicate without first thinking clearly about the subject and the receiver. Part of this analysis must increasingly be about cross-cultural dynamics of our diverse and global workplace. Without such clear thinking, negative verbal and non-verbal ideas and emotions are often communicated unintentionally, but with no less damage.

Despite what has just been said, *Skills of Workplace Communication* is at heart a very optimistic book. It believes that problems have solutions. It believes that thinking and writing skills can be learned or significantly improved. Specifically, this book shows how various writing and communications problems can be solved in a simple, orderly manner using text boxes, checklists, and other tools for improving organization and expression. By following these concrete steps, the writer can achieve the ultimate goal of communication, that is, linking sender, message, and receiver to bring about positive change in the workplace.

I wish to thank my editor Eric Valentine for his initial vote of confidence, as well as his ongoing direction and patience; Alfred Dean Hall for his professional advice and support during a long project; Drs. Joseph and Jack Franzetti for opening a new door in my life; Jessica Ratigan of St. John's University for her invaluable assistance in the creation of charts and illustrations; Mariana Conde and Cheryl Powers of LaGuardia Community College for their assistance in the preparation of the manuscript; Dr. Frank J. Macchiarola, PhD, of St. Francis College for his readiness to help on this and many other projects.

I

Communication: Its Flow and Its Flaws

1

Successful Business Communication in a Competitive Environment

Most people presume that we live, at the onset of the new millennium, in a golden age of communication. In terms of technology, we do. And the age grows more golden every day, because each day brings new and faster machines and software. But this is no golden age in terms of individuals communicating with one another.

It has been over 35 years since Marshall McLuhan warned us that "the medium, or process of our time—electric technology" was changing everything. In *Understanding Media* he told us that "the medium is the message."[1] Today we have come to realize the critical importance of the next step. For successful communication we must focus on the medium, the message, *and* the messenger.

And what is the information and knowledge state of America's potential messengers in the twenty-first century? The Pew Research Center for People and the Press reveals that we may be wired in but we are tuned out. While 79 percent of Americans have cable or satellite television, 84 percent know very little about the Microsoft breakup. And although 59 percent have home computers, 71 percent are unaware of the federal budget surplus. And finally, while 53 percent have cell phones, 56 percent have no idea who Alan Greenspan is.[2]

Even those individuals with the greatest technological skills often fail to communicate successfully. Sometimes it is our very technology that causes this failure. In many cases dashed off, scatter-shot e-mails have replaced well thought-out letters. "There are more avenues to reach people than ever before, but there's no substitute for face-to-face communication" observes Andrew Gilman, a communications consultant in Washington, D.C.[3]

It's not just the medium that is important. The computer doesn't exist in a vacuum; it is used by people. People are the creators and carriers of communication. Ultimately it is people, not machines, that create messages. Corporate and governmental workplaces are changing rapidly. And in this "bricks to clicks" era, corporate managers and governmental supervisors must see to it that the changes are positive. New technologies in the hands of old communicators won't do.

Failure to communicate is not just an annoying inconvenience. It is very costly for companies because it has the following negative consequences: (1) It prevents positive change; (2) it lessens productivity; (3) it leaves employers at a competitive disadvantage; and (4) it diminishes morale. A recent survey by Office Team found that "14% of each 40 hour workweek is wasted because of poor communication between staff and management."[4] That means up to seven workweeks of productivity lost every year. In addition, poor communication, especially when it comes down from management, often causes frayed tempers and lowers morale. It makes "people live with fear, doubt, and confusion" says Peter Giuliano, chairman of Executive Communications Group in Englewood, New Jersey.[5]

JUST HOW HIGHLY DO EMPLOYERS RATE COMMUNICATION SKILLS?

Three thousand employers were asked the following question in August and September 1998: When you consider hiring a new nonsupervisory or production worker, how important are the following in your decision to hire?

Ranked on a scale of 1 through 5, with 1 being "not important" or "not considered," and 5 being "very important."

FACTOR	RANK
Attitude	4.6
Communication skills	4.2
Previous work experience	4.0
Recommendations from current employees	3.4
Recommendations from previous employer	3.4
Industry-based credentials certifying skills	3.2
Years of schooling completed	2.9
Score on tests administered as part of interview	2.5
Academic performance (grades)	2.5

Source: *Census Bureau*[6]

If effective communication is so critical in the workplace, why is it in such short supply? Perhaps as Cassius said in *Julius Caesar*, "The fault, dear Brutus, is in our selves, not in our stars, that we are underlings."[7] Poor communication continues because we tolerate it. We throw up our hands and blame schools or training programs, or secretaries. Or we delude ourselves that everything will be solved by technology.

Here are some popular misconceptions that contribute to poor communication in our technological paradise. They are followed by the truths of today's workplace:

Wishful thinking: "All the rules about communication have changed. E-mail communication doesn't require old-fashioned writing skills."

Reality byte: E-mail is not communication; it is merely a channel for messages. True communication is done not by mere "content providers" but by flesh and blood people who understand the complexity and subtlety of language and ideas. Even in highly technical fields real communicators know that the power of language is not merely its ability to transmit information but to persuade people to act and to foster change.

Wishful thinking: "Computer spell checks can correct any of my writing errors."

Reality byte: Tools such as grammar- and spell-checkers are able to highlight specific problem areas and even prompt revisions. But they don't know what to do with a correctly spelled word that is the *wrong* word. For example, most spell-checks can't figure out whether the word that you need is "effect"or "affect," "illusion" or "allusion."

Microsoft Word's Spell Check will highlight these choices but it has "no spelling suggestions." In other words, you're on your own to figure out which word is correct. Other computer aids are unable to correct many mistakes of grammar and punctuation. And, perhaps most seriously, they are no help in the crucial areas of organization, style, and tone. They may even suggest a substitute word or phrase that would produce verbal gibberish. For example, Microsoft Word has suggested changing the intelligible-enough phrase "some other mistaken notions" to "some other mistook notions," "some other had mistaken notions," or "some other has mistaken notions." On another page it suggests changing antiperspirants to "antipreprints." None of these make any sense at all either in or out of context.

Wishful thinking: "I can always use a form letter."

Reality byte: Form letters lifted from books and computers may supply you with a good format, grammatically correct sentences, and correctly spelled words. But they are usually perfunctory and generic in nature. Their evident lack of sincerity and specificity dooms them to an equally listless reception by their recipient.

The simple fact is that business and government need, seek, and reward people who know how to communicate. Yet, even in this golden age of computer technology they are hard to find. As a result, those managers with the greatest communication skills will be welcomed as valued members of a team that gets things done—a team that makes changes happen in business and society.

MANAGERS, COACHES, AND COMMUNICATION

How often have we all heard employees make excuses such as "I don't have time for the small stuff. That's what secretaries are for." Or managers make statements like "That's what trainers and coaches are for!"

Both are wrong in their own way. A manager's ability to communicate, to organize ideas and choose the precise words to carry each message, can make or break an entire department. Coaches can demonstrate how to write more effectively and even what to write in specific situations, but their help is on a short-term, limited basis. The benefits of skilled coaching must be carried into daily communications.

To what degree can coaches and trainers help in acquiring these communication skills? In January 1999 the *Harvard Management Update* carried an article by Constantine von Hoffman titled "Coaching: The Ten Killer Myths."[8] Here are some of those myths along with the truths behind them.

1. **"Nobody can really define coaching."** Nonsense. Coaching means helping people define clear goals and set a specific time frame in which to meet them. What may throw some managers off is that the heart of the process is a person's potential.
2. **"Coaching is managing with a happy face."** Making sure someone achieves certain performance levels is managing. Helping them handle problems for themselves is coaching.
3. **"Coaching is just another name for mentoring."** Mentoring is a long-term relationship, while coaching is time-limited. A coaching contract is for a specified period of time to work on specific issues with measurable outcomes that we measure every step of the way.
4. **"Being a coach means being a cheerleader."** A coach doesn't just praise an individual's efforts. A coach helps people understand what they need to change in order to attain their professional goals.

5. **"If you successfully coach people, they may leave."** Most employees are looking for people who will invest in their professional development. Coaching is one of the best tools for that. While some employees who achieve new goals will leave, far more will feel greater loyalty to an organization that is interested in their professional development.
6. **"Coaching doesn't add to the bottom line."** The fact is that coaching produces more consistent, replicable results than a lot of other management approaches. Coaching is an investment in a person that's going to really pay off, but not for the next month's numbers—that's not coaching anymore, that's managing, even if you call it coaching.

Concluding key point: Coaching can have a positive impact on performance, but it is not a short-term process. Coaching prospects should be people you think can be even greater assets to the organization than they already are.

Good trainers, must by definition be good communicators. What they have to communicate is twofold: (1) The problems that poor writing skills cause employees and their organizations, and (2) The solutions to these problems on a step-by-step basis.

Faced with this challenge, communications coaches of corporate and governmental managers must be able to answer these three questions:

1. What is the nature of all *human* communication?
2. What are the specific characteristics of *business* communication?
3. What are the principal qualities of *successful* business communication?

Armed with this knowledge, coaches will be prepared to instill this understanding in others. They will be ready to identify the specific steps needed to guarantee successful written and oral business communication. This means communication that is *effective,* communication that produces change. No matter how well intended and planned, change is always difficult. But when improved communication is a shared goal of managers, coaches, and employees it is possible. Each of us is responsible for making this possibility of positive and successful change a workplace reality.

2

Human Communication: Its Basic Flow and Potential Flaws

THE NATURE OF HUMAN COMMUNICATION

All human communication falls into two basic categories: verbal and nonverbal. Each of these breaks down into many subcategories, which are illustrated as follows:

Verbal		Nonverbal
Oral	*Written*	Physical appearance
Speaking and listening	Writing and reading	Body language
		Territory
		Property-Space-Time
		Sensory signals
		Sight Sound Touch Taste Smell

VERBAL COMMUNICATION

Verbal communication includes all messages using words, whether oral or written. It can be either formal or informal. *Formal* communication occurs in management information and directives about policies and procedures. These can be transmitted by written document channels or orally at meetings and conferences. *Informal* communication, what is known as the *grapevine,* is primarily an oral method of transmitting information. It occurs at the water cooler, across the table at lunch, in the carpool, and in the gym.

Oral Communication

Oral communication has two equally important components: speaking and listening.

Oral communication is, ironically, one of the most important yet temporary functions in business. With it we can clarify a problem or situation almost immediately. We have the added benefit of nonverbal clues such as eye contact, body language, pregnant pauses, modulating voice tones, and other physical modes to emphasize or underscore specific points.

Without good oral communication everyday business and governmental communication would slow down to a snail's pace. Everything from questioning fellow workers, to making presentations, handling customer inquiries and complaints, giving directions, and evaluating performance would become completely cumbersome and inefficient.

Good, that is, effective, oral communicators must simultaneously be good listeners picking up visual clues from their audience as they proceed. Without good listening skills, however, even the most carefully prepared and rehearsed oral communication may be ineffective. The intended audience, whether one individual or a thousand, must likewise have good listening skills for the circle of communication to be complete. Poor listening is thought to cause more than half of all communication problems that occur in business and government.

Written Communication

Written communication also has two components: writing, which corresponds to the "speaking" mode, and reading, which corresponds to the "listening" mode of oral communication.

Unlike verbal communication, written communication is permanent—and more difficult. It may be done quietly and with time for reflection and revision, yet by its very nature it is performed in isolation. The writer must function without the spontaneous feedback that nonverbal facial cues and body language may provide.

While written communication includes everything from bulletin board notices to contracts and direct mail, its most frequently used forms are:

1. The *memo.* A written message sent vertically or horizontally between people working within the same organization. Memos are sent by hard copy or *e-mail.*
2. The *letter.* A written message sent horizontally to people outside the company or governmental agency. Letters are sent by traditional hard copy or by *e-mail networks.*

3. The *e-mail.* A computerized communications channel.
4. The *report.* A lengthy, objective presentation of information on a specific subject that enables the recipient to make a decision or solve a problem.

NONVERBAL COMMUNICATION

Nonverbal communication refers to any message that is sent without written words or speech. As shown above, nonverbal communication includes messages that are sent, often involuntarily or unconsciously, by our physical appearance, body language, territory, and sensory signals. It has been estimated that as little as 7 percent of a message is communicated through words. The remaining 93 percent of the message is delivered by one's tone of voice (38 percent) and one's facial expression (55 percent).[1]

Physical Appearance

The first impression we make in business and social situations is our physical appearance. Clothes, posture, grooming, and personal hygiene all combine to make an immediate nonverbal statement. Grandmother was right: always make a good first impression! American culture attaches great, some might say too great, importance on physical appearance. We live in a society where models, both female and male, are celebrities commanding huge paychecks. Magazines, newspapers, television, and Internet websites are saturated with products and advice for both men and women to improve their physical appearance. It goes without saying that the people selling these products are physically peerless.

When 12-Step programs and "fat whacker" pills don't deliver, Americans are opting for plastic surgery, in the form of facelifts, liposuction, and breast enlargements. The American Society of Plastic and Reconstructive Surgeons reports that the number of patients having facelifts rose 50 percent between 1992 and 1997.[2] The same survey revealed that three times as many women aged 19 to 34 had breast-implant surgery. When Nautilus machines and Ab-Blasters don't deliver the prized "six-pack," men are turning more and more to the surgeon's knife for that sculpted body or that commanding jut-jawed chin of authority. If present trends continue, men may someday catch up with women in plastic surgery use.

Why all the hype? Like it or not, shallow and superficial as it might seem, beauty is perceived as being much more than just skin deep. When the whole package—the body, the clothes, the smile, the grooming, the posture—is physically attractive men and women are both seen as more intelligent, more credible, and more persuasive than their unattractive coworkers. The added side effect is that they command higher salaries.

Document Appearance

Positive first impressions are just as crucial in business and government writing as personal appearance. Documents can give the same positive or negative nonverbal messages as their senders' physical appearance. When they are carelessly composed, sloppily formatted, and full of grammatical errors and misspellings they can have the same negative effect on the recipient as a person who walks into an interview with coffee stains on her white silk blouse.

Body Language and Facial Expression

Recognizing the existence of nonverbal communication does not automatically make such messages any easier to interpret. Consider the following situations:

At a dinner party a guest compliments the Merlot being served but drinks very little. Does the host conclude the guest doesn't really like the wine?

At an important sales meeting an account executive is invited out on a 30th-floor terrace to admire the view. After saying "Wow! What a view!" he pulls back abruptly and turns away. Does the host businessperson conclude that the account executive couldn't care less about the spectacular view and is in a hurry to leave?

In both of these cases there is a conflict between what is being said verbally and nonverbally. The speakers are saying they like something, but their body language is saying they don't. Which message is the receiver likely to get? Time and again research shows that the *non*verbal message is believed to be the true one. In the first case the guest really *hates* the Merlot, in the second the account executive is totally *bored* with the treasured view. As matters of fact, the first guest may simply be passing on the Merlot because she has a long drive home later that night; the second guest may be turning away from the view because he is terrified of heights. Unfortunately for the guest and the account executive, any listeners will believe the negative, nonverbal messages in both cases.

Facial expression is one of the strongest components of body language. And it is usually the first to register upon the listener. Whether a frown or a smile the nonverbal message is inescapable. A look, like a picture, can be worth a thousand words. Often the facial expression-message is involuntary, although some people are able to control their facial expression with a "poker face" or Sphinx-like mask. This may not be important on the golf course, but in high figure negotiations such talent may be invaluable.

When your body talks people are listening

BODY MOVEMENT	MESSAGE
You hunch over, leaning forward with your feet squeezed together on the floor, biting your fingernails.	You're weak, afraid, insecure.
You glance sideways, you rub your eyes, cross your arms, drawing back or away.	You're defensive.
You lean forward with open hands, you unbutton your coat.	You're cooperative.
You sit upright, you stand with your hands behind your back, or you even turn your back after speaking.	You're confident—a veritable master of the universe!

Body language and facial expressions often carry different messages in different cultures. Americans are known for the ease and frequency of their smiles. But in other cultures, Teutonic and African for example, this may not be the case. For these a smile, especially when frequent, may be interpreted as a sign of weakness.

Territory

Includes: Property such as real estate that we own or lease, the space within which we operate at any given moment, and how we allot time within that space or zone of activity.

Property

People consider their homes their castles. A burglar may walk unchallenged down a quiet, neighborhood street, but stare down the business end of a shotgun if he decides to slip in to someone's house through an open window! Store owners and their employees view their property in the same way. A customer may freely stroll anywhere in Tiffany's fine jewelry department, but definitely *not* behind the counter!

Space

People consider the physical space around their bodies as a type of territory. Family members and loved ones may come within 1½ to 4 feet without setting off any alarm bells. Friends may come within a foot and a half to four feet, which is considered arm's length, and be comfortable. Any other social intercourse, except for large groups, is usually kept at a distance of 4 to 12 feet. Large groups inhabit what is called public space, the area from 12 feet to the limits of one's sight and hearing.

Likewise people tend to view particular spots or objects as an extension of their personal space. A young son or daughter may watch the game from any chair in the house, *except* "Dad's" club chair or recliner!

The definition of and the amount of space individuals consider their own may vary from culture to culture. In the United States, we view our personal space as a right that must be respected. We view with disdain, even hostility, people who try to cut in on lines instead of waiting their turn. The cause of many cases of "road rage" has been traced to drivers who cut off other drivers or cut in on long tollbooth lines. In other countries, China and Japan for example, space is viewed as everyone's common possession. Hence, they crowd and jostle for space in stores, trains, and lines in a way that might seem hostile to North Americans. Whatever the cultural variation, space exists as an important factor in nonverbal messaging.

Time

The amount of time that we give to a person or situation is often a powerful, if unspoken message. As before, if we tell someone he or she is important or cherished by us, but then turn away, we have just bequeathed an unspoken, negative message. Whether this was our intention no longer matters.

Just as with space, the unspoken message of time varies from culture to culture. North Americans, especially those in big cities like New York and Chicago, are on the short end of the time continuum. They are always in a hurry. In Washington, D.C., it's who you know. In New York it's not just who you know, it's when you know it. And that had better be first. Or better yet, yesterday! South Americans, island people, and Southern Europeans, for example, tend toward the long end of the time continuum. Life is too important to waste rushing around driving oneself crazy. "Slow down and smell the roses. You'll live longer!" Perhaps they're on to something!

In addition to cultural factors one's status within a corporate or governmental organization also affects our notion of time. The higher people are in the hierarchy the less likely you will be to keep them waiting. A new employee who keeps his CEO cooling her heels half an hour for a scheduled meeting is probably not going to get a second chance to do it again. A new employee should arrive not merely on time, but *early*, for such a meeting.

Sensory Signals

Our five senses—sight, sound, touch, taste, and smell—are all-powerful communicators of nonverbal messages.

Sight

Often called the "windows of the soul," our eyes reveal our true state of mind when we speak. Unless we are pathological liars, we find it impossible to look into someone's eyes and tell a whopper. We consider someone to be evasive and crafty when he gives us a "shifty look," that is, doesn't keep eye contact.

Good eye contact elicits trust and confidence. Be careful though: The boundaries of what is considered good eye contact, like most nonverbal communication, vary from culture to culture. You can easily cross the line from a steady gaze that will elicit trust and confidence. Too steady eye contact can be transgressive, even a sign of aggression. Hence the angry expression, "Don't you eyeball me!"

Sound

The level of sound and the intonation of our voice is as much a part of the message as the words we choose when we communicate. A raised voice or a hissing sound can convey as negative a message as any word. Like eye contact, sound is a culturally complex issue. What Americans consider a friendly, jovial level of conversation, Japanese may view as offensive. But, regardless of the culture, the importance of our sense of sound is profound. It is believed that the last sense to leave when we leave this earth is hearing. We all hope to hear the voice of a loved one when we board that last flight.

Touch

Our sense of touch conveys positive and negative nonverbal messages. In normal everyday business situations the hands and arms are the primary vehicles of communication. Note, however, some of the following cultural variations:

CULTURE	STYLE
Asians	Handshaking is so rare that it is uncomfortable in many Asian cultures.
Americans	Prefer a firm, vigorous handshake. President Calvin Coolidge was maligned for having a handshake that "felt like a dead fish wrapped in newspaper"!

British	Soft and gentle.
French	Very brief and light.
German	Very firm, almost brusque.

A handshake or arm around the shoulder can be a potent force in communication. However, they can backfire in an embarrassing way in certain cultures. If one touches or offers a gift with the left hand in a Muslim country, the attempt at friendliness will be viewed as an insult. Why? Because in those cultures the left hand is considered unclean.

Taste

Of the five senses taste is the most solitary and least communicative. Hence, we have such proverbs as "There's no accounting for taste" or "Everyone to his own taste." Culturally speaking it is important to respect the taste of other nations' cuisines and not make offensive facial gestures when the taste of a food is not to our liking.

Smell

The sense of smell, unlike taste, is highly communicative among all living beings. In the animal kingdom and the human, smell is intrinsic to mate finding and love making rituals.

Americans are extremely conscious of body and space odors. We consider body odors and offensive space and territory odors to be a sign of someone or someplace being dirty or lacking in hygiene. We are deluged in print and television ads with an endless stream of body deodorants and antiperspirants. Use them and we will smell like "spring rain" and "mountain air." Or with toothpastes and mouthwashes that will make us "fresh," "mint-filled," and marathon kissable. Or with fragrance candles and plug-in room deodorants that will turn our abodes into "English gardens," "summer eves," and "musk-filled seraglios." We even get seduced and spritzed with perfume sprays in department stores!

To some Asian and Pacific island cultures we must seem phobic, even paranoid. To them body odors are not something to be relentlessly covered up, but a type of bonding shared among friends.

THE CIRCULAR PATTERN OF HUMAN COMMUNICATION

Whether verbal or nonverbal, oral or written, all human communication follows a circular pattern from sender to receiver and back to sender.

In the following case, Linda, the sender, seeks information from Bert, the receiver.

1. The sender has an *idea-information,* which needs to be sent.
   - Linda wants to know if Bert has completed the report for the following day's meeting.
2. The sender finds the *right words* to communicate this message.
   - Many factors will influence Linda's choice of words. Some, such as their respective positions within the organization, will be obvious. Others, such as her education, culture, and experiences, will be more subtle, but no less important.
3. The sender decides how to *channel* the message. Here again, obvious factors such as the physical distance between two parties and the amount of time available will affect the choice of channel. But subtle matters of personality and temperament will also play a significant role in the decision.
   - *Person to person:* Linda and Bert are in the same office and a note of urgency is desired.
   - *Phone call:* The two parties are not in the same office space, but some personal involvement is desired. Linda knows she has a good, even authoritative, speaking voice and presence.
   - *Memo:* Would provide a calmer, more distanced written record, if the two parties did not share a trusting relationship. Time is too short, however.
   - *E-mail:* again, a drier, more distanced channel, in writing with a copy on file.
4. The receiver *interprets* the message. The very same subtleties of personality and temperament, background and culture that influence the choice of channel affect the receiver's *interpretation* of the message received.
   - *Person to person:* Bert may think Linda is being friendly or confrontational depending on *his* background, experiences, and state of mind. However, he is on his way to a meeting.
   - *Phone call:* Provides a quick avenue of response to a relatively simple situation. However, Bert isn't sure if Linda is in her office at the moment.
   - *Memo:* Would provide a written record, but time is too short.
   - *E-mail:* again, time is very limited.
5. The receiver forms and sends a *response.* Bert decides to phone Linda. If she is not in her office, he uses her voice mail.
6. The original sender is now the receiver, beginning the cycle again. If she needs more information, Linda goes through the same steps that Bert just performed.

Interference may block communication at any stage in the sending and receiving of human messages. However, it is most likely to occur at stages two and four of the communications between Linda and Bert.

Why there? Because it is at those particular points that Linda's and Bert's individual frames of reference are most likely to assert themselves.

HOW OUR FRAME OF REFERENCE AFFECTS OUR COMMUNICATION

What exactly is one's "frame of reference"? Webster defines it as the "structure of concepts, values, customs, or views by which an individual or group perceives or evaluates data, communicates ideas, and regulates behavior."

Consider the following case. You're going to buy a car, perhaps a "previously owned" car. You gird yourself for battle, because you know that all used car salesmen are liars. Right? Not according to Timothy C. Gercke, an auto industry educator. When he conducts a training program and shouts "All buyers are—what?" "Liars!" the salespeople shout back, proving that they have learned to adopt the precise opposite frame of reference.[3]

The radically different answers to the following four questions reveal just how much our frame of reference can affect our thinking and behavior.

1. How much money do you think you will need per month to raise a four-year-old child?
2. What is the value of an honest day's work?
3. How much should parents influence their children's dating choices?
4. Which American political party is best for managing the nation's economy?

Concepts

"My 4-year-old needs $4000 per day in child support. Minimum!" Speaker: The wife of a New York City billionaire	"I need to earn $400 per week to support myself and my three kids." Speaker: A single mother living in a small town

Values

"If you work hard enough, you'll succeed." Speaker: Self-made millionaire	"Why work. I have lots of income from my grandfather's estate." Speaker: Self-made millionaire's heir

Customs

"Parents should choose their children's spouses."	"I'll marry whoever I want. It's a free country, isn't it?"
Speaker: The conservative father of a Hindu family	Speaker: An American teenager

Views

"The Republican Party is the best for the economy."	"The Democratic Party is the best for the economy."
Speaker: Lifelong registered Vermont Republican	Speaker: Lifelong registered Chicago Democrat

The speaker of each of the above statements has a different frame of reference. The New York City billionaire's wife views the world through a very different lens than the single working mother of three in a small town. Who we are and where we come from affect the way we look at the world and our place in it. Just when we think we "completely understand" a situation or an issue, we may be startled to be confronted with a wall of opposition.

What went wrong? We didn't realize how much we had allowed our frame of reference to distort our thinking. Our thinking was not clear, it was fuzzy. We thought we had viewed the issue with fiber-optic clarity, instead it turned out we were just hooked up to a rabbit-eared antenna!

Such interference may be mental, emotional, physical, or verbal. It can occur in the sending and the receiving of messages. It can cause problems for both the sender and the receiver of messages. It can block both written and oral communication. These barriers may cause anything from a slight misreading of the message to a total misunderstanding. Misreadings may cause a smile or a laugh; serious misunderstandings can drive a wedge between working partners. Miscommunication is not deliberate; when it is intentional, it is called deception.

Different Ways Our Frame of Reference Can Block Communication

Internal causes

Mental filtering. The meaning of words is in the mind, not in the words. This is what is termed the denotation of words versus the connotation, the strict, literal definition versus the broad area of suggestion and implication. Consider, for instance, the words *house* and *home*. Or *car* and *Rolls-Royce*.

No two people attach the identical meanings to the same words. If Linda asked Bert whether the report was ready, she might mean totally written, printed, and packaged for each person attending the meeting. Bert, knowing that the report was only just written in his computer, might respond "yes," because in his mind printing and packaging are someone else's responsibility. Miscommunication is caused by such differences in our individual frames of reference as personality, culture, education, and social status.

Emotional blockage. Few things twist the meanings of words as much as our emotions. If Linda says to Bert, "Are you ready for this meeting?" she is focused on the word *ready*. Bert, however, may still be smarting from someone else's criticism of his first meeting a year before, and focuses on the words *this meeting*. If he lets his emotions color Linda's question, he may respond with very unproductive and undeserved anger or sarcasm

External Causes

Physical barriers. Poor light in a meeting room, excessive heat or cold, a jackhammer drilling outside, or static on a phone line are all examples of things that can interfere with communication. Similarly, the physical appearance of a person or document may form a barrier. A man who wears chinos and sneakers to address a formal meeting of bankers or a document with faulty grammar and sloppy formatting will probably share the same fate.

Language fences. Inadequate written and oral skills in vocabulary and grammar are widespread barriers to communication. You need the right words to convey your ideas in a specific culture. While unacceptable today, "ain't" was quite acceptable in educated circles of Victorian England.

Listening blocks. Good listening skills are just as important as good writing and speaking skills. Good listening is not a passive endurance contest; it is a proactive skill. Squirming and fidgeting are dead giveaways of a poor listener. But faux good listeners, eyes fixed on the speaker, gaze steady, mind on a beach in Tahiti, may fool some speakers, but not for long. Even a listener who is very attentive but only for the opportunity to jump in with counterarguments to score points is not a good listener.

3

The Flow of Business Communication

THE FOUR PURPOSES OF BUSINESS COMMUNICATION

Whether written or oral, business communication has four main purposes: information, persuasion, results, and public relations and good will. Some type or degree of change is inherent in all of them.

1. **Information.** Among employees of corporations, between the same corporations and their customers and vendors, between government agencies and the public. Includes request and reply memos, procedures and policies memos, letters to customers and suppliers, government publications.
2. **Persuasion.** In addition to the overtly persuasive intent of, for example, sales letters and proposals, there is a subtle element of persuasion in all business communication. In a procedures memo there is the implication that these are the *best* procedures, that they will lead to the *best* results. In a request memo, that these are *reasonable* requests. In a reply memo, that this is a *sensible* response. In a government publication, that the information contained is *current* and *correct*.
3. **Results.** The reason information is being forwarded is either to make the corporation function more effectively or to sell the products of the corporation more readily. Business, like politics, is

neither a philosophical exercise nor an abstract science. Both admire results. One measures results in profits, the other in votes.

4. **Public Relations or Goodwill.** These are make or break goals for all business and government communications. Good public relations is not a cosmetic con-job intended to paper over problems with manpower and material. Good will is the *natural* outcome of good information that is persuasively presented.

THE TWO BASIC PATTERNS OF BUSINESS COMMUNICATION

Business communication, whether written or oral, follows two basic patterns: vertical–horizontal and internal–external.

Internal Vertical Operational Communication

Flows upward and downward between the levels of the organization through memos, reports, meetings, and e-mail. In well-managed organizations, upper-level management gets, and quickly reacts to, a steady stream of information and feedback from lower-level employees.

Internal Horizontal Informational Communication

Flows laterally among workers on a specific level of the organization, for example, between two maintenance supervisors or among several sales managers.

Oral forms: conversations, phone calls, conferences.

Written forms: memos, e-mail, reports, newsletters.

External Horizontal Communication

Flows laterally between a corporation and its suppliers, customers, and the general public. In the case of government agencies the horizontal flow is usually with the public at large, or with a particular segment of the public.

Oral forms: conversations, telephone calls, speeches, press conferences.

Written forms: Letters to customers and suppliers, press releases; government publications.

THE PRINCIPAL QUALITIES OF SUCCESSFUL BUSINESS COMMUNICATION

Whether formal or informal, internal or external, oral or written, business communication succeeds when it achieves its four main purposes: information, persuasion, results, and good will or public relations. The degree to which it succeeds can be measured by the answers to the following questions.

Information

1. Is it accurate?
2. Is it presented in a way that underscores its accuracy?
3. Is the information supported with sufficient data?

Persuasion

1. Is the issue or problem presented clearly?
2. Are there alternative ways of solving the problem?
3. Is the choice of the solution inevitable and inescapable?

Results

1. Are the projected results realistic and attainable?
2. Are the benefits purely financial?
3. Are there other benefits, for example, workplace or environmental?

Public Relations or Good Will

1. How will the recipient, individual or group, receive the proposal under discussion?
2. Will it be viewed as arrogant and self-serving?
3. Will it appear civic-minded, environmentally sound?

HOW CORPORATE MANAGERS AND GOVERNMENTAL SUPERVISORS CAN BE LEADERS IN ACHIEVING THESE COMMUNICATIONS GOALS

Corporate managers and government supervisors in many places today are being taught to take lessons on leadership from Shakespeare.

> "Across the Shakespearean stage strolls every type of human leader, manager, advisor, consultant, communicator. . . ."
> write Norman Augustine and Kenneth Adelman in
> *Shakespeare in Charge*[1]

And Jay M. Shafritz, in his work *Shakespeare on Management*, offers these new ways of looking at two Shakespearean heroes:

> "What is Julius Caesar if not a very hostile takeover attempt by disgruntled stockholders? And is not King Lear a warning to all executives on the perils of divestiture and early retirement?"[2]

Corporate managers and governmental supervisors can take another page from the kings of Shakespeare as a call to leadership. Henry V won the battle of Agincourt for England despite the overwhelming majority of the French forces. His leadership is immortalized in the thrilling words with which he rallied his beleaguered men on the eve of battle:

"Once more into the breach, dear friends, once more,
Or close the wall up with our English dead.
. . . when the blast of war blows in our ears,
Then imitate the action of the tiger;
Stiffen the sinews, summon up the blood, . . .
For there is none of you so mean and base,
That hath not noble lustre in your eyes."
Henry the Fifth. Act III. Sc. 1.[3]

The communications battlefield may be very different, and only metaphorically bloody, but it is still undeniably crucial.

The battlefields of American corporations and governmental agencies are strewn with the legions of failed communicators. Managers and supervisors must master verbal and nonverbal communication themselves before they can lead their departments and agencies. How they can do this is the subject of this chapter.

What is successful communication in a competitive environment? Communication that achieves its purpose concisely, accurately, and with the appropriate tone.

Such effective communication wins allies in the daily contests of business and government. It wins contracts; it maintains accounts; it facilitates the implementation of new programs; it reduces confusion and stress in the workplace. In short, it gets results—and not those career-shaking, unexpected ones.

How can trainers and coaches instill this winning state of mind? First by demonstrating how to remove internal and external barriers in the various modes of verbal and nonverbal communication. Internal barriers such as those psychological and emotional ones that are created when communicators and recipients have different frames of reference. This applies to understandings about culture, gender, sex, and age, as well as economic and physical condition. External barriers such as those caused by personal and document appearance, facial expression and body language, as well as factors of space and time.

Second, by showing the specific steps needed to create effective verbal and nonverbal messages.

These are written and oral communications that possess clarity of purpose, organization, and expression. Verbal includes writing of memos, e-mail, letters, and reports, speaking skills, and listening skills.

Nonverbal includes the physical appearance of documents and territorial and body language.

Winning Pregame Mindsets versus Losing Postmortems

Communication is not a game, but it requires a positive pregame mindset to be effective. Postmortems are best left to county coroners. To be effective communicators we must learn how to break through the invisible walls that can block our messages before they are even sent. Better yet, we must learn how to prevent such walls from ever going up in the first place. As the poet Robert Frost famously put it: "Something there is that doesn't like a wall."[4]

Coaches and poets will both agree that there are ways to prevent walls from arising or to surmount them if they do arise despite our best efforts.

In communication, the two main ways of achieving this objective are:

1. By thinking first of the *receiver* of the message. Who is this person I have to inform, persuade, or entertain? What is his or her frame of reference? Is he of another culture? Is he more educated than I? Less? Does she have time to spare? Or is she in a great hurry?
2. By thinking next of our own *verbal and nonverbal skills.* Do I have a good command of language? Or do I have to improve my written and oral skills? My writing style? My grammar? What about my listening skills? What about my appearance? The appearance of my documents?

The first step in mastering business communication is to make sure the channels are clear. Just as portable phones, televisions, and radios must have clear, static-free channels for their signals to be effective, human communicators must have clear interior and exterior channels for their messages.

A good way to avoid blockage and promote better communication is to focus on what goes on *pre* or *before* speaking or writing.

Four Barriers to Successful Communication

1. **Prejudice.** Being unfavorably disposed to someone or something without any reason, thought, or knowledge. Unreasonable and hostile feelings, opinions, and attitudes based on race, religion, ethnicity, or sexual orientation.
2. **Presumption.** Taking things and people for granted without sufficient inquiry. To assume that something is right or correct without any basis in fact. To offer a guarantee or assurance without justification.

3. **Pretension.** Laying claim to some quality, dignity, merit, or importance beyond anything supported by facts. Assuming an air of importance in an organization or situation. Whether done directly or indirectly by implication, this is an equally off-putting habit or characteristic.
4. **Prevarication.** To speak in a false or misleading manner. To circumvent or avoid the truth. To push the envelope of truth. The roots of this word have to do with being "bowlegged," as from straddling a horse for too long. The picture says it all!

Chapter 4 shows how to avoid these barriers to successful business communication.

Four Promoters of Successful Communication

1. **Preparation.** Getting ready for what is about to occur, whether it's writing a memo, a letter, an e-mail, or a report. Or whether it's a simple phone call, an interview, a meeting, or a speech before a major convention. Simply put, preparation means getting ready for the future.
2. **Precision.** Being "on the mark" or right on target with ideas and expression as opposed to "far afield" or "out in left field." As the Buddha put it two and a half millennia ago, "Let us praise clear thinking, for it burns like a flame through all obstacles great and small." Precision and clarity go hand in hand with preparation.
3. **Presence.** Having the ability to convey a sense of poise and self-assurance. This capacity results from a state of being prepared internally and externally—mentally and physically. Being simultaneously calm yet ready for action gives one what is called a compelling personality. Such a person has that much admired and desired "charisma."
4. **Preference.** This quality of successful communicators works in two ways. It means that, because they have prepared themselves for any situation, they enjoy the ability to make choices. They set the priorities. Therefore, they enjoy a practical advantage over others.

In Chapter 5, we learn how to use these four promoters of successful business communication.

4

Removing Internal Causes of Business Communication Flaws

Business communicators often set sail in a sinking ship. This is because they have internal flaws of thought. These flaws or barriers can scuttle communication. When real communication stops, change cannot occur. There are six major areas of flawed thinking that can stop the flow of communication: ethnocentrism, gender, sexual orientation, ageism, physical and emotional constitution, and lookism and economic status.

COMMUNICATING IN THE MULTICULTURAL AND GLOBAL WORKPLACE

When we think we are the center of the universe, just as the sun is at the center of our solar system, we are considered to be very self-absorbed. We are also victims of solipsism, the theory that only the self exists or can be proven to exist. When we act as though this were in fact true, most sensible people will rightly think we have achieved a level of human vanity worthy of satire.

When we think our own ethnic group or culture is at the center of the universe, superior to all others, we invite the same level of scorn and ridicule. We have become victims of ethnocentrism. This is the belief that one's group or country's way of acting, speaking, dressing, or conducting business is the right way, the best way, and the only way. But there may be even more fundamental differences at work.

Recent studies suggest that cultural differences extend beyond what we think about things to the *way* we think. Dr. Richard Nesbitt, a social psychologist at the University of Michigan, has conducted research comparing European Americans and East Asians, which indicates that people from different cultures don't simply think about different things—they think differently. Easterners appear to think more "holistically," that is, they put much greater emphasis on context and relationship, while Westerners appear to be more "logical" and separate objects from their context.

In one case, students from Japan and the United States viewed an animated underwater scene containing one large fish swimming among smaller fish. Japanese participants made far more observations about the relationships between the fish and the background environment, saying, for example, "The large fish moved past the green seaweed." Dr. Nesbitt reported that American participants, on the other hand, focused directly on the biggest or fastest fish: "That's where the money is as far they're concerned."[1]

Yes, the United States of America is the greatest economic power in the world, but it is not the only power. We now realize that the days when a book titled *The Ugly American* portrayed us as believing the rest of the world must do it "our way or not at all" should be behind us.[2] This is not an idealistic pose, it's good business sense. The United States accounts for a mere 5 percent of the population of the world. In fifty years, we will be only the eighth most populated country on the earth.

Furthermore, the English language is spoken by less than 9 percent of the world's peoples. Even within our own borders English is losing its hegemony. According to a U.S. Census projection,[3] by the year 2050 America's minority groupings will be close to the majority. Currently, this is how our population is broken down:

Non-Hispanic white	53%
Hispanic	21%
Black	15%
Asian	10%
Native American	1%

We Americans are known around the world for our directness and lack of formality, our Teddy Roosevelt–like "rugged individualism" and Emersonian self-reliance, our belief in our ability to control time and nature, our near worship of material goods and profits. Yet we are beginning to realize that other cultures are becoming more and more like us. Marx and Lenin would be in terminal shock if they were around to witness the capitalistic spirit overrunning the old Soviet bloc.

Sometimes ethnocentrism makes it appear as though that 1950s book should be retitled *The Stupid American.* The following story shows that even mighty Wal-Mart can forget that there's a big difference between Arkansas and Argentina.

Selling to Argentina (as Translated from the French)

When Wal-Mart opened its first store in Argentina four years ago it found itself in the unaccustomed role of David—against a Goliath of a competitor in Carrefour, the French general merchandise chain. . . . Wal-Mart entered the Argentine market with a team of American managers and the same basic store model that worked from Des Moines to Dallas.

The meat counters featured American cuts like T-bone steaks, not the rib strips and tail rumps that Argentines prefer. Cosmetic counters were filled with bright-colored rouge and lipstick, though Argentine women tend to like a softer, more natural look. And jewelry displays gave prominent placement to emeralds, sapphires and diamonds, while most women there prefer wearing gold and silver. The first few stores even had hardware departments full of tools and appliances wired for 110-volt electric power; the standard throughout Argentina is 220. Wal-Mart will not divulge any sales or income figures for its Argentine operations, but analysts there and on Wall Street say the company racked up huge losses in its first few years in Argentina. . . .

When Wal-Mart came to La Plata in July, 1997 it avoided making the same mistakes. The aisles were made wider than in the first Buenos Aires stores, and the floor was scuff-resistant tile, not carpet. Metal displays for fish gave way to ceramic tile reminiscent of traditional Argentine fish markets. Wooden wine shelves with overhanging arbors replaced metal racks, a change that bolstered wine sales by 20 percent. . . .

"Let's call it the 'tropicalized Wal-Mart way,' said an Argentine Wal-Mart district manager, with a smile." *The New York Times,* December 5, 1999[4]

Americans are far from alone in their need to guard against ethnocentrism. The experiences in Japanese society of Ana Bortz, a Brazilian television reporter, and David Aldwinkle, an American university professor, make this very clear.

'Japanese Only' Policy Takes a Body Blow in Court

"What Ms. Bortz . . . said she had not been prepared for what was being escorted out of a jewelry store in Hamamatsu City where she lives, because, as the store's owners stated adamantly, they had a policy of refusing people of her nationality. . . .

Ms. Bortz took on the discrimination against foreigners in Japan's courts, and to the surprise of many, not least herself, she won. . . .

> David Aldwinkle, who has lived in Japan for 12 years, has made the notion of bringing multiculturalism to the country something of a personal crusade. . . .
>
> The challenge now for Mr. Aldwinkle is to obtain Japanese citizenship. The process is so exclusive that more foreigners are naturalized each week in the United States than in Japan in an entire year."
>
> *The New York Times*, November 15, 1999.[5]

We must be careful, however, in our effort to understand other cultures. Yes, multicultural awareness and sensitivity are better for human relations and business success. But like most matters in human relations, this is a very complex issue. There are subtle gradations within each culture and we must be careful not to fall into easy generalizations that may increase rather than decrease cultural gaps. Even if we are intending to compliment someone from another culture, we should not slip into stereotypes and think or say, for example, "Isn't that a charming custom the Koreans have!" There are differences and subcultures within all cultures: between rich and poor, urban and rural, educated and noneducated. When confusion and frustration may cause us to criticize another culture's practices, we should continue to focus on the individual we are having a problem with, not the entire society.

Guidelines for Improved Cross-cultural Communication

1. **Appreciate diversity.** Learning about the history of other cultures is a good way to start becoming less ethnocentric. Around the time of the last millennium while people enjoyed coal stoves in China, crystal tableware in Baghdad, and libraries in Ghana, Northern Europeans tried to survive in filthy huts with open fires for heat. Some other examples history teaches us about cultural variations in the past:

   Circa 1005: A aristocratic lady of Venice was insulted because her daughter-in-law from Byzantium in Asia Minor disdained eating with her hands and insisted on using her own "golden instrument with two prongs," otherwise known as a fork. Almost 500 years later, Englishmen at the court of Henry VIII thought visiting Italian diplomats were "lily-livered" because they ate with forks.

   Circa 1110: The Anasazi people of Chaco Canyon built Pueblo Bonito, an apartment complex of 800 rooms with 1,000 "tenants." There wasn't an apartment house to compete with this native American achievement for another 750 years.

   Circa 1255: A common item in the Arab world—soap—is finally produced in England. Three hundred years later, when bathing was still thought to be unhealthy, Queen Elizabeth I was viewed as a bit eccentric because she bathed monthly.

2. **Relate to the individual.** While it is important to learn the general characteristics of other cultures, especially if we hope to do business with them, we will always deal with individuals, not groups. Positive stereotyping can be just as counterproductive as negative stereotyping. In England one will definitely find Londoners who do not have a "stiff upper lip" and are very emotional. Similarly, in Italy one will find many Romans who do not "speak with their hands" and are far more reserved than anyone from the British Isles. While we can't become fluent in the language of every country with which we may do business, we can learn some basic phrases such as *thank you, good morning, please,* and so forth. This is a part of being respectful and relating to an individual from another culture.
3. **Be respectful.** Every culture has contributed to the ebb and flow of human endeavor. The great Roman Empire that built cities, roads, and aqueducts across Europe, Africa, and Asia Minor is now only a memory residing in ruins and museums. Yet its system of law, its architecture, its literature, are alive in America and in many parts of the world today. No culture has a monopoly on good or evil. We sit rather than squat; therefore, we think millions of people on the planet are more primitive. Is there any basis in fact for this judgment? Aren't American children quite happy squatting? We think that a good, firm handshake is the right way to greet a businessperson. If the truth be told, handshaking originated as a way of demonstrating that one's hands were free of such civilized things as rocks and other weapons. Still think bowing is an essentially inferior way of greeting someone?
4. **Practice clarity.** In speaking and writing it is more critical than ever to present a clear message when addressing someone from another culture. It is relatively easy to buy something in any country on the planet using our own native language. But we can only sell something or some idea to those from other cultures when we use their language. Using "their" language requires understanding of their cultural language as well as their spoken language. In toll-free telephone jargon, 1-800-FLY-4444 might seem harmless enough for an airline advertisement. But as some airlines learned to their regret a few years ago, it was like using the number 1-800-FRIDAY-THE-13TH in English. The reason? In many Asian cultures the number four suggests death.

Sometimes practicing clarity has more to do with how carefully you use your own language. The author of the following statement would be understood by most Americans but not by the recipient in Singapore: "We were really caught flat-footed when your request arrived. I showed it around but no one could make heads or tails of it. If we act immediately we might end up the creek without a paddle. So please give us the straight scoop so we can hit a home run instead of striking out. I'll touch base with you on this problem early next week."

Some confusing messages heard around the world:

"Bring your ancestors back from the dead with Pepsi."
This was how the slogan "Come alive with Pepsi" was translated in Thailand.

"New York City is so much better than it was a few years ago. But there are too many prostitutes outside all those magnificent skyscrapers."
An Italian tourist's conclusion about women taking smoking breaks outside office buildings.

"Nothing sucks like an Electrolux."
An advertisement in Britain for Electrolux vacuum cleaners.

"Please leave your values at the front desk."
Sign in a hotel elevator in Paris.

"The manager has personally passed all the water served here."
Sign at the front desk of an Acapulco hotel.

To avoid unintended communications failures such as these, here are some suggestions for improving clarity in cross-cultural messaging:

- Use plain English in short, simple sentences (no more than 15 words). Avoid proverbial expressions and slang or sports and military metaphors.
- Speak slowly and pronounce your words as clearly as possible without being patronizing. Pause frequently to check for eye messages, especially that glazed-over look.
- Provide a written account of the key points of the discussion for members of your audience or group to take with them for review.
- Avoid trying to inject humor into the discussion. Much humor is untranslatable across cultures, as it is between generations.

Being a good multicultural communicator requires sensitivity to language. The best way to avoid blunders in this area is to choose words and phrases that are objective and neutral. Except in certain situations where the context may require it, there is no need to mention ethnic or racial factors.

Insensitive or biased expression	Improved expression
They interviewed a Chinese lawyer.	They interviewed a lawyer.
An African American named Jim Hibbert was selected for the position.	Jim Hibbert was selected for the position.

Communicating Across Genders

Gender issues constitute the second group of barriers to successful communication in the workplace. The basis of this obstacle is the belief that certain abilities are the exclusive province of one sex or the other. Men are the stronger sex, women the weaker. Men go out to work, women stay home. Women who go to work, as opposed to swinging in a hammock all day at home, should do only certain types of work. Men who lose their tempers in the workplace are admirable alpha-males, women who raise their voices are PMS-challenged bitches.

If you think this problem has gone away in the age of the Internet, think again. Internet broadcasting giant Pseudo Programs has been hit with a $3 million lawsuit charging that women at the company are treated like "bimbos." It further alleges that women are made to work apart from the men in a separate office.

There may still be "boys in the mailroom" and "gals in the typing pool," but not because that's the only place they should or can be. Even the so called glass ceiling, that supposedly invisible level of management beyond which women could not rise, has definitely been shattered. Deborah C. Hopkins, for example, a senior executive with the Boeing Company, has been named chief financial officer of Lucent Technologies as of April 25, 2000. Lucent is America's number one maker of communications equipment.[6]

The appointment of Carly Fiorina as president and CEO of Hewlett-Packard, the world's second largest computer maker, was described in *The New York Times*, July 20, 1999:

Hewlett-Packard Picks Rising Star at Lucent as its Chief Executive

PALO ALTO, Calif., July 19—Abandoning a long tradition of picking its leaders from within its own ranks, the Hewlett-Packard Company announced today that it had chosen as its next chief executive a woman who earned her power and reputation in the telecommunications industry. . . .

The unanimous decision by the board to choose a woman with an undergraduate degree in medieval history and philosophy to head Silicon Valley's pioneering technology company was widely hailed as a step for gender equality in an industry that is still largely dominated by men. However, Ms. Fiorina, who now heads a $20 billion division of Lucent, is already one of the nation's highest-ranking female executives. And today

> she sought to play down the role of gender in her new role. "I hope we are at a point that everyone has figured out there is not a glass ceiling," she said in response to a question. "My gender is interesting but really not the subject of the story here."[7]

Sexist or gender-biased language continues to be a problem in business messaging. This is language that stereotypes or reveals prejudice based solely upon sex and power. When we use such language we are implying that these factors are more important than an individual human being's ability and contribution to a team effort.

Such insensitivity can be directed against men or women. Consider an advertisement created for the American Civil Liberties Union for a campaign against racial profiling by police officers. It shows a white face and a black face, side by side, followed by the question: Which man looks guilty? as if only men commit crimes.

In male-dominated societies and workplaces women are far more often the victims of insensitive language. But substituting one bias for another, such as in changing history to *herstory,* is not the recommended way to go.

In the United States the equality of the sexes in the workplace is a continuing goal. In corporate more than governmental America, the goal is well along the way to being achieved. In other parts of the world such as India, women have ironically achieved greater political power, even when they continue to lack corporate power. Regardless of the power equation it is always better from a personal as well as a business standpoint to use language that is sensitive to gender issues.

Some ways to avoid these language barriers include omitting the male–female pronouns by changing the construction of the sentence, using the plural they instead of the singular *he* and *she.*

Sexist or gender-biased expression	**Objective improved expression**
The congressman will see you now.	The member of congress will see you now.
How many man-hours will this job take?	How many working hours will this job take?
I invited the executives and their wives.	I invited the executives and their spouses.
If a customer has a question, she has the right to an answer.	A customer who has a question has the right to an answer.
Every supervisor must inform his department.	All supervisors must inform their departments.

Communicating Beyond Sexual Orientation

In North American society questions of male and female sexual orientation are said to be in the *post-Stonewall* phase. This refers to demonstrations that took place in New York City in July 1966 to protest continual police harassment of homosexual gathering places. Gay men and women are demanding and receiving equal rights, including employment opportunities in business and government. Jokes based upon sexual orientation should be as unacceptable in the workplace as any other form of bias.

Language with sexual-orientation bias	**Neutral bias-free expression**
We have a first-rate lesbian accountant.	We have a first-rate accountant.
There are five people on the team: three men and two gay technicians	There are five people on the team, including two technicians.

Communicating without Age Bias

Although it is commonly thought to be a problem affecting the elderly, ageism is often a bias directed against the young. Until they are 25 or even 30 years old, young men pay higher auto insurance premiums. This is supposedly because they are more likely to have accidents. Then why don't the elderly pay higher rates? Aren't they more subject to reduced vision problems and slower reflexes? And doesn't the senior citizen discount discriminate against the young?

Whatever the answers to these questions and until we achieve a Utopian society, it is wise to avoid ageist language. Unless it is relevant to a particular issue, for example a legislative committee meeting on Medicare benefits, or a panel discussion of attention deficit hyperactivity disorder, there is rarely any need to refer to a person's age.

Age-biased communication	**Objective age-free expression**
Some restaurants have reduced-prices for elderly customers.	Some restaurants have discounts for Seniors.
She looked like a feisty old woman.	She appeared to be a strong woman.

Communicating without Disability Bias

As with age there may be certain situations, such as government agency meetings on access for the handicapped, where mention of physical disabilities may be necessary. Otherwise, carry the "people are people" rule of human relations into the way you communicate about disabilities, whether physical or emotional. The days of President Franklin Delano Roosevelt's invisible wheelchair and leg braces are beginning to be left behind. It is no longer startling to see models with disabilities in television, such as the Ikea ads, and in print advertising, for example, the Land's End catalog.

Disability-biased expression	**Improved objective language**
David suffers from multiple sclerosis.	David has multiple sclerosis.
Jennifer is afflicted with AIDS but her disease doesn't interfere with her work.	Jennifer has AIDS, but her condition doesn't affect her job performance.
Ryan is burdened with the manic-depression defect, but it doesn't poison the atmosphere of the workplace.	Ryan's bipolar personality has not affected his workplace contributions.

The preceding five categories of bias are not the only negative ideas and stereotypes that linger in our subconscious. There is a newly coined term known as "lookism," or judging women and men by the attractiveness of their appearance alone. And there is the ancient tendency noted by Stendhal in *The Red and the Black* to judge the poor as incapable of having opinions as worthwhile as the financially fortunate: "How can he [Rousseau] reason about anything when he has not an income of a thousand ecus?"[8] We all experience many stumbling blocks and barriers along the road to better communication. Underlying all of the proposals for improved expression is the time-tested fact that dealing with people as individuals rather than stereotypes guarantees better communication.

The same Shakespeare who is being used as a type of corporate management consultant on military and kingly leadership said 402 years ago, we are all human beings ". . . fed with the same food, hurt with the same weapons, subject to the same diseases, healed with the same means, warmed and cooled by the same winter and summer." *The Merchant of Venice,* Act III, Sc. 1.[9]

5

Removing External Causes of Business Communication Flaws

Compared with internal blockage, external barriers to effective communication are easier to identify and cure. They include the following three areas, which are part of what was discussed earlier as nonverbal communication: personal and document appearance, facial expression and body language, and space and time factors. These are called areas of nonverbal communication because, whether we intend them to, they all carry silent messages to the receiver. Remember the party guest who didn't drink the Merlot and the account executive that pulled back from that spectacular 30th-floor balcony? Both persons communicated an unintended negative message.

REMOVING BARRIERS CAUSED BY PERSONAL APPEARANCE AND THE APPEARANCE OF DOCUMENTS

If it is true that "a picture is worth a thousand words," it is also true that it may take a thousand words to undo the negative impression caused by a poor or inappropriate appearance. To borrow a thought from *King Lear*, while "robes and furred gowns" may not in fact hide all sins, "through tattered clothes small vices do appear."[1] Let's consider how a tattered appearance affects our perceptions of people and documents and how a great appearance can send a strong nonverbal message.

First impressions count. Is this unfair? Probably. Is it a fact? Definitely. As noted earlier, our society places great importance on physical appearance. Television and print advertising are filled with beautiful young women and handsome, athletic looking young men. Some newspapers have devised variations on the old inquiring photographer. They have features such as a "Guy-ger Counter" that have roving panelists rate men at their "messed—and sometimes, best." The categories include "hair, physique, accessories, and overall outfit." The ratings go from "No chemistry" to "Oh, baby"!

In the workplace, whether corporate or governmental, physical appearance is crucial. When the whole package—body, clothes, grooming, and posture—is in place, a person is seen as more intelligent, more credible, and more persuasive. This is a powerful message.

Posture

One's posture is probably the first nonverbal message anyone can send. Even when too far away for someone to notice a person's clothing and grooming, that person's posture is making a positive or negative statement. Even from a distance an individual can project authority and self-confidence—or weakness and timidity. Good posture begins *inside* the body. The first of the promoters of successful communication is *preparation.* By preparing our mind before stepping into workplace situations we can improve our posture. A rigid, overly poised appearance, however, will seem artificial. The goal is to appear confident without resorting to a West Point cadet's posture, and to appear relaxed without throwing a leg over the side of the boss's armchair. We are not usually the first ones to notice our own posture, so asking a friend's opinion and practicing in front of a mirror can be very helpful.

Body

Although genetics determines some of our bodily characteristics, much is left to the will of the individual. Diet and exercise are medically proven ways of staying in shape. Smoking, excessive alcohol, and high-fat foods damage the body internally and externally. Most gyms and health clubs have information on healthy eating habits that should be joined with exercise to improve the health and appearance of the body.

Clothes

Just as genetic factors determine some physical traits, the size of one's wallet will dictate some but not all clothing decisions. Quantity is not as important as quality. A few high-quality outfits will create a much better impression than closets of low-quality apparel. We all know that not every big spender is considered well dressed. The most important thing is to dress appropriately for the occasion. Stay away from clothing *du jour*, the latest trends. Simple, classic styles and colors are always appropriate. Avoid flashy jewelry and loud colors.

Grooming

A classic wardrobe on a good body does not in itself guarantee a positive first impression. Personal grooming and hygiene require careful, daily attention. Cleanliness, most of all extending to skin, nails, and hair, is essential. But well-groomed hair is immediately noticed. Avoid hairstyles that call attention to themselves. "Big hair, no money" is not a desirable first impression. Finally, men and women both need polished shoes to complete their wardrobe and grooming.

REMOVING BARRIERS CAUSED BY FACIAL EXPRESSION AND BODY LANGUAGE

Facial Expression

As stated earlier, in any given message the actual words spoken comprise on average only 7 percent of the total meaning. We interpret or infer the remaining 93 percent from the speaker's facial expression and tone of voice. This is why we can coax a smile from a small child by saying the most reprehensible things with a smile and a soothing tone of voice. Even as adults, when we hear unwelcome messages from a speaker with a soothing voice, we are unlikely to become as agitated and hostile as we might have when hearing it from a panicked voice.

When there is discrepancy or confusion between the spoken words and unspoken facial expressions and body language, we trust the physical rather than the verbal message. Why? Because we instinctively feel that nonverbal, physical cues are more immediate and uncontrolled. We believe they are the genuine barometers of what is going on inside the speaker's head. Therefore, they are truer and more trustworthy.

Guidelines for Effective Facial Expression

- One's face is like clothing. Wear a calm, poised expression—a classic suit or outfit—for most situations.
- A smile is an accessory. It should be used in moderation, however, especially in other countries where a more sober, straight-faced look is the norm. Even in the United States, when used inappropriately or excessively, a smile can be interpreted negatively. It can

suggest airheadedness or vacuity rather than warmth and friendliness.

- Reflexive scrunching or raising of the eyebrows can be distracting. This habit can signal confusion or disdain rather than attentiveness.

Eye Contact

Good eye contact is the first element in effective facial messaging. Unless dealing with a sociopath, the eyes are considered the "windows of the soul." Under normal circumstances they tell us something about the speaker's attitude, sincerity, and truthfulness.

Guidelines for Effective Eye Contact

- Establish and maintain good eye contact. Americans should follow this as a general mode of communication. Good eye contact will show the listener or audience that one is interested in them and their concerns.
- Strong eye contact is an acquired skill. Americans tend to value strong eye contact. This is not true of all cultures. Among most Asians it is considered rude and invasive. If you question a woman from a Hispanic culture and she turns her eyes down or away, do not jump to the conclusion that she is lying or being evasive. She is most likely just being polite. Her traditions have taught her that strong eye contact is too forward or bold.

Successful eye contact must be done in conjunction with body language. Strong eye contact will not be effective if it accompanies a squirming body with a rapid, high-pitched voice.

Body Language

The face and eyes are not the only nonverbal message givers that human beings have. The body—its overall posture, the arrangement of arms, hands, and legs—speaks volumes. We can learn much about what is going on inside someone's head by paying careful attention to body language. We can learn to read body language like a book: Changing body movements become like new paragraphs or chapters. By reading body language correctly we can avoid the disaster of becoming the book that is closed after the first few pages. None of us wants to be the book that is told by its cover.

Negative Body Language to Avoid

- Arms crossed over one's chest: signals defensiveness and resistance.

- Hands clasped behind one's back: signals frustration, possibly anger.
- Steepling fingers: signals a barrier or shutting off of a message receiver.
- Placing one's hand over one's mouth: signals disapproval or intent to deceive.
- Tapping or drumming fingers: signals restlessness and impatience.
- Sitting with hands clasped behind one's head: signals overconfidence, even arrogance.

Guidelines for Positive and Effective Body Language

- To show interest, understanding, or agreement: nod head slowly up and down.
- To show interest and relaxed comfort: lean closer to receiver or audience.
- To show receptivity, sincerity, and openness: open palms of hands.
- To show thoughtful evaluation: move hand to cheek or to chin with thumb and index finger cupping chin.
- To show a positive attitude and involvement: make embracing gestures with hands.

REMOVING BARRIERS CAUSED BY SPACE AND TIME

When the subject is communications between people, space and time are not philosophical abstractions. Like the face and body, they can carry very strong nonverbal messages.

Space

We inhabit a given space physically and psychologically. The way we use space tells a lot about us personally and culturally. We use and order the space around us in a way that makes it a type of language analogous to body language. And like other languages the use of space varies from one culture to another.

Some Tips for the Successful Use of Space as Language

- If you wish to set a tone of sincerity and intimacy usually reserved for immediate family members and loved ones, move within a radius of 1½ feet from the person you are communicating with. You may wish to enhance the note of deep sincerity by placing your open hand on the back of the elbow of the person.
- If you wish to create an atmosphere that is not intimate, yet is friendly, move within a radius of 1½ to 4 feet from the person you are communicating with.

- If the desired atmosphere is merely a social one within a business context, use a communication radius of 4 to 12 feet.
- If the situation calls for a large group presentation, keep the audience at least 12 feet away while communicating.

Time

The way we use time, like the way we use space, sends strong nonverbal messages. The language of time, as with most nonverbal communication, also varies between and within different cultures. North American cultures tend to be much more time-conscious than southern European and Middle Eastern cultures. Furthermore, within a culture such as the United States, there is a far greater emphasis on time in New York and Chicago than in Southern cities like Jackson, Mississippi, or St. Augustine, Florida.

To understand the messages we give each day with the language of time, we only have to think of how we prioritize our daily schedules. Do I frequently arrive late for work? This is sending a negative message to superiors. Am I always on time for staff meetings? This reveals respect for one's fellow workers. How long do I take to respond to memos? Letters? E-mail? The amount of time reveals the degree to which we control our workplace demands. Do I keep people waiting when they have appointments with me? If we do this as a matter of habit, we are showing passive–aggressive tendencies. Such behavior sends very negative nonverbal messages.

Some Tips on Effectively Controlling the Language of Time

- Make and be faithful to a daily schedule.
- Prioritize your agenda. If you have had someone travel two or three hours to meet with you, allow extra time in your schedule.
- Forsee the unforseen—allot time on your daily agenda for unexpected problems or delays. Show common courtesy—everyone's time is valuable. If a meeting or phone conversation is running long, send word to whomever is next on your schedule.

Once our frame of reference has been cleared of internal and external barriers to successful communication, we are ready to let effective verbal messages flow within a static-free and noise-free environment.

II

Becoming a Successful Business Writer

6

The Foundations of Effective Business Writing

When external and internal barriers are recognized and removed, the writer is free to focus on the positive flow of communication. Mastering written communication means achieving the ability to create written messages that can create change. These can only be messages that possess clarity of purpose, organization, and expression. With successful written communication we can bring about change for the better. Without it we are stuck with the status quo. If all we have to offer is the status quo, who needs us?

Every message we create represents an opportunity for positive change. This means change for the better, a chance to gain something either personally or financially. Good verbal communication will win allies, admiration, and trust. It will also earn financial rewards in increased sales and profits, or a better budgetary bottom line. Good verbal skills are not a matter of genes—either you have them or you don't. They can be learned and developed by following clear goals and procedures.

THE PRINCIPLE PURPOSES OF BUSINESS COMMUNICATION

Let's stop a moment to recall the four principal purposes of business communication. All involve change in one form or another: information, persuasion, results, and public relations or good will.

These four goals can only be achieved if they answer the following questions posed in Chapter 3 for each goal.

Information

1. Is it accurate?
2. Is it presented in a way that underscores its accuracy?
3. Is it supported with sufficient data?

Persuasion

1. Is the issue or problem presented clearly?
2. Are there alternative ways of solving the problem?
3. Is the choice of solution inevitable and inescapable?

Results

1. Are the projected results realistic and attainable?
2. Are the benefits purely financial?
3. Might there be other benefits—for example, workplace and/or environmental?

Public Relations or Good Will

1. How will the recipient, individual or group, receive the proposal under discussion?
2. Will it be viewed as arrogant and self-serving?
3. Will it appear civic-minded, environmentally sound?

Recalling how each of these goals is preceded by a series of questions reminds us that it is always necessary to think *before* communicating. Doing this will enable us to determine our purpose and decide on a plan of organization and expression. This in turn will ensure us the results or *after* that we desire.

THINKING IN THREES FOR BETTER COMMUNICATION

The patterns of thought that we need to follow are three-dimensional in time and place. They provide the following triple foundations of successful communication.

Here are three ages of communication: yesterday, today, and tomorrow.

Here are three phases of written communication: purpose, organization, and expression

Here are three stages of written communication: thinking, writing, and rewriting.

The following diagram shows how this communication triple play works.

Required Focus	Think About Yesterday	Create Today	Prepare for tomorrow
All Communication	People and Issues	**Change**	Good Will
All Written Communication	People and Issues	**Write to Change**	Rewrite to Improve Results and Good Will
All Oral Communication	People and Issues	**Speak to Change**	Question to Improve Results and Good Will

This diagram reminds us that no communication exists in a vacuum. All communication has a "before." Or to put it another way, every message we set out to transmit "today" has a "yesterday." There is a background history to all communication, even so-called "cold calls." Similarly, all communication has an "after" or a "tomorrow." There are always results or outcomes of any communication. Sometimes, unfortunately, these are unintended. These are the ones we can learn how to minimize or prevent altogether.

Before creating any message, whether written or oral, we should stop for a moment and consider the background as well as the consequences of any planned act of communication. For example, before proposing a new way of handling customer complaints, questions such as the following about the issue and the people involved should be asked.

1. **Who** will be the recipient of this message? Have you been working with these people a long time? Have your relations been amiable or have they been strained?

How can this message improve your working relationship with this person or group? How can this message avoid strains caused in the past?

2. **What** is the nature of this message? Does it concern an issue that has been a problem in the past? Have you proposed solutions in the past either orally or in writing?	How can this message be made more effective than past ones? Can you word your proposals more clearly to increase their effectiveness?
3. **When** do they have to receive it? Have customer complaints suddenly reached critical mass? An air of crisis and the need for group support would call for one-on-one meetings or group sessions, depending on numbers.	Can you defuse the crisis situation? If so, will this buy you some time to craft your message more effectively? Or will the delay lessen the note of urgency and diminish the end result?
4. **Where** are the recipients located? If there are four or less people in the adjacent office,, person-to-person talks will work best. If there are 400 people in five departments, a memo or e-mail would be more practical.	Can you build a feedback system into the small-office, person-to-person communication, as well as into the much larger corporate or government workplace?
5. **How** should I package this message? Memo? E-mail? Phone call?	Phone calls work well for a few recipients. E-mail provides speed. Memos work well for larger groups and when a written record is needed.

FUNDAMENTALS OF EFFECTIVE WRITTEN COMMUNICATION

Writing is not a one-stage operation. Whether it is a memo, an e-mail, a letter, or a formal report that we set out to create, all written communication must go through three stages in order to be successful:

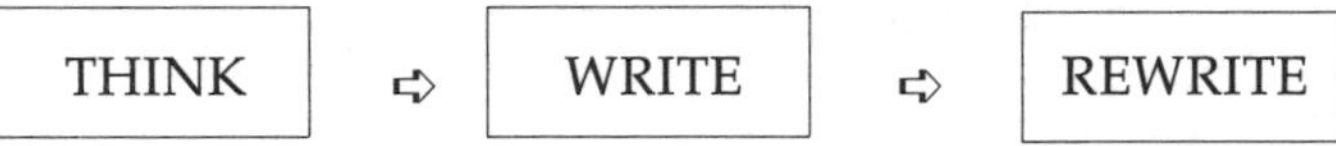

Whenever and whatever we write in the workplace, it will eventually be read by someone. Whether those readers are a room away or a world away they will be receiving our message in their own workplace. We will not be present simultaneously the way we would be in oral communication to interpret voice and body clues to the reception of our message. We send out a written message to fly or crash on its own. It's got to be right the first time.

Every individual who sends a message in the workplace automatically becomes an expert. The sender is assumed to be more knowledgeable than the receiver, at least as far as the particular communication is concerned. Therefore, the reader is depending on the sender to present a clear message. Most business communication fails in direct proportion to the degree with which it ignores the reader.

Some of the ways we can ignore readers include:

- Talking over their heads
- Talking down to them
- Using technical jargon and lingo
- Omitting crucial details

Once we have determined precisely who the audience for this communication is, our writing has to target this individual or group directly. The attention of the recipient must be gained immediately by showing that he or she has a stake in our message. In a very real way our message has to become our reader's message. The reader shouldn't even stop to think, "What's in it for me?" The benefits should be obvious and should begin to appear in the first sentence.

READER-BASED WRITTEN COMMUNICATION

To achieve this goal requires morphing or transforming writer-based communication into reader-based communication. This process has four stages:

1. Focus on reader benefits and shared goals
2. Organize a reader-based structure
3. Provide a cue-based navigation system
4. Develop a persuasive argument

Stage 1: Focusing on Reader Benefits and Shared Goals

Successful communication is focused on the receiver, not the sender. When I send a written communication the message is from me, but not *about* me. It's about *you.* Over 200 years ago Ben Franklin had the idea of reader benefits in mind when he said, "To be good [writing] ought to have the tendency to benefit the reader." In the year 2000, Robert Pittman, president of America Online, said that he and Gerald Levin, chairman and CEO of Time Warner, were merging two companies that "are a lot alike. What we both think about is the consumer, what people are doing, and how do we serve them and create new value."[1]

Senders of written messages can demonstrate their focus on reader benefits and shared goals in two areas: in the content of the message being delivered, that is, its ideas; in the words the message uses to present those ideas, that is, its form of expression.

Today's aggressive marketers know that they do not even have to wait for the recipient of their communications to open their mail. The reader benefits are clearly emblazoned right on the envelope.

Introducing the "It's All Yours" Platinum Ultima Card

- Pre-Approved with no Annual Fee
- Credit Line Up to $50,000
- Balance Transfer Savings
- Exclusive Money Saving Offers

Thomas Impartial
909 Buckeye Court
Indianapolis, IN 46260

0% APR

THAT'S RIGHT, ZERO

In order to determine the right content of a planned message we first have to determine the precise purpose of the particular message we are about to send. Which one of the four purposes of business communication listed above: information, persuasion, results, and public relations and good will, do we primarily wish to achieve with the present communication? Often, all four are involved to a greater or lesser degree. But which one is most important at this time?

Once our purpose has been determined, we have our goal. Adapting the goal to the reader is the act of creating a shared goal. The reason for writing and the reason for reading become one. However, just because we want to persuade does not mean our reader wants to be persuaded. Here are some ways to bring the writer and the reader together by creating shared goals.

- Learn as much as possible about the needs of the reader.
- Think of needs that the reader may not be aware of.
- Evaluate how to meet or fulfill those needs.
- Suggest how you can help your reader attain these goals.

A shared goal can be a powerful motivation for the receiver of a message to read and remember what the writer has to say. The average reader may have a blizzard of letters, memos, and reports on his or her desk. The opening statement and shared goal the writer presents should motivate the receiver to read *this* memo or letter first and carefully.

A shared goal can also make comprehension easier. People understand and retain information and ideas that fit in with what they already know. For example, everyone in the corporate world today knows the terms *enter* and *delete*. For those in international banking, the acronym *SWIFT* would be a familiar term for a messaging system for overnight transfers of funds. However, if we start using terms like *remote triggering* and *MPS* (messages per second), we will undoubtedly cross a shared line and lose most of our audience: that woman whose desk is already piled high with banking letters and reports.

When we offer our readers a shared goal, one for which they already have a framework, we help them turn our message into something meaningful to them—something they can use to bring about positive change.

The form or expression of business writing must also be reader-based. This means that our choice of words and use of language should demonstrate clearly that the reader is the focus of our message. One of the easiest and most effective ways of doing this is by simply remembering to use the word *you* instead of *I* or *we*. Here are some examples that show the difference. If you were the reader, which one do you think would grab your attention and hold your interest?

Writer-based expression:	Because we want to update our mailing lists and reduce our postage costs, we need you to complete this survey.
Reader-based expression:	You can get your discount catalogs and special-sales notices earlier by simply filling out the enclosed card.
Writer-based expression:	I have the pleasure of announcing that we have approved your application for our training program.
Reader-based expression:	You will be happy to learn that you have been chosen to join our new training program.
Writer-based expression:	Because we want to keep our history of making famous brands available at reduced prices,, we do not give cash refunds.
Reader-based expression:	You can enjoy the twin benefits of getting famous brands at reduced prices and store credit for all returns.

Stage 2: Organizing a Reader-Based Structure

Using reader-based language is the first step. To be effective it has to accompany a reader-based structure. Most of us set out to communicate with our reader by writing reader-based documents, but we often end up writing as if we were our own audience. We end up talking almost exclusively about ourselves, our needs, our interests, our problems. In the following case the manager of a large brokerage office in Seattle requested a solution from an employee named Arthur to the problem with Mark's journal approvals. This is the response she received:

> Gentlemen:
> For a number of weeks we had a problem with approving journals in the Seattle office. The problem was with Mark approving journals as ADM. MANAGER. We took many swings at the bat, from many different angles to solve this problem.
>
> Mark would start off his day as ADM. and soon become OPS during the day's operations. The reason for this was SMART had two managers listed as Branch Managers at start of day. Hence it was operationally necessary to sign them both out.
>
> Now here is the twist to all of this and the ugly consequences that resulted. Vince is the Assistant Manager in Seattle. SMART listed him as Branch Manager. Compliance listed him as non-existent. Process Manager had Vince as an Ops Manager. That's the gun of the issue and the following paragraph the ammunition. At some point during the business day it was necessary for Matt (Ops MGR.) or Mark (Adm. MGR.) to sign both Branch Managers out of the office (SMART) for ck payouts. This caused a chain reaction, Vince (in SMART) is BRM. When Vince is signed out it needs to assign a level change so it looks to Compliance (where Vince does not exist). At this point Process Mgr. Joins the picture and says Vince is Ops. Mgr. and assigns Mark that level.
>
> The cure—Vince is now Assistant Manager. He is no longer a BRM in SMART and Process Mgr continues to view Vince as Ops. Mgr. (which is correct!)
>
> The problem was with Mark approving journals as ADM. MANAGER. I am happy to report a solution has been found and implemented.

Aside from its careless formatting, grammar, and spelling, this memo does not have a reader-based structure. There is a logic organizing this document, but it is the logic of a story told from the writer's perspective and memory. The memo seems designed to satisfy the writer's need to explain what went wrong and why. The reader's needs have not been considered, if at all, until the very end. If the receiver is still reading this memo at this point, her eyes have glazed over. She probably regrets having asked Arthur for a solution in the first place. Ninety percent of this memo is about how the problem arose. The solution that was asked for is just a throwaway in the last line.

You can usually recognize writer-based prose by one or more of the following features:

1. A self-absorbed focus on the writer.
2. A narrative organization focused on the writer's own discovery process.
3. A survey structure organized around the writer's information.

Narrative style has its place, but it is hardly ever in business and persuasive writing. Effective business communicators know that they must reorganize their information and knowledge of an issue to suit the reader's needs.

Creating Written Communication That Is Reader-Based

People often ask "How can I make my memos, letters, and reports more reader-based? I've always written this way. Until now I thought it was okay." The fact is that, as long as the writer has a clear goal and a logical method, the writing can change for the better. It can become more effective and successful. Here are three important steps that can be taken:

1. Each document should be organized around a problem or goal that is shared with its intended reader, instead of around the writer's own discovery process or around the issue itself.

   With this goal or thesis as the starting point, the message's key ideas can be grouped or prioritized. The major and secondary topics must be determined and the relationship between them made clear to the reader. Writers will find this method useful to organize individual sections and paragraphs as well as an entire document, as in the following alphanumeric outline.

ALPHANUMERIC OUTLINING STYLE

TITLE:

Central idea: a one-sentence summary of the contents of the document to follow

I. **INTRODUCTION OR FIRST MAJOR TOPIC**
   A. **First subordinate unit**
      1. Evidence, example
      2. Evidence, example
   B. **Second subordinate unit**
      1. Evidence, example
      2. Evidence, example

II. **SECOND MAJOR TOPIC**
   A. **First subordinate unit**
      1. Evidence, example
      2. Evidence, example
   B. **Second subordinate unit**

1. Evidence, example
2. Evidence, example

III. **THIRD MAJOR TOPIC**
(as needed)

2. Make conclusions explicit. When we leave it up to our reader to draw inferences from what we have written in our document, he or she could very well draw a different set of conclusions than what we had in mind. This unplanned outcome could point to faulty reading comprehension on the part of the receiver or a lack of clarity in our messaging. In either case the best way to avoid such problems is not to leave conclusions to chance. Make them explicit.
3. The primary and secondary ideas have been outlined and prioritized based on the goals shared with the reader. The desired conclusions have been determined. What has to be done now is to make that organization vivid and clear to the reader. This is done by giving the receiver cues, in effect leading the reader where you want him or her to go.

Stage 3: Providing a Navigation System for the Reader

If we are really serious about communicating with our readers we have to guide them through our documents. We need to set up signposts that help the reader see what is coming and how it will be organized. This means creating expectations at the beginning of the journey and fulfilling them along the way. Furthermore, we want the reader to know which of our points are major and which are subordinate, and how they are related to one another. Doing this will be like taking the reader on a journey using a high-tech navigation system.

Some or all of the following signpost units may be used depending on the type, length, and complexity of the document you are creating.

Signposts that predict your major points:

Title

Table of contents

Abstracts

Introduction

Headings

Issue or purpose statement

Topic sentences for paragraphs

Signposts that summarize or illustrate your points:
- Sentence summaries at ends of paragraphs
- Conclusion or summary sections

Signposts that guide the reader visually:
- Pictures, graphs, and tables
- Punctuation
- Varying fonts, underlining, and numbering
- Varying formatting with indentation, spacing, rows, and columns

Signposts that guide the reader verbally:
- Transition words
- Conjunctions
- Repetitions
- Pronouns
- Summary nouns

Stage 4: Developing a Persuasive Argument

In business we usually write because we want change. We want to make something happen or be known. And we want results whether they be information, persuasion, or good will. You might say that there is an element of persuasion underlying all of these. We want our reader to do something or think in a certain way—usually our way. But simply expressing our point of view is rarely enough, because it may conflict with the way the reader already sees things. How do you turn things around so that you and your reader share results as well as goals? This is the art of persuasion.

Persuasion is not the same thing as winning an argument or debate. Arguments can be won by force. (Hence all the military and contact-sport metaphors heard around cafeterias and boardrooms.) In such a case, while you may have changed your adversary's behavior, you haven't necessarily changed his or her mind. In a debate your objective is to score points. It is a contest with a winner and a loser decided by an impartial judge. In American political debates the winners and losers are determined by polling audience reaction or by the urgent judgment calls of spin-meisters.

In real-world communication, especially business communication, the goal should not be to defeat an opponent or to score points. This is negative thinking. The more positive goal is to affect the reader, to change his or her existing condition, whether that condition be ignorance of a subject or a different view of a subject. Following are three possible outcomes or goals when there is a difference of opinion on a course of action to be taken or a change to be undertaken:

1. We will totally change our readers' mind or attitude so that they see the issue exactly as we do. We simply substitute our perception for theirs. Unless our audience is totally ignorant and we are the recognized leading authority on the subject, this is an unrealistic outcome to expect.
2. The second possible resolution of a difference of opinion is the opposite, that is, no change at all. Unfortunately this is probably the most common outcome. What we may perceive to be the best or most "correct" arguments, don't always win. The "no change" eventuality may be a very pragmatic reason for making the third alternative your customary goal.
3. A third alternative is to modify or change our reader's viewpoint, to add to or clarify it. We can do this by adding new information or offering a different way of looking at an issue. We do this whenever we draw a distinction, for example between compromise and surrender. As a writer, modifying or adjusting your reader's viewpoint is the most reasonable goal you can have. You are showing respect for your readers' point of view while aiming to tilt it in your direction.

However, we often encounter a great roadblock on the road to modifying a reader's viewpoint. There may be emotional or psychological forces at work. Office politics or other barriers to successful communication may exist.

Many people consider any change on their part as a threat to their own security and stability. People consider their points of view as part of themselves, part of their identity, part of how they have brought order into a chaotic world. Asking people to change or disturb this order in any significant way can make them anxious and resistant. The more urgently the message giver argues, the more firmly the recipients may dig in their heels.

When this happens the crucial question for the writer is, "How can I convince my readers to listen to my position and perhaps even modify theirs without making them feel threatened?" If this is allowed to continue, communication may simply crash and burn.

If readers feel they are understood—that their position is honestly recognized and respected—they are far less likely to feel threatened. Feeling less threatened allows them to relax their self-defensive posture. They feel they can afford to listen freely and consider another way of thinking or looking at things.

Carl Rogers, the developer of Rogerian argument, recommended the following rule of thumb:[2] Before the writer presents a position and point of view, he or she should be able to recount the receiver's position back to him or her in such a way that he or she agrees with your version of it. In this way, the writer proves that a genuine and ongoing effort has been made to understand the receiver's perspective.

With written communication we do not have the tools of facial expression and body language to reassure our receiver. We can't use the winning smile or comforting arm around the shoulder. Are there other ways to achieve the same effect with written communication?

There are two ways to achieve the goal of keeping your communication highway open.

First, the writer can use the introduction to each document, including the shared goal, to show the reader that there is a real understanding of his or her position and goals. This is the moment to show empathy, to look at the issue from the readers' vantage point and assert how the particular message is relevant to them.

Second, the writer can avoid categorizing people and issues. This divides people into warring camps, polarizes the issue, and stifles communication.

In conclusion, changing writer-based messaging into reader-based communication opens the lines of communication between writer and reader. When the lines are open we can achieve the four goals of business communication—information, persuasion, results, and good will. We can bring about the changes we seek.

7

Achieving the Style and Tone of Effective Business Writing

Now that we have a new understanding of how to change writer based communication into reader-based communication, we are ready to focus on the first major area of verbal business communication. This area is effective business writing, writing that can make change happen. Change of some sort is always on the sender's agenda, whether that change be an addition in information, a reason for persuasion, or an increase of good will. To achieve any of these goals the sender needs three things: a clear purpose, a clear organization, and a clear form of expression.

SENDER'S GOALS	⇨	**CHANGE** IN INFORMATION, PERSUASION, GOOD WILL
SENDER'S NEEDS	⇨	**CLARITY** OF PURPOSE, ORGANIZATION, EXPRESSION

Experienced communicators see writing not as a set of rules but as a living organism. There is a series of steps by which it comes into being and maturity. Writing starts with a focus on the people and issues involved. It moves on to the actual composition of the sentences and paragraphs of the document. Then it undergoes revision to sharpen its clarity and tone. Here are the stages of conception, composition, and revision, or what we need to do to create a winning document:

1. Change attitudes of people and perceptions of issues
   By choice of language:
   - The "you" view
   - Positive expression
   - Clear and concise language
2. Compose document to achieve changes desired
   Overall organization—outlining based on placement of central idea:
   - Front loading: direct method
   - Back loading: indirect method

   Paragraphs:
   - Topic sentences
   - Transition words

   Sentences:
   - Active voice, action verbs
   - Passive voice
3. Revise documents
   - To improve clarity
   - To increase results
   - To increase good will

The first of these stages, changing the attitudes of people and the perception of issues by choice of language, is the subject of this chapter. Creating and revising the total document will be the subject of Chapter 8.

The time before we create any message is the most critical moment of the whole process. This is when we focus on the people and issues where we want to see some changes made.

CHANGING THE ATTITUDES AND PERCEPTIONS OF READERS

Before creating any message we have to stop and consider the background as well as the consequences of our planned message. To help make the right decisions at this crucial stage we should ask some key questions. For example, who will be the recipient of this message? Is it an individual or a group? If the answer is just a name, the boat chosen to navigate through a communications channel has just sprung a leak. The writer needs to ask more specific questions about the frame of reference of the intended audience, such as:

1. Have I been dealing with this person or persons only recently or for a long time?

2. How familiar am I with my receiver's culture, beliefs, and attitudes?
3. Have our relations been amiable or strained?
4. Do I expect my message to be welcomed or rejected?
5. Is my message likely to be forwarded to another audience?
6. If so, what reception do you expect your message to receive from that secondary audience?

Focus of change: How can this message improve my working relationship with this person or group? How can the present message build on gains or avoid strains caused in the past?

The next step is to clarify the nature of each message. This will be the area of purpose—what the sender wants to see changed.

1. What is the nature of the change?
2. Does it concern an issue that has been a problem in the past?
3. Have my prior proposals been received warmly or coolly?

Focus of change. How can this message deal with the issues as effectively as past ones? Or how can a writer word proposals more clearly and more positively to increase their effectiveness and, therefore, their acceptance?

CHOOSING THE RIGHT LANGUAGE FOR CHANGE

Be Personal

"It's strictly business, nothing personal" is a sure way to spring another leak in your communications boat. Everything that matters is by definition personal. An impersonal sales letter is almost a contradiction in terms. An impersonal "thank you" or congratulatory note is about as welcome as a pink slip.

The receiver of any message should be made to feel important as an individual human being, not a number. And each reader *is* important. This is the person whose ideas, opinions, or practices the writer seeks to change. A good rule of thumb to measure the personal component of our writing is a variation on the Golden Rule: Write to others as we would have them write to us.

Here are two ways writers can begin communicating in a more personal manner:

1. By trying to spend more time thinking about the reader than about what the writer has to say. This means focusing on the "you"

instead of the "me." Doing this will make it easier to accomplish the next step in writing more personally.

2. By imagining, almost in an exaggerated way, the self-interest of the reader. Writers who are truly alert to this aspect will strengthen the impression that the reader is considered an important individual. This is always a good starting point.

There are many options in the actual words and phrases used to show that the writer is truly reader-directed. The simplest way is to remove oneself, the "I" or "we" at the beginning of the sentence and substitute the "you" for the person the message is directed at.

"Me/we" view:	I need the entire sales staff to complete the attached questionnaire about safety in the workplace.
"You" view:	Your safety in our workplace will be increased through your input into the questionnaire.
"Me/we" view:	We have approved your consumer loan application.
"You" view:	Your consumer loan application has been approved.
"Me/we" view:	I am happy to announce that we have instituted a new training program to improve employee letter writing.
"You" view:	Enhance your letter writing skills by attending the new training program.

Be Positive

The simple act of changing from the "I/we" view to the "you" view makes written communication more positive from the very start. Being positive is always desirable, unless we want to burn our bridges behind us. Burning bridges, however, means that all hope has been given up for any change for the better. Positive thoughts, on the other hand, lead to positive words. And positive words generally lead to positive actions.

Although its negative tone wasn't funny at the time, today we can probably laugh in sympathy at a slash-and-burn letter Mark Twain wrote over 100 years ago:

> To the Hartford Gas Company
> Hartford, February 1, 1891
> Dear Sirs:
> Some day you will move me almost to the verge of irritation by your chuckle-headed Goddamned fashion of shutting your Goddamned gas off without giving any notice to your Goddamned parishioners. Several times you have come within an ace of smothering half this household in their beds and blowing up the other half by this idiotic, not to say criminal,

custom of yours. And it has happened again today. Haven't you a telephone?
Ys
S L Clemens

Similarly, let's look at a letter from the manager of an electronics store to a customer who complained that a printer she had recently bought didn't work:

Dear Madam:

I am in receipt of your letter in which you state that the printer you purchased from us recently failed to meet the warranty requirements.

You claim that the printer failed to do the things you say our salesperson promised it would do.

Possibly you misunderstood the salesperson's presentation. Or perhaps you failed to follow instructions properly. We positively know of no other customer who has made a similar complaint about the printer. The feeling is that it will do all that is stated if properly used.

However, we are willing to make some concessions for the alleged faulty part. We will allow you to return it; however, we cannot do so until you sign the enclosed card and return it to us.

Sincerely yours,

The tone is unmistakably negative. "State" and "failed to meet" in the opening paragraph imply there's some doubt that the claim is valid. In the second paragraph, "you say" suggests the salesperson didn't make the statement at all. Such phrases as "you misunderstood," "you failed to follow instructions," and "if properly used" tell you in so many words that you're not too bright. And to wrap it up, the writer uses the negative "we cannot . . . until" instead of the positive "we will . . . as soon as."

Most letters aren't this negative, of course. But it doesn't take much to offend. Any of these negative words or phrases, in themselves, could have spoiled the tone of an otherwise effective letter.

Let's take a look at some examples of the negative approach. In each case, the negative thought (emphasis added by the author) has been converted into a positive one.

Negative:	Since you *failed* to say what size you wanted, we cannot send you the shirts.
Positive:	You'll receive the shirts within two or three days after you send us your size on the enclosed form.
Negative:	We *cannot* pay this bill in one lump sum as you requested.
Positive:	We can clear up the balance in six months by paying you in monthly installments of $20.

Negative:	We're sorry we *cannot* offer you space at $200 per square foot.
Positive:	We can offer you excellent space at $300 per square foot.
Negative:	We are *not* open on Saturday.
Positive:	We are open from 8 AM to 8 PM daily, except Saturday and Sunday.

Be Clear and Concise

Getting our reader on our side with personal and positive language is a first step; keeping them there is achieved by a clear and concise message.

Clarity is the bedrock of successful business writing. Without clarity none of our goals will be achieved. Clear writing is easily understood and unambiguous. It is plain and direct. It is free of obscurity and confusion. Misunderstandings are costly to companies and their employees. Lack of clarity causes employees to lose patience and productivity, and companies to lose money. Whether the message is a purchase order for a new telecommunications system or preliminary test-marketing results, understanding the message on the first reading is essential.

Clarity, like anything having to do with communicating, begins in the mind. It is revealed in our choice of language as well as our mastery of the basics of grammar.

Conciseness is next in importance to clarity. We do not live in leisurely times. Everyone is on the run, cell phone firmly in ear. People appreciate messages that are brief and to the point. Some of the most influential and memorable documents of Western civilization are models of brevity: the Ten Commandments has 132 words; the Bill of Rights has 462 words; and the Gettysburg Address has 272 words. While some of the most forgettable documents are very long: Abraham Lincoln's Gettysburg Address followed Governor Edward Everett of Massachusetts, who went on for two hours. Does anyone remember even one phrase of the thousands of words he said? The United States Department of Agriculture needs 14,054 words for its publication on cabbage. Anyone interested?

Railroad magnate Cornelius Vanderbilt, who created one of the greatest fortunes in American history, needed only 22 words when he wrote this unforgettably clear and concise message to some associates who had attempted to cheat him:

> Gentlemen:
> You have undertaken to cheat me. I won't sue you, for the law is too slow. I'll ruin you.
>
> Yours truly,
> Cornelius Vanderbilt

Here are five ways to make business writing more clear and concise:

1. **Choose concrete not abstract words.** Concrete words refer to actual, material things. These are what can be perceived by our senses, what can be scientifically verified and measured. Abstract words refer to ideas and generalities. They often cause confusion and misunderstandings because they refer to qualities and characteristics that are subjective and open to debate and disagreement. Here are some examples of the difference:

ABSTRACT–VAGUE	CONCRETE–SPECIFIC
In the near future	By 5:00 PM Friday
Considerable savings	A 40 percent reduction
Home-office machine	Epson 1440 printer
At a later date	March 17
Beverage	Chateau Petrus 1955
Businessperson	Deputy Director of Housing

2. **Use plain everyday words.** Short and simple words are the fastest and surest carriers of your message. You use them confidently and your reader grasps their meaning quickly. Some business writers mistakenly think that if they use long words they will dazzle their readers. What they end up doing is annoying the very people they thought they would impress.

   The greatest and best example of language choice that defies clarity is "legalese." Even lawyers have to admit that most of their "herewiths," "heretos," "thereins," and "ipso factos" do not increase communication at all.

   One person who waged war on what he called the "junk antiques" of lawyers' writing was David Mellinkoff. A lawyer himself, and writer of such books as *Language of the Law* and *Dictionary of American Legal Usage,* Mellinkoff was an early force for simplifying insurance policies and other consumer documents. He also argued for streamlining state and federal legislation, and adding writing classes to law school requirements. When New York State passed a law in 1981 requiring that consumer agreements be written in a "clear and coherent manner using words with common and everyday meanings," Mellinkoff went after the government writer. "Common and everyday are redundant," he said.

   David Mellinkoff's solution for "legalese" was simple. "The most effective way of shortening legal language," he wrote, "is for judges and lawyers to stop writing."[1]

   Managers and supervisors can't simply stop writing, but they can use clear, everyday language. Here are some examples of long words drawn from Latin roots of ancient Rome. They are followed by short action words from the Anglo-Saxon and Teutonic roots of the English language.

NEEDLESSLY LONG	SHORT AND CLEAR
antecedent	prior
ascertain	learn
definitive	final
enumerate	list
interrogate	ask
modification	change
predicated	based
recapitulation	review
remuneration	pay
subsequent	after
termination	end

And here are some examples of "legalese" that we can all communicate very clearly without:

LEGALESE	PLAIN ENGLISH
aforementioned	said earlier
aforesaid	said earlier
annexed hereto	added, attached
appurtenant	additional
ascertain	find out
attached herewith	enclosed
furtherance	promotion
hereby	by this action
hereinafter	later
I am in receipt of	I have
notwithstanding	in spite of
pending your reply	until I hear from you
thereinafter	later
wherefore	for that reason

Below are some examples of old-style corporate and governmental writing. Unfortunately, the type of writing they contain, as out of date as it might be, is still around. Following each example of the old and musty is a rewritten update in the kind of plain English that would have pleased David Mellinkoff.

INSURANCE INDUSTRY

Old Style: It is the express intention of the undersigned to create an estate or account as joint tenants with rights of survivorship and not as tenants in common. In the event of the death of either of the undersigned, the entire

interest in the joint account shall be vested in the survivor or survivors on the same terms and conditions as theretofore held, without in any manner releasing the decedent's estate from any liability provided for in the next preceding paragraph.
(The only help computer spell-checks will give you with this one is that "theretofore" is not in the software's dictionary and that the sentence is too long.)
Clear, concise, plain English: Other signers share your interest equally. If one of you dies, the account will continue and the other people who've signed the document will own the entire interest in it.

BANKING INDUSTRY

Old style: For value received, the undersigned jointly and severally hereby promise(s) to pay. . .
Clear, concise, plain English: To repay my loan I promise to pay you . . .

Following is an agreement on safe-deposit boxes that a bank actually asked bank customers, not lawyers, to sign.

The liability of the bank is expressly limited to the exercise of ordinary diligence and care to prevent the opening of the within-mentioned safe-deposit box during the within-mentioned term, or any extension or renewal thereof, by any person other than the lessee or his duly authorized representative and failure to exercise such diligence or care shall not be inferable from any alleged loss, absence, or disappearance of any of its contents, nor shall the bank be liable for permitting a co-lessee or any attorney in fact of the lessee to have access to and remove the contents of said safe-deposit box after the lessee's death or disability and before the bank has written knowledge of said death or disability.

This mind-numbing 119-word sentence can be reduced to the following 52-word sentence without any loss of legal and technical requirements.

Our liability with respect to property deposited in the box is limited to ordinary care by our employees in the performance of their duties in preventing the opening of the box during the term of the lease by anyone other than you, persons authorized by you, or persons authorized by the law.

GOVERNMENT AGENCY

Old style: Notice of Eligibility, Denial or Pending Status
Tax Dependency Form

Clear, concise, plain English: Action taken on your food stamp case
Student Tax Report

3. **Use long and technical words sparingly.** There will be cases where there is simply no short simple word to convey your meaning. Better then to use the long word than replace it with many short words. Use "refinancing," for example, rather than "obtaining a lower rate of interest on an existing loan."

   Technical language can be very useful even essential in some professions. Law, health maintenance organizations, accounting, computer systems, and government title programs often have a language all their own. But clarity exits and confusion enters when a doctor tells a child that her black and blue mark is a sub-dural hematoma. The message is clear: use technical language at will with members of your own profession. With those outside your business or profession use it very cautiously and with an introductory explanation.
4. **Avoid slang and buzzwords, clichés, acronyms, and Instant Messenger abbreviations.** These are words and phrases that can cause communications barriers like the ones discussed in Chapter 4. Their meanings are often understood only by a small group; therefore, they are not good vehicles of communication. In addition, they do not survive being passed to secondary audiences and other cultures.

   Slang and buzzwords, which come naturally to oral communication, do not function well in business writing. Business writing is often informal, but it should be standard written English easily understood by your reader. The principal reasons for avoiding slang and buzzwords are:

   - *Slang is substandard and idiomatic.* It is the jargon of a particular group. Your primary audience, the readers directly targeted by your business message, may understand that your phrase "clip joint" refers to an overpriced restaurant or service establishment. But what if your document is passed on to a secondary audience? Will those readers mistakenly think that a "clip joint" is some sort of architectural term? Or is it medical one?
   - *Slang words and phrases have a short life span.* "Hoist with his own petard"[2] was once a colorful expression meaning to get caught in one's own trap. Today, it would only make sense to a student of archaic language or to someone who knows the fate of poor Polonius in *Hamlet*.
   - *Buzzwords are meant to impress the reader with the importance of the writer.* The writer is trying to show how "in the know" he or she

is. Buzzwords represent writer-based communication instead of the reader-based writing we must achieve.

The computer age has spawned an entire lexicon of new words known as "geek-speak." In our technology-obsessed culture the digerati speak a language that exalts the machine and has nothing but contempt for flesh and blood human beings who are known as "wetware." Writers and artists are dismissed as "content providers" who may need to take a "bio-break," that is, use the bathroom.

Use expressions like the following only in very informal messages:

SLANG EXPRESSIONS	BUZZWORDS
a can of worms	agnostic
canoodle	bottom line
curry favor	granular
in your zone	herding cats
keep it on the down low	interface
keep your nose clean	no-brainer
low-hanging fruit	paradigm
the low down	parameter
to the max	policy wonks

GEEK-SPEAK

Domainist: Someone who judges others by their e-mail addresses; especially someone who looks down upon anyone who posts from public Internet providers like aol.com.

Showstopper: Refers not to a spectacular moment of live theater that astonishes a delighted audience, but in Microsoft language "a function, object, or issue important enough to jeopardize a ship date or schedule," that is, a "really big bug."

Net.gods: Not mere mortals, these are leaders of the cyber-universe.

Sheepies: Not net.gods, not even human.

Client/server action: Sex.

Treeware: Printed books, magazines, and newspapers; also known as "dead tree editions."

Meat-jail: The human body.

Clichés are tired, worn out words and phrases. While easy for writers to use, they are stale from overuse. They are not reader based because they give most readers the impression that the writer couldn't be bothered choosing language for the particular reader. In a word, clichés are impersonal.

Acronyms are words formed from the initial letters of words in names or phrases. Some, like ATM for automated teller machine, are universally understood. Others, like STAT (which is actually a shortened form of the Latin word "statim," meaning "immediately"), are best left to actors playing doctors on television.

Instant Messenger abbreviations are similar to acronyms. They are shortened forms that combine words and numbers to form words in cyberspace. They are the buzzwords of online chat rooms and are not considered business-like writing.

Typical clichés and acronyms to avoid:

CLICHÉS	ACRONYMS
If I can be of further help . . .	ASAP
If you have any other questions . . .	FEMA
I would like to take this opportunity to . . .	OPS
Thank you for your consideration . . .	OSCIA

Some Instant Messenger abbreviations to avoid, except in very informal e-mails:

CYBERSPEAK	TRANSLATION
A 404	clueless
brb	be right back
BDU	big dumb user
cul	see you later
cya	see you
cul8r	call you later
g2g	got to go
lol	laugh out loud
nm	not much
wsup	what's up?
24-7-365	twenty four hours a day, seven days a week, three hundred sixty five days a year . . . (continually)

5. **Avoid dangling participles and misplaced modifiers.** These grammatical errors have caused problems for readers long before there was such a thing as cyberspace. Usually the problem is a participle or participial phrase found at the beginning of a sentence, which modifies a different part of the sentence than the writer intended it to. In the sentence, "Rising in the distance we saw the Washington Monument," the participle *rising* seems to modify the sightseers. But this nonsensical meaning is unintended. The writer means to say that it was the Washington Monument that was rising in the distance.

Every *ing* word or participle does not have to be avoided at the beginning of a sentence. In usage some are really independent phrases or are functioning like conjunctions. The meaning of the statement, "Generally speaking, the proposal was acceptable," is clear to any reader despite the opening dangling participial phrase. Use a common sense approach: If the dangling participle causes confusion or unplanned humor, reconstruct the sentence.

6. **Avoid noun phrases.** A noun phrase, usually consisting of three words—an article, a noun, and a preposition—is usually a weak and wordy substitute for a strong action verb. In 1998 a federal relief worker stated that the government would get help to the victims of a hurricane in Puerto Rico "when we get them within the scope of our evaluation." Perhaps the hurricane victims would have gotten relief sooner, if she had simply said, "When we evaluate them." In the following lists the noun phrases are slow and wordy; the single-word verbs are clear, concise, and vigorous.

SLOW NOUN PHRASE	ACTION VERB
Conduct an investigation of . . .	Investigate
Have a discussion about . . .	Discuss
Make a schedule for . . .	Schedule
Prepare a plan for . . .	Plan
Put an end to . . .	End

7. **Remove redundancies and compound prepositions.** Like wordy noun phrases, redundancies and compound prepositions are expressions that use several words instead of single ones. Unfortunately, their use is widespread in corporate and governmental writing today. A look at the following examples will reveal redundancies that defy logic and compound prepositions that waste the time of both writer and reader.

REDUNDANT EXPRESSION	CONCISE SUBSTITUTE
Along the lines of . . .	Like
At this point in time . . .	Now
At which time . . .	When
Consensus of opinion . . .	Consensus
Due to the fact that . . .	Because
Contributing factor . . .	Factor
End result . . .	Result
Few in number . . .	Few
Free and clear . . .	Clear

In the event that . . .	If
Past history . . .	History
The manner in which . . .	How
With regard to . . .	About

Choosing language that will make it easier to change perceptions of people and issues should not be considered a simple list of do's and don'ts. It should be a reminder to drive carefully and be wide awake on the communications highway. Clear and concise language is a continual goal for reader directed business writers. It also provides the basis for the entire document.

8

Organizing and Developing the Total Document

In Chapter 6 we studied the triple foundations of effective business writing and how to change writer based communication into reader-based communication. In Chapter 7 we learned how to choose the kind of clear and concise language all business writers need to achieve their goals of information, persuasion, and good will. Now we will see how to organize and develop the total business document to bring about whatever changes we seek.

Chapter 6 demonstrated that effective business communication is reader-based not writer-based. It also showed that such reader-based communication goes through four stages.

1. Focusing on reader benefits and shared goals.
2. Organizing a reader-based structure.
3. Providing a cue-based navigation system.
4. Developing a persuasive argument.

In Chapter 7 we studied various ways for the business writer to improve their focus on reader benefits. One way was by making our writing personal. The other was by starting sentences frequently with the pronoun "you," instead of "I," to demonstrate that we are reader-directed.

We also saw in Chapter 7 that when they are not reader-based, business writers will reveal the following flaws: a self-absorbed focus, a narrative organization focused on the writer's own discovery process, and a survey structure organized around the writer's information.

This chapter will show how the writer can avoid these three flaws by organizing a reader-based structure. The first step in this process is to determine your central idea.

HOW TO DETERMINE THE CENTRAL IDEA OF YOUR DOCUMENT

Everything in nature serves some purpose. Nature almost never does anything just for fun. Likewise, before we begin to create any business document we must first decide our purpose. This will become the central idea of the document.

The central idea of a business message should always be the specific *answer* to the question: What exactly do I want changed?" The answer to this question will be a clear and complete statement that will function as the central idea or thesis of the entire document. Phrases will be of little use, as they will only give the topic or area of change. A phrase will be vague; the writer needs a clear map to reach each destination.

Vague topic:	Releasing clients' names
Specific central idea:	Releasing our clients' names would violate their right to privacy
Vague topic:	Liquidating assets
Specific central idea:	If we must liquidate, we have to sell the following assets first.

Secondarily your central idea should answer the following two questions: Who will be affected by this change? and How will they be affected by this change? Changing people is not a realistic goal. We may set out to change people's perceptions of things, but setting out to change people is not a profit making goal of business or a sensible mission for government.

Our goal is to change *things*: procedures, profits, systems, people's perceptions. What we want changed and how we think it would best be changed will cover a broad continuum from very positive to very negative. As a result, business messages will fall into three categories:

1. Very positive, that is, brimming with good news about issues and people. The change desired in such situations will not be to make them negative, but to make people aware of the good news or to congratulate those who helped to cause the good news.
2. Neutral, that is, with no clearly positive or negative issues.

3. Very negative, that is, dealing with problems and losses, with resulting negative effects on people involved.

CHOOSING THE RIGHT PLACEMENT OF EACH CENTRAL IDEA FOR CHANGE

These notions of positive and negative will determine where to place the central idea, that is, whether to frontload it or backload it.

How do I frontload my central idea? Placing the central idea at the beginning of the document achieves this objective. The most direct frontloading lets the central idea stand alone as a one-sentence first paragraph. However, a writer can also frontload by placing the central idea in the first paragraph with additional sentences.

When should I frontload my central idea?

1. Whenever there is positive or good news to deliver to the targeted reader.
2. When agreement or approval is expected from the intended reader.
3. Whenever there is neutral or purely factual news to be delivered.
4. When there is no reason to expect controversy or hostility from the specific reader.

Why should I frontload my central idea? Here are two of the many advantages of presenting the central idea directly.

- It proves the writer is focused on the reader. In business everyone's in a hurry. By stating the central idea immediately, whether it is a routine request or any other common business communication, the writer saves the reader's time. On the other hand, if the writer makes the reader go on a hunting expedition for the purpose of every communication, a barrier to successful communication is erected.
- It reduces the risk of miscommunication. If the central idea is buried somewhere in the third or fourth paragraph of a message, the message may be lost. The reader may pick up some idea in the second paragraph, for example, speed-read the rest of the document and miss the point the writer intended to make.

How do I backload my central idea? This is done by stating it indirectly and by placing the central idea toward the end of the document, but not in the concluding paragraph.

When should I backload my central idea?

1. When there is negative or bad news to deliver to the targeted reader.
2. When disagreement or disapproval is expected from the reader.
3. When reader reaction can't be predicted.

Why should I backload my central idea? There are two major reasons for backloading negative or bad news:

- It proves the writer is focused on the reader. Backloading or indirect messaging of bad news shows that the sender has considered the receiver's reaction to the negative news being delivered. Receiving bad news is disturbing enough. It doesn't have to be worsened by bad delivery. With very few exceptions negative news should be delivered in the most positive way possible.
- It keeps the door open for future communication. By delivering bad news in an indirect, even positive way, the sender avoids slamming the door on the receiver. The writer may not be able to grant the current request but may be able to grant future ones and continue to do profitable business.

What are some specific ways to backload negative news? While positive language is always the goal in business writing, there are often negative situations to deal with. In such cases choosing positive language is not enough. The negative or potentially negative central idea must be placed in such a way that the least damage or ill will is caused.

When a message is so negative that it has to be backloaded, the sender can do this by using one or all of the following methods. Any or all of them will have the effect of making the bad news seem less personal. They will also reduce greatly any confrontational note.

1. *In the document.* By placing the central idea of the negative or bad news toward the end of the document but not in the last or concluding paragraph. This will avoid closing the message on an unhappy note.
2. *In the paragraph.* By putting the bad news at the end of the chosen paragraph.
3. *In the sentence.* By positioning the bad news in the subordinate or dependent clause of a complex sentence, instead of the main or independent clause. This will reduce the force of the negative news.
4. *In the verb.* Express the bad news in the passive form of the verb, not the active. This will make the bad news appear less personal or confrontational.

5. *By implication.* Avoid any specific statement of the bad or negative news. Instead of stating what you cannot do, say what you can do. Your reader will conclude that what he or she wants is not on your can-do list.

HOW TO DEVELOP A READER-BASED STRUCTURE FOR EACH CENTRAL IDEA

Structure refers to the organization of the entire document. In architectural terms it is like constructing a building. Every building has:

- a purpose,
- a number of floors,
- a number of units per floor.

Every business document, whether it's a memo, a letter, or a report has:

- a purpose: this is expressed in the central idea.
- a number of paragraphs: these include the introduction, one or more paragraphs of development, and a conclusion.
- a number of sentences within each paragraph.

How Do I Develop a Central Idea in a Frontloaded Document?

The informal list. This refers to an initial group of ideas on the subject of the communication that the writer thinks most important to develop a specific central idea. Making and critically reviewing such lists are done in three stages:

1. Making an informal list: the process of writing always involves choices. After determining the particular central idea the writer must decide how to expand or develop it. This is done by making a list of the reasons and examples that might best convey the central idea to the reader. The writer might come up with a dozen ideas for a long document such as a report. If it is a memo or letter, the writer might come up with six or seven ideas.
2. Narrowing this list: looked at from the reader's point of view the writer reduces these six or seven ideas to those that will best convey the central idea. The original six or seven ideas may at this point be shortened to three ideas.
3. Arranging these ideas in order of importance to the reader: first, second, and third.

Ways of arranging an informal list of ideas. Here are some ways to organize or arrange the ideas or elements of an informal list:

Chronological:	From the distant to the recent past to the present to the future Background, present status, and prospects
Spatial:	By location: regional, national, global Mid-Atlantic, Pacific Northwest, New England; Italy, France, China; South America, Europe, Pacific Rim
Logical:	Different choices relative to the central idea Cause and effect for troubleshooting manuals Comparison-contrast for measuring one unit of a company against another or one company against another Classification and division for showing different units according to a consistent principle, for example, showing the divisions of a company according to their function Illustration for giving concrete examples of abstract or technical concepts
Problem–Anaysis–Solution:	Description of a problem, why it exists, what can be done about it
Order of importance:	From the least important to the most important, which is climactic order, or from the most important to the least important, which is descending order.

The number of paragraphs. If the writer develops these three ideas in the same paragraph, a brief, three-paragraph frontloaded document will be created.

Introduction
The **central idea** of the entire message:
Central idea includes some direction for the reader:
1. First idea in a word or phrase
2. Second idea in a word or phrase
3. Third idea in a word or phrase

Development of first idea

Development of second idea

Development of third idea

Conclusion: Rephrase central idea in an action-request time frame

If the writer decides that each of these three ideas needs fuller explanation, he or she would place each one in a separate paragraph and produce a five-paragraph or longer frontloaded document.

Introduction
The **central idea** of the entire message:
Central idea includes some direction for the reader:
First idea in a word or phrase
Second idea in a word or phrase
Third idea in a word or phrase

Development of first idea

Development of second idea

Development of third idea

Conclusion: Rephrase central idea in an action-request time frame

How Do I Develop a Central Idea in a Backloaded Document?

The informal list

1. The writer makes an informal list of the main points connected with the central idea, as would be done for a frontloaded document. These will include the main reasons for the negative news that is about to be delivered.
2. The list is whittled down to the ones that will have the most significance for the intended reader.
3. The reduced list is arranged in the order of importance from the reader's perspective: first, second, third, and so forth.

The number of paragraphs. If the writer places these three ideas into one paragraph, a three-paragraph, backloaded document will result.

Introduction The **central idea** of the entire message: Central idea includes some direction for the reader: 1. First idea in a word or phrase 2. Second idea in a word or phrase 3. Third idea in a word or phrase

Development of reasons First idea and reasons Second idea and reasons Third idea and reasons **Central idea** expressed indirectly or implied

Conclusion: A forward-looking closing statement is made

Now let's apply this method to an actual writing situation. You are a member of the Environmental Protection Committee of a county government. You have been asked to summarize the potential problems that will arise if the Stellar Oil Company is allowed to begin drilling in a populated area and recommend a course of action. The company intends to begin by erecting a 130-foot derrick and follow this by drilling as many as 30 wells. The company has been a major contributor to your party's political campaigns.

1. *Begin by making an informal list of potential problems*
   Pollution of ground water
   Union problems
   Pollution of the air
   Possible spills
   Tax rates
   Waste disposal problems
   Carcinogens
   Possible accidents
   Increased truck traffic
   Political fundraising
   Increased noise
   Smells
   Loss of property values
2. *Narrow the list down to environmental issues*
   Pollution of ground water ✓
   Union problems
   Pollution of the air ✓
   Possible spills ✓
   Tax rates
   Waste disposal problems ✓
   Carcinogens ✓
   Possible accidents ✓
   Increased truck traffic ✓
   Political fundraising
   Increased noise ✓
   Smells ✓
   Loss of property values
3. *Arrange the edited list in order of importance for the reader.* Because the chair of the environmental protection committee is your primary intended audience, you decide to arrange your list in climactic order from the least to the most important issue.

   - Increased noise
   - Increased traffic
   - Pollution
4. *Fit in the remaining items under these three headings.*
   1. Increased noise
      a. Nearby hospital
      b. Nearby school
      c. People in neighboring homes

2. Increased traffic
   a. Trucks bringing in equipment
   b. Trucks carrying away oil
   c. Workers arriving and leaving
3. Pollution
   a. Air
   b. Ground
   c. Water

5. *Assemble the three-paragraph document.* The following three environmental issues should be considered before the oil-drilling project is approved: the risks of environmental pollution, an increase in noise, and an increase in automobile and truck traffic.

   - Drilling operations will be conducted from 8 AM to 7 PM. The neighboring county hospital and elementary school both need a degree of quiet to be effective. Although many people are at work between those hours, many others earn their living at home.
   - Furthermore, increased truck traffic would make surrounding streets more noisy and dangerous. Pedestrians and drivers would have to be extra cautious to avoid encounters with large trucks bringing in equipment or hauling away oil and other products. The oil workers' cars and trucks would further increase traffic in this quiet area.
   - Most of all, the inevitable problem of pollution would affect all those living within the area surrounding the project. Site preparation, drilling, and production operations would pollute the air by emitting hydrocarbons and odors. Oil spills might contaminate the ground and water. For these reasons the Environmental Protection Committee should consider industries such as computers or light manufacturing for this sensitive area.

There are a number of areas in the county that would be suitable for your Stellar Oil's operations. Let's schedule a meeting in the first week of June to discuss some of these possibilities.

Introducton Background or reasons for your unwelcome central idea Includes some direction for your reader: First idea in a word or phrase Second idea in a word or phrase Third idea in a word or phrase

Development of first ideas

Development of second ideas

Development of third ideas

Central idea expressed indirectly or implied

Conclusion

Make a forward-looking closing statement

If you decide that each of these three ideas needs fuller explanation, then place each one in a separate paragraph and produce a five-paragraph or longer document.

Once we have a front- or backloaded structure for a document, we can consider the ways of creating more effective paragraphs and sentences to embody our message.

9

Making Your Ideas Flow Easily Through Your Paragraphs

Becoming an effective business writer takes careful planning and deliberate steps. It is a process that begins in the mind by focusing on the reader—how our written communications will benefit our reader and how we can jointly achieve the goals that we share.

Building on this solid foundation of reader-based communication, the writer can acquire the style and tone of a successful business writer by using language that is clear, concise, and positive.

In Chapter 8 we saw how to put this language to use by developing a total document around a central idea. Communicating a positive or neutral message to our reader calls for a direct or frontloaded organization of our paragraphs. Communicating a negative or bad news message, on the other hand, requires an indirect or backloaded paragraph structure.

Now we will study in detail how to make the central idea of a total document flow through individual paragraphs. This will be a flow directly *down from* the central idea in the frontloaded pattern or a flow *away from* the central idea in the backloaded pattern. This will give the document more effective paragraphs—the ones that will bring about the changes the writer seeks.

THE CHIEF QUALITIES OF EFFECTIVE PARAGRAPHS IN BUSINESS WRITING

A paragraph is a group of related sentences that develop one central idea. Although there is no absolute rule for length, it is usually 5 to 12 sentences long. In business writing the average is 8 sentences.

Whether they appear in a frontloaded or backloaded business document, whether they are in a memo, a letter, or a report, all effective paragraphs have four main characteristics: topic sentence, unity, brevity, and coherence.

Topic Sentence

Just as every document needs a central idea, every effective paragraph needs a topic sentence. Topic sentences are often confused with topics. A topic is an area of discussion; a topic sentence is a precise, summary statement of what will be said about a topic in the paragraph that follows.

The topic sentence serves as the central idea of the paragraph. To function properly and work for you, it must be *complete* yet *limited*. This means it must be a complete sentence: it must have a subject and a verb, and express a complete thought. It must also be limited in that it covers only the one specific idea that will be handled within the paragraph. In the first of the following examples, releasing clients' names might cause many problems, but the complete topic sentence limits the paragraph to the violation of the privacy issue alone.

Vague topic:	Releasing clients' names
Complete topic sentence:	Releasing our clients' names would violate their right to privacy.
Vague topic:	Liquidating assets
Complete topic sentence:	If we must liquidate, we have to sell the following assets first.

A good topic sentence controls all of the other sentences in the paragraph. The remaining sentences exist in a direct plus or minus relationship to the topic sentence. They will either support or limit the topic sentence. In addition, an effective topic sentence gives direction and tone for the reader.

Positioning the Topic Sentence in the Paragraph

- *Front door.* Taking the reader into account, if the message of the paragraph will be taken as good news, the writer would use the direct pattern or frontloading method. This means putting the topic sentence at the beginning of the paragraph, just as one would put a good news central idea at the beginning of a total document. The same thing would be done with neutral or strictly informational news.

Here is a paragraph with a front door topic sentence:

Our Year-End Summary of Charges can help simplify your record keeping and tax preparation. Maintaining accurate records can be a time-consuming process. At the beginning of each calendar year, you will receive a complete summary of all Blue Diamond charges made during the previous year. Charges billed during the previous year are itemized by category, such as merchandise, airline, or restaurant, with a detailed report showing totals within each category.

- *Back door.* If the reader is likely to be unreceptive or even hostile to the message of the paragraph, the sender places the topic sentence at the end of the paragraph, just as would be done to backload negative news toward the end of a total business document.

Maintaining accurate records for business and tax purposes can be a time-consuming process. Wouldn't it be easier if, at the beginning of each calendar year, you received a complete summary of all charges made during the previous year? Wouldn't it be even better if charges billed during the previous year were itemized by category, such as merchandise, airline, or restaurant, with a detailed report showing totals within each category? *For a relatively small annual fee our Year-End Summary of Charges can help simplify your record keeping and tax preparation.*

- *Swinging door.* If the sender wants to present contrasting facts, ideas, or possibilities, he or she would want to position the topic sentence mid-paragraph. Doing this will allow it to function like a swinging door. The reader will first see reasons *for* a certain course of action, then the reasons *against*. In between appears the swinging door topic sentence signaling for the reader that he or she is faced with choosing among possibilities.

Maintaining accurate records for business and tax purposes can be a time-consuming process. You have to keep copies of all records and receipts and then sort them out by category. *For a relatively small annual fee our Year-End Summary of Charges can help simplify your record keeping and tax preparation.* When tax time comes around, at the beginning of each calendar year, you will receive a complete summary of all charges made during the previous year. And all charges billed during the previous year will be itemized by category, such as merchandise, airline, or restaurant, with a detailed report showing totals within each category.

Unity

Once a good topic sentence is in place, the writer has to stay focused on it, for the writer's own sake, and for the reader's. To guard against the all too human tendency to drift or get sidetracked by constant interruptions of daily life, writers should always check paragraphs for unity. This process will help to guarantee that the topic sentence, every sentence in the body of the paragraph, and the concluding sentence all relate to the one main idea

Brevity

William Faulkner and Henry James are great writers but not models for drafting business reports. Unless the sender of a communication is in the most delicate negotiations, where subtle distinctions are required, clarity and ease of understanding are the primary goals. For these reasons paragraphs are kept short in all business writing. Eight sentences should be the average length with none over 12 sentences.

Coherence

A paragraph coheres, or holds together, when its sentences are arranged in a clear, logical order and when its sentences are connected like links in a chain. Doing this not only helps the writer, it makes the message reader-based. An orderly presentation of ideas within each paragraph makes it easier for the reader to follow and more pleasant to read than a maze of disjointed sentences.

Achieving paragraph coherence through logical order

Creating and editing an informal list before writing a paragraph is one way to achieve paragraph coherence and unity, just as an informal list can be an effective way to begin planning an entire document. After making some notes or ideas, but before writing the paragraph, the writer should decide which ideas to present to the reader first, which second, which third, and so forth, according to some logical order.

Depending on each reader, each subject, and each writer's purpose, there are many possible orders for logical paragraph development, just as for total document development. This section will explain three basic patterns for ordering ideas: time order, space order, and climactic order.

Time order. One of the most common methods of ordering sentences in a paragraph is time, or chronological order. This pattern moves from past to present or present to past, so it serves well for historical overviews, as well as procedures and instructions memos, letters, and reports.

> The company was started by H.F.S. Morgan in 1910. Like Walter P. Chrysler, he trained to be a railway engineer but became an early motoring enthusiast. He died in 1959, having run the company for half a century. Peter, his son, became managing director in 1957 and chairman two years later. Now 80, Peter still goes to work each morning.

The events in this paragraph are clearly arranged in the order of time. They are presented as they happened, chronologically. Throughout the paragraph the reader is given signals to emphasize the chronological order. This is done with the underlined key words, such as the dates, and transition words, such as "half a century," "later," and "now," which emphasize time order and guide the reader from event to event.

Space order. Another useful way to arrange ideas in a paragraph is space order. With this method a person, place, or thing is described graphically: from left to right, top to bottom, foreground to background, and so on, as the underlined do in the following paragraph:

> As the new classic residences of 2000 Ocean Boulevard are near completion, the opportunity to own them is also drawing to a close. Just a few of our most desirable condominiums remain. Oversized windows reveal sweeping lake and ocean views. Museum-quality floors gleam under 10-foot ceilings in grand rooms of prewar-style proportions. In a separate wing, bedroom suites are ideal for relaxation and repose. A handsome lobby opens unto a private dining room ready for catering large parties. For added convenience owners may purchase studio suites located on the second and third floors. A rooftop garden and Olympic sized swimming pool complete a picture of unprecedented luxury.

This paragraph uses space order. The first sentence clearly places the setting, an oceanfront condominium. The third sentence moves the reader's eyes to the ocean views as seen from the interior windows. The fourth sentence looks at the floors and ceilings; the fifth sentence . the bedroom wings. The seventh entence guides the reader to the lobby; the eighth sentence to the second and third floors, and and the last sentence to the rooftop garden and pool.

Opening words and phrases such as "oversized windows," "in a separate wing," and "a rooftop garden" signal the reader to look at different spaces and floors of the building.

Climactic order. Ideas in a paragraph can also be arranged in order of importance, or climactic order. This can be done by starting with the most important ideas and ending with the least, or by beginning with the least important and building to the climax of the most important one. Order of importance is especially useful in business situations requiring persuasive writing. Beginning with the most important ideas gets the reader's attention and makes her or him want to continue reading.

Sometimes, however, the sender may want to add some punch and surprise to the paragraphs. When this is the goal, the writer will begin with the least important idea and build to a climax by saving the most important idea for last. This method can prevent the tendency of some writers to start with a bang and dwindle away to a whimper.

> "City workers have had no real wage increases in recent years," the union leader said. "We have answered the city's call time and again for cooperation. City workers have taken benefit reductions, and deferred funds owed to us. Now it's time for the pendulum to swing the other way. We municipal employees want our fair share of the pie. We've earned it. We've waited 20 years. Now we're going to get it, even if we have to go out on strike!"

The ideas in this paragraph are explained in order of importance from the least to the most important. The movement is from general statements to highly emotional threats or forecasts. Notice how underlined words, such as "now" and "even if," guide the reader to the climactic ending "go out on strike!."

Achieving coherence through related sentences

In addition to arranging ideas in a logical order, carefully linking each sentence to the next will give the reader coherent paragraphs that are easy to follow. There are three basic ways to do this: by repeating key words and by substituting pronouns, by substituting synonyms, and by using transitional words and expressions.

Repetition of key words and substitution of pronouns. Connect sentences within a paragraph by repeating key words and ideas. This was done in the above paragraph where "city workers" was repeated twice and the pronoun "we" was substituted for "city workers" six times. Here is another example of coherence, this time by repetition and substitution of the underlined words:

> A grand jury is an investigative body composed of members elected from the community. It serves as a buffer between the state and the citizen. The prosecutor, in many cases, brings before the grand jury the evidence gathered on a particular case. It must then decide if sufficient evidence exists to hand down an indictment—the indictment being a formal charge against an accused person written by the prosecutor and submitted to the

> court by the grand jury. With the indictment issued, the prosecutor can proceed to the arraignment.

In this paragraph the words "grand jury" are repeated three times, the words "indictment" and "prosecutor" three times. To avoid unnecessary repetition, which can become boring if overused, the pronoun "it" is substituted for "grand jury" twice.

Use of synonyms and substitutions. When the writer does not wish to repeat a key word or use a pronoun, he or she can make the paragraph more coherent with synonyms and substitutions. In the earlier paragraph, for example, "municipal employees" was substituted for "city workers." Instead of a synonym the writer can substitute other words that describe the subject. Writing about Carl Icahn, for example, one could refer to him as "the famed corporate raider." Such substitutions provide a change from constant repetition of a person's name or a single pronoun, which can become tiresome for the reader.

Use of transitions. Skill in using transitional expressions is vital to coherent writing. Transitional expressions are words and phrases that point out the exact relation among paragraphs and ideas in the total document, and among sentences in each paragraph. Words like "therefore," "however," "for example," and "finally" are signals that guide the reader from idea to idea and sentence to sentence. Without them even orderly paragraphs with good ideas can be confusing and difficult to follow.

> The position of sales manager requires academic and practical work experience in general retail sales. While a college degree is desirable, at least one year of successful sales experience in each of three capacities is required. First, the candidate must show knowledge of cash and register management. Second, the candidate must have demonstrated in past work experience superior leadership and supervisory abilities. Finally, the candidate must possess a record of reliability and diligence. After interviews have been concluded, the company will make hiring decisions within 10 days.

The underlined transitions above link the sentences in a chronological order or time sequence. They also help to stress the purpose of the paragraph stated in the opening topic sentence.

Below are commonly used transitional expressions grouped according to the signal the writer wishes to give the reader.

Signal	Transition Words and Expressions
Addition or reinforcement	Also, in addition, too, and moreover, besides, further, furthermore, equally important, next, then, finally, likewise

Cause	Because, for, for this reason, since
Comparison	All, both, similarly, likewise, in the same way, in comparison
Concession	Of course, to be sure, certainly, naturally, granted
Contrast or contradiction	Actually, as opposed to, but, however, yet, nevertheless, on the other hand, conversely, in contrast, on the contrary, still, although
Emphasis	Above all, especially, in fact, indeed
Example or clarification	For example, for instance, thus, in other words, namely, specifically, to put it another way
Place or space	In the front, in the foreground, in the back, in the background, at the side, adjacent, nearby, in the distance, there, here, above, below
Repetition	Again, as stated before, in summary, to repeat
Result	Therefore, thus, consequently, so, accordingly, due to this
Space	Above, adjacent to, alongside, around, below, beyond, down, forward, here, in front of, next to, on top of, over, there, under
Summary	In conclusion, finally, as a result, hence, in short, in brief,
Time	First, second, third, next, then, finally, before, soon, meanwhile, later, during, subsequently, immediately, at length, eventually, in the future, previously, currently

10

Writing Clear, Forceful, Reader-Based Sentences

Sometimes, after focusing on reader benefits and shared goals, organizing a reader-based structure, and providing a cue based navigation system through the various paragraphs, a business document fails to communicate the intended message. The writer is left wondering why he or she didn't succeed in bringing about the change in people and issues that was sought. Perhaps it was the individual sentences. Would Hamlet have called them "weary, stale, flat, and unprofitable"?[1]

To make sure that our sentences complete the goals set in Chapter 6 to persuade the reader, it is necessary to create sentences within those paragraphs that will have clarity, strength, and interest for the reader. This chapter will show how to create effective reader-based sentences by answering these two questions: What are the different ways to structure my sentences? and What methods can I use to enhance the style of my sentences ?

THE DIFFERENT WAYS SENTENCES ARE STRUCTURED

A clause is a group of words with a subject and a verb. The subject is the *who* or *what* word that performs the action. The verb expresses the action or state of being that the subject is performing or experiencing.

If a clause can stand alone as a complete idea, it is an independent clause. All sentences contain two basic elements: a subject and a verb.

Sometimes, as in commands or urgent requests such as "Come here!" "Hurry!" or "Please!" one of these elements will be understood, but not expressed.

If a clause cannot stand alone as a complete idea, it is a dependent clause.

There are three types of sentences:

- **Simple.** A simple sentence contains an independent clause, with a subject and a verb that can stand alone as a complete idea.

The committee took a vote.	The council proposed a tax increase.
Three members abstained.	The voters rejected it at the polls.

- **Compound.** A compound sentence contains two independent clauses that are joined by placing a comma and a coordinating conjunction between them.

  The committee took a vote, but three members abstained.
  The council proposed a tax increase, but the voters rejected it at the polls.

  Coordinating conjunctions used to join two independent clauses include:

  and but for nor or yet so

- **Complex.** A complex sentence contains an independent clause and a dependent clause joined with a subordinating conjunction. The main or independent clause can stand alone, but the subordinate clause cannot; it depends on the main clause to complete its meaning.

  The president can call the meeting to order *if* there is a quorum present.
  There will be a quorum, *when* three more members arrive.

  Subordinating conjunctions used to join a dependent clause to a main clause include:

	as long as	for	provided that
after	as far as	how	since
although	as though	in order that	so
as	because	if	so that
as if	before	just as	

as soon as		once	that
though	whatever	whether	whose
till	when	which	whereas
unless	whenever	who	while
until	where	whom	why
what		whomever	whoever

Non-conjunctions are transitional words and phrases. These words do not join a sentence. Usually they start new sentences and follow periods or semi-colons.

accordingly	however	meanwhile	soon
afterward	in conclusion	moreover	suddenly
at last	in short	nevertheless	then
consequently	in the first place	next	therefore
earlier on	in the past	now	third
finally	in the second	on the contrary	to summarize
first	place	on the other hand	today
for example	in the third place	otherwise	tomorrow
for instance	instantly	second	years ago
furthermore	later	some time later	yesterday

Understanding the basic ways that sentences are constructed and how to use conjunctions will help the writer avoid the two most common errors of sentence construction: run-on sentences and sentence fragments.

Run-on sentences are caused when a writer follows one independent clause with another without using a coordinating conjunction.

Sentence fragments arise when a dependent clause is left to stand out in the cold by itself.

In the first complex sentence above, the clause "if there is a quorum present" is only a part or fragment, not a complete thought. It makes sense only when joined to the main clause: "The president can call the meeting to order *when* there is a quorum present."

The following chart summarizes the five ways of constructing sentences based on coordination and subordination of ideas.

Coordination

	, and	
	, but	
	, for	
Pattern 1 Independent clause	, nor	independent clause
	, or	
	, so	
	, yet	

Pattern 2	Independent clause	; ; consequently, ; furthermore, ; however, ; in addition,	independent clause
Pattern 3	Independent clause	; indeed, ; in fact, ; moreover, ; nevertheless, ; then, ; therefore,	independent clause

Subordination

Pattern 4	Independent clause	after although as (as if) because before if since unless until when(ever) whereas while	dependent clause
Pattern 5	After Although As (as if) Because Before If Since Unless Until When(ever) Whereas While	dependent clause,	independent clause

WRITING MORE FORCEFUL AND POLISHED READER-BASED SENTENCES

Understanding the different ways to construct sentences will help the writer focus on the following ways that sentences can be made more effective in business writing.

1. Limit sentence length

2. Preserve their unity
3. Vary sentence length and structure
4. Observe parallelism
5. Use active and passive voice deliberately

Limiting Sentence Length

Chapter 7 discussed how to communicate with the reader using words and phrases that are clear, concise, and positive. It is important to put that knowledge to use in composing sentences. Communications technology by itself cannot help; even when it alerts the reader to a potential problem the writer must know which alternative to choose. Often, despite the computer's suggestion the writer wants the highlighted passage to remain exactly as written. Furthermore, and more to the point, there were great and concise communicators before there were any computers.

In 1998 a Federal Emergency Management spokesperson was asked how soon the federal government would get help to hurricane victims in Puerto Rico. Here was her answer:

> After we have had sufficient time to examine the parameters of the present weather-related conditions we will get these people within the scope of our evaluation and determine how best we can deploy our emergency management resources.[2]

In 1933 President Roosevelt used these words to describe economic conditions in Depression-ravaged America: "I see one-third of a nation ill-housed, ill-clad, ill-nourished."

The 1998 government spokesperson would probably have changed President Roosevelt's clear and concise words into something like this:

> It is evident that a substantial number of persons within the Continental boundaries of the United States, as well as Alaska and Hawaii, have inadequate financial resources with which to purchase the products of agricultural communities and industrial establishments. It would appear that for a considerable segment of the population, possibly as much as 33.3333% of the total, there are inadequate housing facilities, and an equally significant proportion is deprived of the proper types of clothing and nutriment.

Too long for you? At 78 words this passage would hardly merit an award from a government bureaucracy that can produce a 308-word sentence on a single civil-service regulation.

Fortunately, thanks no doubt to continued prodding by people like David Mellinkoff, government and business have slowly begun to recognize this language problem. In 1981, for example, New York State passed a law requiring that consumer agreements be written in "a clear and coherent manner using words with common and everyday meanings." Aside from he fact that "common" and "everyday" are redundant, it was a good start.[3]

Instead of waiting for more directives, try the following simple rules for length:

- Keep sentences short—no more than 18 words. This makes it easier to hold the readers' attention. If a look at the staccato evening news on network television isn't convincing proof that America's attention span is shrinking, perhaps these statistics from the American Press Institute will.

  If a sentence is 8 words long the writer can count on 100% comprehension by the average reader. Once it goes over 28 words the writer stands to lose 50% of the audience.

- Use the computer's spell and grammar checker to determine the number of words in sentences and the number of sentences in paragraphs.
- Stay with one idea per sentence. This is good advice for most business and government agency writing. If there is a reason to combine ideas in a sentence, the writer should observe the guidelines that follow for keeping such sentences unified.

Preserving Sentence Unity

The simple act of keeping sentences short will help preserve sentence unity. However, the nature of some material and the desire for variety may sometimes inspire longer sentences.

When there is reason to combine ideas into a longer sentence, make sure those ideas are related.

> *Unrelated combination:* "We appreciate the affirmative vote from our policyholders and urge you to keep all documents."
> *Related combination:* "We appreciate the affirmative vote from our policyholders and the final approval by regulators."

- When combining related ideas use one of the patterns of coordination and subordination shown above. The following combination uses the independent clause followed by a dependent or subordinate clause.

Two simple sentences: "We appreciate the affirmative vote. We were able to change our company."
Combined sentence using an independent clause followed by a dependent or subordinate clause: "We appreciate the affirmative vote, which enabled us to change our company."

Varying Sentence Length and Structure

Sometimes there seems to be no need or reason to combine sentences in a given paragraph. Should a few be combined anyway? The answer is "yes." Experienced writers have learned that doing this will keep their readers from getting dulled by sameness of length and monotony of structure. Here are some ways to keep a reader's interest alive with a variety of sentences.

- *Mix long and short sentences.* Beginning writers tend to overuse short, simple sentences, which quickly become monotonous. Accomplished writers know that by alternating long and short they will keep reader interest.
- *Use a question, command, or exclamation.* The most commonly used sentence is the declarative sentence, which is a statement. However, a carefully placed question, command, or exclamation is an effective way to achieve sentence variety.

Question:	"Have you considered changing your health insurance company?"
Command:	"Act before March 1st to lock in this rate."
Exclamation:	"Congratulations!"

- *Vary the beginnings of sentences.* Every sentence doesn't have to start with the subject—a noun or an article–noun construction. Use different parts of speech to begin sentences. A writer can achieve variety by beginning, for example, with an adverb or a prepositional phrase.

Usual article–noun subject beginning: "The company slowly began to accept the inevitable."
Beginning with an adverb: "Slowly, the company began to accept the inevitable."

- *Use different methods to join ideas.*
  1. Merge ideas with a compound predicate. A sentence with a compound predicate contains more than one verb, but the subject is not repeated before the second verb.

Separate sentences: "We value your trust. We renew our dedication."
Sentences joined with a compound predicate: "We value your trust and renew our dedication."

2. *Merge ideas with an* -ing *modifier.* An excellent way to achieve sentence variety is by occasionally joining two sentences with an *-ing* modifier. An *-ing* modifier indicates that two actions are occurring simultaneously.

   Separate sentences: "The chairperson looked around the conference table. She saw many puzzled faces."
   Sentences joined with an -ing *modifier:* Looking around the conference table, the chairperson saw many puzzled faces."

   When using *-ing* modifiers be careful not to create confusion with a dangling modifier. This would have occurred, for example, if you had written, "The chairperson saw many puzzled faces looking around the conference table."

3. Merge ideas using a past participle as a modifier. A sentence that contains a *to be* or helping verb and a past participle can be changed to one with a past participle modifier.

   Separate sentences: "Car drivers are shocked by high gas prices. Some drivers have decided to carpool."
   Sentences joined with a past participle modifier: "Shocked by high gas prices, some drivers have decided to carpool."

4. Merge ideas with an appositive. To combine two short, choppy sentences use an appositive, that is a word or group of words that renames or describes a noun or pronoun.

   Separate sentences: "Carlotta is the new head of human resources. She is an accomplished public speaker."
   Sentences joined with an appositive: "Carlotta, the new head of human resources, is an accomplished public speaker."

5. Merge ideas with a relative clause. Relative clauses can add sophistication to your writing. A relative clause begins with *who, which,* or *that* and describes a noun or pronoun. It can join two simple sentences in a longer, more complex sentence.

   Separate sentences: "Enclosed you will find your initial transaction statement. It is being issued by the new publicly traded company."

Sentences joined with a relative clause: "Enclosed you will find your initial transaction statement, which is being issued by the new publicly traded company."

Almost all of the preceding ways to achieve variety of sentence length and structure are demonstrated in the following letter.

Dear Shareholder:

Congratulations! Enclosed you will find your initial transaction statement, which is being issued by the new publicly traded company, Caravaggio Financial Services, Inc. It is a confirmation of the number of shares you now own, and no further action is required on your part.

We appreciate the affirmative vote from our policyholders and the final approval by regulators, which enabled us to convert from a mutual company to shareholder ownership. We believe this was an important and critical step to ensure the future success of our company.

As a publicly traded company, listed under the symbol "CFS" on the Toronto Stock Exchange, we begin the new millennium with a more flexible form of organization that will enable us to deliver quality, reliable insurance and investment products, while striving to meet our commitment to deliver outstanding shareholder value.

During the past 75 years, we valued the trust placed in us by our policyholders and customers. Now, we also value your trust as a shareholder. With your continued support, we renew our dedication to serve you today and in the future.

Sincerely

Michael M. Caravaggio, Jr.

Observing Parallelism

Parallelism is another effective way of being reader-oriented. Parallelism, or parallel construction, is the balancing of two or more words, phrases, or clauses. To put it another way, words, phrases, and clauses that serve the same function should be put in the same grammatical form—nouns, verbs, participles, and so forth. Because parallelism makes a list or series of ideas easier to understand and follow, it is a good idea to employ it with numbered or bulleted lists in your memos, letters, or reports.

Unparallel sentence structure: Some people think the tax code is too complex, favors the rich, and it needs to be changed.

Unparallel structure: Some want the federal budget surplus used to lower tax rates by doubling the child tax credit and to boost the deduction for married working couples. Eliminating the Social Security earnings limit is another way.

Parallel structure: Some want the federal budget surplus used to lower tax rates by doubling the child tax credit, boosting the deduction for married working couples, and eliminating the Social Security earnings limit.

Always use parallelism in a bulleted or numbered list, for example:

Here are three of the proposals for using the federal budget surplus to lower taxes:

- Double the child tax credit.
- Boost the deduction for married working couples.
- Eliminate the Social Security earnings limit.

Using Active and Passive Voice Deliberately

Voice refers to the interaction of subject and verb. When the subject performs the action of the verb, the sentence is in the active voice. When the subject receives the action of the verb, the sentence is in the passive voice.

Active voice: The senior analyst researches and designs compensation systems.
Passive voice: Compensation systems are researched and designed by the senior analyst.

The active voice is recommended for business writing for several reasons:

- The active voice is more reader-based. It makes it easy for the reader to see "who did what" or what something means.
- The active voice is also reader-based because it is more clear and concise. To form the passive voice you must use some form of the verb *to be* with the main verb. This is why it takes more words to say the same thing in the passive voice.
- The active voice makes the writer seem more vigorous and in charge.

There is, however, one very useful function for the passive voice in business communication. This function appeared in Chapter 8 as one way to backload negative news. Because it dilutes the force of the sentence, the passive voice is ideal when you are dealing with difficult people and issues. The passive voice will make the bad news appear less personal or confrontational.

> *Active voice—negative news:* "Some employees have complained about the new policy."
> *Same news—passive voice:* "Some complaints have been received about the new policy."

Chapter 8 demonstrated how to organize a total business document around a central idea; Chapter 9 how to make ideas flow through a document. Chapter 10 has provided the techniques needed to complete the document and achieve its goals. The business and government writer can now say:

1. I know how to make the central idea of my total document flow through individual paragraphs. I can make it flow directly *down from* my central idea in the frontloaded pattern or flow *away from* my central idea in the backloaded pattern. Now my documents will have more effective paragraphs—the ones that will bring about the changes I desire.
2. I know how to create sentences within those paragraphs that will have clarity, strength, and interest for my reader.

III

Memos, Letters, and E-Mail

11

Writing Memos and Letters that Achieve Your Goals

The goal of Part III is to apply the principles of reader-based communication to a variety of typical writing situations that managers and employees face every day in business and government. Chapter 11 concerns the basic purpose, organization, and expression common to both memos and letters. Chapter 12 will demonstrate ways to organize, write, and revise a variety of memos that have either good news or simple routine information to convey. These are called frontloaded, or direct, messages. In Chapter 13 we will organize, write, and revise a group of memos that have negative news. These are termed backloaded, deferred load, or indirect messages. The same steps will be followed for letters in Chapters 14 and 15.

Memos, whether hard copy or e-mail, are the primary form of internal communication within corporate and governmental offices. They are used for vertical and horizontal communication whenever face-to-face communication is impractical or a permanent record is desirable. Vertically memos go up and down the corporate ladder: from managers down to employees and upward from employees up to management. Horizontally they flow back and forth among fellow employees. They can even be used for external communications with customers, suppliers, or other interested outsiders.

Memos are informal, versatile, and infinitely adaptable for senders and receivers. They can run for several pages but are usually just one to two pages. With today's workplace pressures the shorter or more concise the better. Lincoln's Gettysburg Address, cited as a model of concise force in Chapter 7, fits on one page. The Declaration of Independence will fit on two pages. Whether short or long, memos have primary and secondary functions.

Primary functions of memos include: informing people about situations and issues and changing people's perception of ideas and issues.

Secondary functions of memos include:

- Communicating responsibility and deadlines for actions
- Establishing a file record of decisions, agreements, and policies
- Serving as a vehicle for short reports or as a basis for formal reports and internal proposals
- Helping to bring new personnel up to date
- Replacing personal contact with people you have personal difficulties with. For example, the Schubert brothers, who were leaders of the American theater for over 40 years, often refused to talk to each other. They communicated with memos. If you have to go this route extra care must be taken to maintain a positive tone at all times.
- Handling people who make a habit of ignoring spoken directions. Even presidents of the United States sometimes have their spoken wishes ignored. President Kennedy handled such a problem between him and the State Department with memos. "I have discovered finally," he said, "that the best way to deal with State is to send over memos. They can forget phone conversations, but a memorandum is something which, by their system, has to be answered."

Memos can also be an effective means of stopping unjustified, time-consuming requests. When someone makes what you consider an unwarranted demand or request, tell her or him to put it in a memo—"just for the record." This tactic can save a lot of wasted time and energy.

Letters, whether mailed through the postal service, faxed, or e-mailed, are also a crucial form of communication in business and government. They remain the key form of external communication with customers, suppliers, governmental agencies, or other interested outsiders.

Letters, like memos, have the primary functions of informing people about situations and issues and changing people's perception of ideas and issues. But they also fulfill a variety of other functions:

- Following up on oral discussions by clarifying or confirming points discussed or agreed on.
- Replacing oral discussion when personal contact has proven problematic, for example, in collections and disputes.

- Creating a permanent or file record. Signed letters containing prices and warrantees may be legally binding when sent to a customer, so they require greater care even than memos and e-mails.
- Promoting action by individuals, companies, and government agencies.
- Selling services, products, and ideas either one on one or through mass mailings.

THE ORGANIZATION, FORMATTING, AND WRITING OF MEMOS AND LETTERS

Both memos and letters should follow the triple plays shown in Chapter 6 that apply to all forms of business communication.

Three Ages	**Three Phases**	**Three Stages**
Yesterday	Purpose	Think
Today	Organization	Write
Tomorrow	Expression	Revise

Memos and letters for business and government are built upon three ages:

Yesterday. No communication exists in a vacuum. The memos and letters written every day in every organization always have a background of people and issues. Before writing, it is important to stop and consider the relevant people and issues. What was said in the past on this matter? Who said it? What was decided? What action was taken? By whom?

Today. When the writer has the answers to these and other questions, he or she appreciates how much the *yesterday* influences "today's" writing task. The greater our awareness of yesterday, the keener our focus will be today. The keener our focus is today the more likely we are to achieve the changes that we seek.

Tomorrow. What is written "today" will have results tomorrow. While we always want these to be positive, sometimes they are not. We may not seek negative outcomes but they happen. These are the unintended results of workplace messages. The goal is to write *today* with sufficient clarity and purpose to produce only positive results. *Tomorrow* often consists of *two* audiences or sets of readers. What we write today will affect our intended reader, which is our primary audience. But that same reader may pass our message on to others; and they become our secondary audience. What effect will our writing have on them? We always want positive results with any audience.

Memos and letters are developed in three phases:

Purpose. Memos and letters have the same four purposes as every other form of business communication: information, persuasion, results or changes, and good will or public relations

These purposes exist to a greater or lesser degree in every business document. For example, when we set out to create a procedure memo, we have to provide information about the procedures to be followed. At the same time we must persuade our readers that the steps we propose are viable. If we do this we have a much better chance of getting the results or changes we desire. And we will leave our readers with a feeling of good will toward our organization and ourselves.

No matter how complex or subtle its ideas the purpose of a memo or letter should be reducible to one clear central idea. If this cannot be done, chances are the document will lack unity and make comprehension difficult for the reader.

Writing a concise yet specific subject line is the first step in limiting your memos and letters to a single topic. This does not mean the document cannot cover a number of different points. It means that the writer must decide what the main idea is and subordinate the remaining ideas to it. At this point the writer may want to review the outlining method explained in Chapter 6.

Organization. Memos and letters will be more effective when they arrange their ideas in a reader-based structure by selecting one of the following patterns of development:

- *Chronological:* by following a time order, such as distant past to recent past to present to future, to show how a government program such as Social Security or a corporation's response to sexual harassment in the workplace has evolved.
- *Spatial:* by following a pattern of place or location, such as the regional, national, and global sales of a corporation or the distribution of assistance through the International Monetary Fund.
- *Logical:* by following one of the following patterns:
  1. Cause and effect: useful, for example, in trouble-shooting manuals.
  2. Comparison-contrast: effective for measuring units of a company against each other, or measuring one company against another.
  3. Classification and division: for showing different units according to a consistent principle, for example the divisions of a company according to their functions.

4. Illustration: for showing concrete examples of abstract or technical terms.

- *Problem–analysis–solution:* for describing a problem facing a corporation or government agency; why it exists and what can be done about it.
- *Order of importance:* according to order of importance from the least to the greatest, which is climactic order, or from the most important to the least, which is descending order. This logical order works especially well in tandem with the preceding problem–analysis–solution pattern. For example, you are writing about the possibility of a work stoppage in the automobile industry or a major urban hospital system. You could use ascending order for a list of the weakest to the strongest measures that could be taken. Or you could use descending order and go from the most stringent measures down to the mildest.

Expression. Purpose and organization alone do not guarantee a successful memo. If a purposeful and logically organized memo or letter is written with a writer-based style instead of reader-based, the document will probably lose much of its persuasive force. As a result an opportunity for positive change may be lost.

Memos and letters are created in three stages:

Think. The thinking stage of writing includes considering the "yesterday" of people and issues and deciding on the primary purpose of the memo or letter you're about to write. The thinking stage of an individual document reflects upon the four phases of purpose, information, persuasion, changes or results, and good will or public relations and moves forward with the following four questions:

1. *Information from the reader's perspective:* What are the facts or issues as my reader sees them?
2. *Persuasion:* What do they mean as I see them? Precisely how do our views differ?
3. *Changes or results:* How do I change my reader's perception to work together with mine?
4. *Good will or public relations:* What do we do together now to reach our shared goal?

Write. To supply the answers to these questions in a reader based memo or letter, the writer will need to use: correct formatting, logical organization, and effective expression.

Revise. The roots of the word *revise* mean not simply to "correct" or "edit" but to "see again." Seeing a document again means stepping back from it and rereading it as if someone else wrote it. Most writers do this in two ways:

1. As they write, by changing and improving the content and expression sentence by sentence or paragraph by paragraph.
2. After they write, by changing and improving the content and expression of a complete first draft.

The Format or Physical Appearance of Memos

Headings

Memos are written either on standard printed forms or with letterheads printed or generated with computer templates. You can use those provided by companies such as Corel or Microsoft, or design your own.

Regardless of the type of stationery, all memos have the following headings:

TO: Write the name and job titles of the receiver as well as those who will receive a copy of the memo. Place job titles either on the same line as the receiver's name separated by a comma, or on the following line.

FROM: Write your full name and title on the same line, separated by a comma, or on the following line. Most writers initial their name as a sign that whether they have typed the memo they are in fact the sender and are responsible for its contents.

DATE: Write the date by using the short numbered version or by spelling out the full name of the month. The latter way is recommended to avoid confusion in other parts of the world.

SUBJECT: Write the purpose or central idea of your memo using all capital letters. A vague phrase or topic is not a reader-based subject line. While a complete sentence is not necessary, make sure you write a clear, specific, easily understood thought. When you do this you are telling your reader in a very concise way what is to come. Many newspaper headlines provide models of good subject lines, for example: "Power Authority Set to Choose Buyer of Two Reactors Today."

If you find it difficult to limit your subject to no more than two lines, you might not be ready to write yet. Try going back to your purpose in writing the particular memo.

What follows are some examples of subject lines.

Writer-based subject line: DRESS CODE
Reader-based subject line: APRIL 15 CHANGE IN DRESS CODE

Writer-based subject line: TAX CONSEQUENCES
Reader-based subject line: INFORMING INVESTORS OF TAX CONSEQUENCES

Writer-based subject line: EMPLOYEE BENEFITS
Reader-based subject line: CHANGES IN EMPLOYEE BENEFIT ADMINISTRATION

ENCLOSURES: when needed, the enclosures, sometimes known as attachments, should be briefly listed at the end of your memo, below your signature.

SIGNATURE: you may choose to sign your memo instead of initialing your name on the "From" line. If so, omit a printed name block.

Following is a standard memo format without letterhead:

MEMORANDUM

To: All Pittsfield Corporation employees
Director, Human Resources

Date: October 21, 2000

From: Michael J. Barrett MJB

Subject: CHANGES IN EMPLOYEE BENEFIT ADMINISTRATION

The Format or Physical Appearance of Letters

Letters generally offer a greater choice in formatting than memos. Formatting refers to the arrangement of the following individual elements of a letter:

1. Letterhead or return address
2. Date line
3. Inside address
4. Salutation or greeting
5. Optional subject line
6. Body or paragraphs
7. Complimentary close
8. Signature
9. Writer's printed name
10. Reference initials
11. Enclosure line
12. Copy line

The full-block and partial-block are the most common formatting choices, while some writers and companies choose the simplified or the indented forms. These are summarized below.

1. **Full block.** All of the individual elements are arranged flush left on the page, single-spaced, with a line skipped between each of the individual elements. Examples of the full block style appear on pages 114–15, 178–79,186–87, and 205.
2. **Partial or semi-block.** All elements except the return address and date, the complimentary closing, signature, and printed name are flush left. Everything is single-spaced except for the double spacing between paragraphs. Pages 174–75, 209–10 and 215–16 give examples of this partial block style.
3. **Simplified style.** A full block format that omits the salutation and complimentary closing lines. However, it includes a capitalized subject line like a memo without printing the term *Subject.* It skips three spaces after the subject line before beginning the body of the letter; and skips four spaces after the body before printing the writer's name and title in capital letters on the same line. This style, fostered by the Administrative Management Society, is closer to the memo format and is more suited to business-to-business communication than business-to-customer writing. Examples of the simplified letter style can be seen on pages 180–81 and 195–96.
4. **Indent style.** Exactly like the partial block style with one exception. It indents each paragraph of the body of the letter five spaces instead of skipping a line between paragraphs. Although the indented style is losing favor, an example of it is shown on page 191. If you use the indented style, do not double space between paragraphs. This is redundant.

A business letter using full block formatting style:

Seraphic Motor Sales, Inc.
1654 Longleat Drive
P.O. Box 550
San Giovanni, CA 91101

May 1, 2000

Mr. Edmund Sydney
1605 Elizabeth Drive
Torrance, CA 90509

Dear Mr. Sydney:

Thank you. . . .

Thank you for selecting a Seraphic Certified Previously Owned Vehicle. Seraphic, long proud of building the finest vehicles in the world, now sets a new standard for previously owned vehicles.

For your valued opinion. . . .

We are interested in hearing from you, our valued customer, regarding your experience with Seraphic Certified. We would appreciate your taking just a few moments to complete the enclosed questionnaire. Your comments will help us continue improving Seraphic's renowned level of service and satisfaction.

Again, thank you for choosing a Seraphic Certified Previously Owned Vehicle. We trust that you will enjoy the quality and security of Seraphic Certified for many years to come.

Sincerely,

Philip Spenser

Philip Spenser
Corporate Manager
Previously Owned Vehicle Operations

CEP: ajt

Enclosure

Graphic highlighting

Refers to the use of **bold face**, *italics*, and <u>underlining</u> as well as numbers and bullets to highlight the division of main and subordinate ideas in your document. As people's schedules get steadily tighter, business writers today use more graphic highlighting than ever before. As in the above letter, graphic highlighting is used to focus the reader immediately on the key points of the document.

Properly used, graphic highlighting can help you to organize, arrange, and emphasize your key points. More importantly, graphic highlighting gives your readers the cues they need to navigate easily and quickly through your document.

Bold. Heavier, darker typeface useful for bringing your reader's attention to: the principal sections of a memo, letter, or report; the leading words of numbered or bulleted lists.

Italics. Slanting typeface used for a variety of purposes:

- Titles of books, magazines, and newspapers; computer software; websites
- Foreign language words used in an English sentence
- Names of aircraft, spacecraft, specific ships, and trains
- Words as words, for example, the words *yesterday, today,* and *tomorrow.*

Underlining. In handwritten or typed papers underlining is used in place of italics. It is sometimes used to emphasize words or ideas. However, this function can be distracting to your reader if overused.

Bullets. Used to highlight different or equal aspects of a topic. They can be used whenever there is no time order and no need to refer to the individual entries later in your document.

Numbers. Used to list subdivisions of a main idea when there is some chronological order involved or order of importance. Numbers are also used instead of bullets when you need to refer to the individual points later in the document.

The Choice of Language and Expression

Diplomatic or political savvy. One important way that memos and letters demonstrate how reader based they truly are is by their level diplomacy or political savvy. Writers of such messages don't lie; they don't avoid difficult situations. But they are shrewd and prudent in a common sense way; they are canny and tactful.

A politically wise hospital superintendent, for example, would not send out a memo recommending that very old and chronically ill patients not be resuscitated after heart failure. If she thought such actions were right, a more tactful thing to do would be to tell her staff orally or mark such a memo "private" and distribute it accordingly.

Conversational tone. Most business writing today, except for formal reports and proposals, is conversational in tone, but in a descending scale. Letters, while still conversational, are more formal than memos. E-mails are the least formal. Like good conversation effective memos are friendly, filled with personal references, and with few exceptions, informal in language and tone. E-mails once considered out of reach for any norms of grammar and language are beginning to find limits of their own.

Every memo or letter is a personal contact. Within limits of diplomatic or political common sense, let your writing style express your personality. Even a routine form memo or letter can be made more personal and conversational if you use the receiver's first name in the opening sentence.

Use personal pronouns such as "you" and "yours" frequently. If you have negative news, however, use "you" and "yours" not to assess blame but to suggest positive aspects of the bad news situation. Use pronouns such as "we" infrequently, and "I" even more sparingly.

Concise style. Most memos and letters can be polite, savvy, conversational, and informative and still be brief. Longwinded, background-filled narratives are not the way to go. Follow the guidelines for plain English language developed in Chapter 7.

Freedom from internal barriers. Neither memos nor letters can be effective when they directly or indirectly make people feel unwelcome or like outsiders. As discussed in Chapter 4, all forms of business communication should be free of ethnocentrism, sexist or gender-biased expression, sexual orientation judgments or innuendoes, age-biased expression, denigrations of physical and emotional constitution, and economic status.

The Opening or Introductory Paragraph

Once you have a clear, specific subject line, expanding it into a complete sentence will give you a central idea for your direct opening paragraph. This sentence should give direction or tell your reader where you are going. For this reason it is sometimes said to contain the *controlling* idea of the entire message. Expressed in your introduction or opening paragraph it will function as the central idea of your entire document.

If you are writing an indirect message this central idea will be deferred until a later paragraph. But it will still be the controlling or central idea of your message.

Longwinded opening:	"I would like to begin this memo by reviewing the issues and concerns addressed in our recent meeting."
Concise opening style:	"Here are the three points we agreed to implement on April 5th."

The Development or Body of Memo and Letters

Memos and letters are organized in the two ways, described in Chapter 8: frontloaded or backloaded.

Routine memos that are typically frontloaded:

1. *Information and procedures memos:* announcing a new or revised company plan or policy; explaining new procedures to be followed

2. *Request memos:* for information, suggestions, permission to change procedures
3. *Reply memos:* approving requests, explaining procedures
4. *Confirmation memos:* of oral agreements, orders, or changes

Routine letters that are usually frontloaded:

1. *Order letters:* placing or replying to orders for products or services
2. *Claim letters:* requesting replacement of defective products or compensation for poor service
3. *Information and action letters:* requesting information about products or services

Frontload all memos and letters that contain positive, neutral, or only somewhat negative news by placing the central idea at the beginning of the document in two ways:

1. Give your reader your main point or reason for writing in a concise, direct, and specific subject line.

Vague subject line:	OFFICE EXPENSES
Specific subject line:	PROPER AUTHORIZATION OF OFFICE EXPENSES
Vague subject line:	PHILOSOPHY AND POLICY
Specific subject line:	UPDATE OF NOVEMBER 11, 1999 EMPLOYMENT PHILOSOPHY AND POLICY STATEMENT

2. Expand the subject line into a fuller statement or central idea in the opening paragraph of your memo.

Unclear opening paragraph:
Recently I've been getting requests from employees asking why it seems to take so long to get some of their expenses paid back. I've come up with some possible solutions that I wanted to go over with you.
Direct, frontloaded opening paragraph:
Please submit all requests for reimbursement of office expenses according to the following procedures.

Unclear opening paragraph:
In January I issued a memo outlining our Equal Employment posture towards employment applicants and for our present em-

ployees in regard to promotion, compensation, and otherwise providing terms, conditions, and privileges of employment.
Direct, frontloaded opening paragraph:
The purpose of this memo is to repeat the March 17 Equal Employment philosophy and policy statement and expand on nondiscrimination factors of age and disability.

Routine memos that are usually backloaded or indirect:

1. Memos rejecting ideas and requests
2. Memos declining invitations
3. Memos giving bad news to employees

Routine letters that are typically backloaded or indirect:

1. Letters refusing requests for information—action
2. Letters declining invitations
3. Letters denying claims and adjustments

Defer or backload all memos and letters that contain seriously negative news for the receiver by deferring or placing the central idea at a later stage in the message. This doesn't mean that we should leave our readers completely in the dark at the beginning of such a document. Get to the bad news gradually and objectively.

An ancient Chinese proverb says, "Don't use a hatchet to remove a fly from a friend's forehead." In other words, it's enough that our readers are about to get some bad news, there's nothing to be gained by antagonizing them with a combative or demeaning subject line.

On the other hand, we shouldn't be so indirect that our opening paragraph becomes an unmagical mystery tour.

1. State your main point with neutral, objective, unemotional language in the subject line.

Emotional, combative subject line:	RECENT UNWORKABLE PROPOSALS
Indirect, deferred load subject line:	FLEXTIME SUGGESTIONS
Emotional, negative subject line:	LAST YEAR'S DISAPPOINTMENTS
Indirect, deferred load subject line:	YEAR-END REVIEW

2. Expand the subject line gradually. Follow the principles of writing a reader-based document. Show that you are aware of and value

your reader's opinion, even when you have come to a different conclusion about its merits.

- Adopt a personal tone and avoid any direct mention of the problem/issue in your opening paragraph.
- Instead mention shared goals and other understandings that you have in common.
- Give reasons for the unhappy change or decision you are about to reveal
- Treat the change as something that involves and affects you, the sender, and the receiver.
- Offer alternatives or face saving proposals.

Direct, combative opening paragraph:

Last week you submitted to me some ideas for changing schedules, which just won't work. I wish to point out to you now why your flextime proposals will cause problems for everybody.

Indirect, deferred load opening paragraph:

Jennifer, thanks very much for forwarding your proposal for a flextime schedule for your department. I appreciate the creative input. I can always count on receiving fresh new ideas from you.

Direct, sour opening paragraph:

Last year we had some really disappointing results in several areas that are important if we are going to avoid being also-rans in our industry.

Indirect, deferred load opening paragraph:

Last year our industry was faced with many challenges. Thanks to our continuing spirit of dedication and teamwork we rose to those challenges and improved our position in many areas.

The Closing or Conclusion of the Memo or Letter

Whether frontloaded or backloaded, all memos and letters have a wrap-up or conclusion that is placed in its own separate paragraph.

Closing a frontloaded memo or letter. Frontloaded communications can conclude as clearly and directly as they began by using the following methods:

- Refer briefly to the central idea as it appeared in your subject line.

- Politely tell the reader what mental and physical actions you want, for example, a decision, a choice, a meeting, a phone call, a hard copy written response, or an e-mail.
- Suggest a time frame for these mental and physical actions, that is, give the date by which you would like these actions to be started or completed. By doing this you are specifying when you expect to achieve your shared goals.

Closing a deferred load memo or letter. The care you have taken in delivering negative news indirectly should extend to the conclusion. The more unwelcome the news you gave your reader, the more important it is to end on an upbeat, pleasant note. Most of all make it clear that the matter is concluded.

- Extend best wishes or, depending on the situation, suggest other avenues that your reader might pursue.
- Remain confident that your decision was correct. Don't refer back to the bad news or apologize. Apologizing suggests doubt in the wisdom of your decision.
- Avoid clichéd endings that may only prolong the unpleasantness. The decision has been made. Closing with expressions such as, "If there are any further questions, please do not hesitate to call me," will probably appear insincere anyway.
- Remember that even negative news can be presented with reader benefits and shared goals in mind. If nothing else the shared goal is to move on.

Revise. Before printing and sending off your document it should be revised. You may have already done much of this sentence by sentence or paragraph by paragraph as you wrote. However, it is still necessary to reread the entire message with a critical eye. Rewriting is the twin of improved thinking. It requires us to be truly open-minded and objective.

This process works best when we allow some time to pass before rereading what we have written. The reason for this is that when we are not so close to what we *intended* to say we can judge more clearly if we *actually wrote* what we intended. Whenever possible, let your document rest; then reread it imagining yourself as the person receiving the memo or letter. Your goal will be to improve your document in two areas:

- *Content.* Review your message to make sure that it is:
  1. Reader-based with shared goals
  2. Has correct language usage and grammatical accuracy
  3. Shows a cue based organization of ideas in paragraphs

4. Displays correctness and variety of sentences

- *Expression.* Review your message and remove any of the following:
  1. Internally caused barriers to successful communication discussed in Chapter 4: ethnocentrism, sexist or gender-biased expression, sexual orientation judgments or innuendoes, age-biased expression, physical and emotional constitution, and economic status.
  2. Externally caused barriers to successful communication listed in Chapter 5: incorrect formatting of your document, absence or inappropriate choice of graphic highlighting.

Revising what we have written is always hard work. In a sense it requires us to redo the job that we thought we had just completed. Not just do it over, but do it better. Is it worth the effort? Clearly it is worth it, because we believe we have a responsibility to think and communicate effectively.

Using the Channel of E-mail for Sending Memos

In just a few years e-mail has become one of the most popular forms of business communication for internal and external communication. Computer networks connect senders and receivers of messages using telephone lines.

The *e* in e-mail, contrary to popular belief, does not signify electronic mail. It was coined by Steve Dorner of Urbana, Illinois, the inventor of the e-mail software used by millions of people, as a tribute to the great American writer Eudora Welty. This should remind us that just zapping out e-mails with no regard for grammar, organization, and expression is not a good idea.

Another reason for not sending e-mails indiscriminately is that they might well be monitored. According to the American Management Association the percentage of employers that store and review e-mail messages has grown from 14.9% in 1997 to 38.2% (est.) in 2000.[1]

What companies look for in e-mail messages…and why

Messages with *.exe* attachments, like animated movies or any attachment larger than a megabyte	They overload networks, slow computers, and could crash the system.

Subject lines with the designation *Fwd* or *Re* appearing several times in one message	These are likely to be forwarded jokes and back-and-forth chats.
Scores of messages sent in one day by a single employee to people outside the office	They overload the system and suggest the sender is goofing off.
Headlines with phrases like *Job Hunt* or *Resume Enclosed*	No explanation necessary.
Words like *confidential* and *proprietary*	Company secrets may be divulged, even inadvertently.
Racial slurs or words like *sex* and *babe*	Off-color or ethnic jokes can be grounds for lawsuits.

The channel of communication might be new but, like it or not, some of the old rules remain. Why? Because whatever channel we use, we are still sending a message. Whether we are using an antique typewriter or keyboarding an e-mail, our message must be reader based. It must be clear and well organized to convey our ideas. It must be concise and courteous in language and expression or it might not be welcomed by our readers. If this happens the advantages of e-mail will be outweighed by its disadvantages. Then we might as well go back to the typewriter.

Advantages of e-mail:

- It is fast
- It can send messages to many receivers simultaneously
- It is cheap
- It is convenient

Disadvantages of e-mail:

- It is often carelessly written
- It can cause communication glut
- It is almost eternal
- It can become a form of entertainment, legitimate or otherwise

Standard e-mail headings. Although systems differ, the following are the standard elements:

To: the e-mail address of the receivers

Cc: stands for the courtesy copy that will go to the names listed on this entry
Bcc: stands for blind courtesy copy. Since this information is kept from the people indicated as receivers the practice of sending blind copies is considered duplicitous or unethical. However, diplomatic or political common sense sometimes requires it.
Subject: this entry line serves the same purpose as the subject line in memos and some letters. It gives the central idea, or at least a preview of the central idea, of the whole message.
Attachments: this line is used for entering any files that you wish to send with your message.
The message: this is the content or message you wish to send by e-mail.

The golden rules of reader based e-Mail

Just as the "old" rules of organization and expression have not been fossilized by the new channels of communication, the basic human need for common sense and courtesy has not been outdated. It is not wise to deliver bad news badly and it is not wise to use new channels of communication badly. Neal L. Patterson, CEO of the Cerner Corporation learned this when he fired off an e-mail on March 13, 2001 loaded with words like "SICK" and "NEVER" shoulted in all capital letters and closing with threats of reduced employee benefits and layoffs. When the e-mail was posted on Yahoo, a message intended for company managers quickly became available to over 8,000 employees worldwide as well as stock analysts and investors. Result? The stock value of the company crashed 22 percent in three days.[3]

The fact that commonsense ideas are being ignored on all levels is clear not only from stories like this, but from the increased monitoring of e-mails in corporations and government agencies.

1. *Be courteous in expression.* The fact that we have a new channel of communication doesn't mean we should do in e-mail what we would never do face-to-face, or in a memo or letter.

   Demanding, ordering, or screaming is no more acceptable in e-mail than it is in speaking or in more traditional channels of written communication such as memos and letters. Instead of commanding someone to visit your website, ask politely with the simple, never outdated word *please.*
2. *Be correct in language.* Far from absolving the senders of e-mail messages, this new channel of communication should challenge the sender to be scrupulously correct in several areas.

   Carelessness and errors in sentence structure, grammar, and spelling are more glaring in proportion to the sophistication of the channel. Someone receiving your error-filled e-mail is likely to think, "With all the technology at his disposal you'd think he could tell the difference between *there* and *their*!"

Avoid cyberspeak in business e-mails. The use of *cul8r, lol,* and other cyberspeak expressions in a business setting will make your message look like adolescent chatter. After learning how to avoid legalese and other types of jargon, don't fall victim to a new form of the same old problem. Speak in plain English. Doing this carries with it the added advantage of confidence that your primary and secondary audiences will understand your message.

3. *Use a standard format.* There's room for variations in this still emerging channel, but a salutation or greeting as well as a closing is still preferred. It's also a good idea to use some type of subject line, as you would do in all memos and some letters. This simple reader-based addition will help your reader focus immediately on the purpose of the e-mail.

12

Writing and Revising Neutral and Good News Memos

CREATING FRONTLOADED INFORMATION AND PROCEDURE MEMOS

The single greatest purpose of business memo writing is to provide information and explain procedures. Like all memos they are sent through three channels: hard copy, fax, and e-mail. These are almost always internal, vertical communications sent down from upper management to lower-level employees or up from employees to management.

When we write such memos we want to get right to the point. This is why they are frontloaded or direct in organization and expression. However, they should not be abrupt or condescending in any way. Like all successful business communication they should always be courteous and positive in tone.

Information and procedure memos, like all expository writing, have three parts: introduction, development, and conclusion. Since they are frontloaded, information and procedure memos place the central idea up front in the introduction.

INTRODUCTION	**Picks up** the subject line preview **Expands** the subject line into a fully stated central idea
DEVELOPMENT	**Gives** the specific items of information **Gives** the reasons if necessary

CONCLUSION { **Refers back** to the central idea
Cues desired mental and physical action

1. *Central idea.* The process of creating a successful information memo begins with the choice of a central idea. This idea, which embodies the purpose of the memo, first appears in condensed form in the subject line. Then it is stated more fully in the opening paragraph of a frontloaded memo.
2. *The informal list.* With your central idea clearly in mind, make a list of the reasons and examples that might convey your central idea to your reader. Narrow the list down to the reasons and examples that will *most* clearly convey your central idea.
3. *Organizing the list into paragraphs.* This edited or final list will become the items in the bulleted or numbered list of a short memo or the paragraphs of a longer memo.
4. *Closing.* The final paragraph refers the reader back to the central idea of the opening and directs the reader toward some mental and physical action.

CREATING THE INFORMATION MEMO

Now let's see how we go about writing a specific information memo. Charles De Tore, president of Universal Insurance, has learned that some criticism has appeared in print. The article did not mention his company by name but implied that Universal has a growing number of present and former employees, as well as shareholders, who question its commitment to equal opportunity employment.

Situation: Charles J. De Tore, President of Universal Insurance, has learned that questions have been raised in the industry, and repeated in the press, about his companies' adherence to equal opportunities statutes. He wishes to restate and reinforce Universal's dedication to these statutes. Charles begins creating an informal list about the situation he needs to make a statement about as well as his needs and purpose. Then he needs to narrow the list down to create a central idea.

Situation:
1. Critics are questioning our commitment to equal opportunity hiring practices. ✗
2. We already established a policy last November. ✓

Need or purpose:
1. Inform upper-level people about continuing questions. ✓

2. Change their perception of the issue; make need more urgent. ✓
3. Set stage for the future observance of this policy. ✓

Creating the central idea: After reviewing the five entries on situation and need or purpose, Charles decides that perhaps the first entry about critics should be deleted. While he wants to be direct, he doesn't want to emphasize or begin on a defensive note. Next he will combine the four checked items into one clear summary statement of what's to come:

> REISSUE AND UPDATE OF NOVEMBER 11, 1999, EMPLOYMENT PHILOSOPHY AND POLICY STATEMENT

Now the writer expands this central idea from his subject line into his first paragraph.

> I think it is important at this time to repeat what I wrote on November 11, 1999, when I issued a memo outlining our Equal Employment posture, both toward employment applicants and for our present employees in regard to promotion, compensation, and otherwise providing terms, conditions, and privileges of employment. At this time I wish to repeat this philosophy and policy and expand upon nondiscrimination factors (i.e., age and disability).

Charles makes an informal list of possible reasons and ideas to develop and support his central idea.

1. We don't practice or tolerate discrimination. ✓
2. I stated this clearly in November. ✕
3. Critics are uninformed, have some other agenda. ✕
4. Always comply with all laws—federal, state, etc., about discrimination. ✓
5. Hiring is based on company needs and applicants' abilities. ✓
6. Firing never based on discriminatory motives. ✓
7. Have an obligation to our shareholders to employ the most qualified. ✓

The writer has edited or narrowed down this informal list to achieve single topic unity: looking over the list, he decided to omit items 2 and 3. They're not reader-based; they just show the writer's annoyance and impatience. They're also somewhat negative.

Rearrange the narrowed down informal list according to one of the logical patterns:

- *Chronological:* by time order

- *Spatial:* by a pattern of place or location
- *Logical:* by one of the following patterns:
  Cause and effect
  Comparison-contrast
  Classification and division
  Illustration
- *Problem–analysis–solution:* a problem, why it exists, what can be done about it
- *Importance:* order of importance from the least to the greatest, which is climactic order, or from the most important to the least, which is descending order. This logical order works well in tandem with the preceding problem–analysis–solution pattern.

Charles decides to use a combination of problem–analysis–solution and order of importance. He sees the problem as a continuing question about his companies' commitment to equal opportunity employment practices. What can be done is to make a clearer restatement of their philosophy and policy. This statement will be written in descending order from the most important down.

1. We have an obligation to our shareholders to employ the most qualified
2. Hiring is based on company needs and applicants' abilities
3. We don't practice or tolerate discrimination
4. We always comply with all laws—federal, state, etc., about discrimination
5. Firing is never based on discriminatory motives

Now the writer has all the elements needed to write the *first draft* of an information memo.

TO: Regional Vice Presidents
Executive Council
Operating Committee

FROM: Charles J. De Tore, President

DATE: March 17, 2000

SUBJECT: REISSUE OF NOVEMBER 11, 1999, EMPLOYMENT PHILOSOPHY AND POLICY STATEMENT

I think it is important at this time to repeat what I wrote on November 11, 1999, when I issued a memo outlining our Equal Employment posture. This related to our policy toward employment applicants, which in turn relates to what is used for our present employees in regard to promotion, compensation, and otherwise providing terms, conditions, and privileges of employment. At this time I wish to repeat this philosophy and policy and expand upon nondiscrimination factors (i.e., age and disability).

This issue concerns people looking for employment with our company and people who are already employed by our company in regard to promotion, their rate of pay, etc. It also covered terms, conditions, and privileges of employment.

At this point in time, I would like to repeat everything I previously said on this issue. In particular, I would like to repeat this philosophy and policy and tell you more about certain non-discrimination factors.

Each and every one of you are requested to take all possible steps to guarantee that the following is in spirit as well as in form the policy which governs all our actions.

Universal Insurance Companies
Employment Philosophy and Policy

> We have an obligation to our policyholders to determine realistically any needs we have for employees and we must select those who are in our eyes the best qualified personal to handle there insurance business.
>
> The company's personal requirements and each individual applicant's qualifications will be the sole basis for how we hire, promote, compensate, and provide terms, conditions, and privileges of employment.
>
> Fulfilling those obligations we won't practice, tolerate, or condone discrimination because of someone's race, color, or religion. Nor will we tolerate discrimination based on age or disability.
>
> Every law, whether federal, state, or urban, about employment will be complied with at all times.
>
> We will not in any eventuality hereinafter terminate any person to make room for someone else based on such reasons. In the same manner we have not heretofore tolerated any discrimination against prospective employees based on race, color, or religion.

The Vice President, acting at my behest, will continue to work together with you in the establishment and maintenance of employment procedures consistent with and in support of the aforementioned policy.

Charles J. DeTore

President

Revising the Information Memo

Spell-check has not highlighted anything on this memo. This doesn't mean that it is error free. Actually there are three errors of language and grammar in this memo. *Personal, there,* and *company's,* are correctly spelled, but they are the wrong words. In the first and second policy paragraphs, *personal,* an adjective, is used when the noun *personnel* is needed. *There,* a demonstrative pronoun, is used incorrectly, instead of the possessive pronoun *their*. In the second paragraph of the policy statement, the singular possessive *company's* is used instead of the plural possessive *companies'*.

If a careful review shows no errors of language and grammar, the remaining elements of content and expression should be reviewed. This review will show where to revise and improve the first draft.

Formatting revisions

- Headings: All headings are correct except for the following two:
  Subject line. The subject of this memo could be more accurately termed a *reissue and update* rather than simply a *reissue,* because the author states in the second paragraph that he will "expand upon" some nondiscrimination factors.
  Signature line. When a memo is signed the printed name block is usually omitted.
- *Single topic.* The memo does deal with a single topic, namely a reissue and update of an existing policy. The single nature of the memo could have been underscored by the use of transition words and phrases.
- *Graphics.* The five elements of the employment philosophy and policy are indented and could also be numbered for additional emphasis and ease of reference later. In addition, memos are usually aligned left on the page rather than justified left and right as done here. Bulleted or numbered lists should use parallelism, that is, beginning each entry with the same part of speech.

Language and expression revisions

- *Diplomatic and political savvy.* Diplomatic awareness was shown in the earlier decision to omit any reference to outside criticism. However, the choice of the term *posture* in the opening is questionable. To some it may suggest an external, artificial appearance as opposed to a real commitment.
- *Conversational tone.* This type of information memo might call for a less conversational tone than usual in memos. Contractions such as *won't* are usually acceptable and even preferred but in this formal statement of policy *will not* is probably more appropriate.

Legalese words and phrases such as *heretofore, hereinafter, at my behest,* and *aforementioned* in the closing should be changed to plain English.

- *Concise style.* Many sentences contain redundancies and wordy writing such as "at this point in time," "relates to what is used for," "in any eventuality."
- *Parallelism and variety.* Parallelism, or beginning each entry of a bulleted or numbered list with the same part of speech, could be improved in the five-item philosophy and policy list. Variety of sentence length and structure could also be improved.
- Internally caused barriers to successful communication was discussed in Chapter 4. The memo is free of any direct barriers such as ethnocentrism, sexist or gender-biased expression, and age bias. However, it fails to include sexual orientation bias. Also, it might show even greater objectivity by putting the nondiscrimination list in alphabetical order

Organization revisions

- *Introduction.* This memo did not open effectively because it was writer-based instead of reader-based. This is revealed in two areas. First, it opens with all *I*s and no *you*s. In addition, it took four paragraphs to expand its subject line into a clearly stated central idea. What needs to be frontloaded or stated directly can be done in one or at most two paragraphs.
- *Development.* There is a logical pattern of development based on chronology, that is, past, present, and future. There is also an implied problem–analysis–solution pattern at work, which could be more effectively organized.
- *Conclusion.* The last paragraph refers back to the subject of the memo, but might have more impact if a time frame were included.

Here is how this information memo would read if all the suggested revisions were followed.

TO: Regional Vice Presidents
Executive Council
Operating Committee

FROM: Charles J. De Tore, President

DATE: March 17, 2000

SUBJECT: REISSUE AND UPDATE OF NOVEMBER 11, 1999, EMPLOYMENT PHILOSOPHY AND POLICY STATEMENT

Today we are reissuing the Equal Employment Policy statement that you received on November 11, 1999. As you will recall, that statement covering present employees and new job applicants specifically referred to promotion and compensation, and other terms, conditions, and privileges of employment important to all of us.

Today I wish to repeat this philosophy and expand on nondiscrimination to include factors of age and disability. Together we will take every possible step to assure that this policy governs our actions in spirit and in fact.

Universal Insurance Companies
Employment Philosophy and Policy

1. We have an obligation to our policyholders to select the best qualified personnel to handle their insurance business.
2. We will hire, promote, compensate, and provide terms of employment solely on the basis of the companies' personnel requirements and each individual's qualifications.
3. We will not practice or condone discrimination because of age, color, disability, national origin, race, religion, sex, or sexual orientation.
4. We will comply with the letter and spirit of all national, state, and local employment laws.
5. We will not terminate any competent person to make room for another on the basis of any of these reasons.

You can count on the Vice President of Human Resources to work with you in maintaining employment procedures consistent with this philosophy and policy.

We will review the success of this policy at our May 1st meeting in Houston.

Charles J. DeTore

CREATING FRONTLOADED REQUEST AND REPLY MEMOS

Request and reply memos form the next category of routine, internal business communication. They achieve their purpose best when they are frontloaded or direct. However, reply memos that deny or refuse requests may be backloaded. This may be advisable when political or diplomatic wisdom suggests an indirect or deferred pattern.

Typical requests are for information, suggestions, ideas, favors, and permission to change procedures. Reply memos are commonly used to approve requests and clarify policies and procedures.

Request memo situation: Robert Holinshed, the Director of Media Relations for a large state university, needs more specific information to respond to numerous media and alumni organizations questions on the status of campus construction projects. He has decided to go directly to Cecilia York, the Chief Operating Officer, with his needs and request.

Thinking stage.

1. I have already issued some memos about progress on the Master Plan construction and improvements projects. I think I also saw a University letter about this. She seems to get irritated when I keep calling to ask additional information.
2. I'm still getting questions from big alumni donors, the press, faculty union, and students groups about parts of the projects that I can't answer clearly.
3. I need to get her to realize that additional clarification and progress reports are needed on an ongoing basis.
4. If I am successful with my requests both of us will be better off.

Central idea. Embodies the purpose of the memo. The central idea first appears in condensed form in the subject line. Then it is stated more fully in the opening paragraph of a frontloaded memo.

Robert Holinshed, the Media Director's central idea will be: "I would like to receive a complete update on the status of the construction and renovation projects going on."

The informal list. With this central idea clearly in mind, he makes a list of my key points, as well as the reasons and examples that might express his central idea. Then he'll narrow the list down to the reasons and examples that will *most* clearly convey his central idea to Cecilia York, his primary audience.

1. Some new residence halls already built. Opening date? ✓
2. What about the ones still under construction? Completion date? ✓
3. Any construction of academic facilities? Changes in existing facilities? ✓
4. Cafeteria in Erasmus Hall. Renovation complete? ✓
5. When will new Albert dining hall be ready? ✓
6. Parking lots: main campus lots, temporary lots? ✓
7. Recreational facilities: those in Alumni Hall? The tennis "bubble"? ✓
8. Basketball and football schedules for next year? ✕
9. Change location of Annual Sports Dinner? Dissatisfaction expressed over last year's site? ✕

10. What is the construction schedule for the new University Center? ✓
11. Garage opening date? Number of spaces? ✓

Organizing the list into paragraphs or graphically highlighted units. After reviewing his list, Robert decides which entries will stay and which will be deleted. He then rearranges the narrowed-down informal list according to one of the logical patterns: chronological, spatial, logical, problem–analysis–solution, order of importance. For this memo the logical pattern would be primarily *spatial,* that is, organized by visualizing the different locations on the campus that are under construction and renovation. Then *chronological,* that is, according to which project in each location of the campus will be finished first, second, third, and so on.

Buildings
1. Opening date of new residence halls already built?
2. Completion date of the ones still under construction?
3. Construction schedule for the new University Center?

Parking lots and garages
1. Status of main campus lots and temporary lots?
2. Garage opening date? Number of spaces?

Recreational facilities
1. Recreational facilities: those in Alumni Hall? The tennis "bubble"?

Academic facilities
1. New construction? Existing facilities change or expansion?

Closing. The final paragraph refers the reader back to the central idea of the opening and directs her toward some mental and physical action.

INTRODUCTION	**Picks up** the subject line preview of request **Expands** the subject line into a fully stated central idea
DEVELOPMENT	**Makes specific** requests **Gives reasons** for specific requests
CONCLUSION	**Refers back** to the central idea **Cues** desired mental and physical action for a reply

Following is the first draft of this request memo:

TO: Cecilia York
Chief Operating Officer

FROM: Robert Holinshed
Director of Media Relations

DATE: June 14, 2000

SUBJECT: MASTER PLAN CONSTRUCTION AND RENOVATION

I continue to be hounded for information on the many projects underway on the Madison campus. Yesterday, for example, I had a call from Matt Barton, Chair of the Chicago Alumni Association. I'm sure you know that he and his family have been substantial donors for many years. Also, his alumni group is one of the largest contributors to the university.

I am called to respond to numerous media and alumni organization questions on the campus construction and I have to do this in as forthright and expeditious a manner as possible.

I need much more specific information about the status of all these many projects, so I have initiated and developed for your perusal a listing of some of these questions that need to be addressed ASAP prior to the major summer alumni reunions and before the homecoming weekends as well.

1. Buildings

- Is there a scheduled opening date for the new residence halls that are undergoing final, finishing touches? If there is, can you tell me what it is so that I can pass the word and respond with greater clarity to calls and letters?
- I see that the residence halls under construction have a long way to go. Do you have a completion date for these yet?
- I also need to know more precisely the construction schedule for the new University Center? When will it be ready?

2. Parking lots and garages

- I need to know the status of the main campus lots. By this I mean the permanent ones. As you know some are no longer accessible due to the ongoing construction. People are also calling about the temporary lots that are intended to alleviate the problems with the permanent ones.
- What is the scheduled opening date of the new garage? Do you have a number handy for the number of spaces it will include?

3. Other facilities

- Matt Barton is particularly interested in recreational facilities, especially those in Alumni Hall? What can I tell him about that project?

- Others have called about the tennis "bubble." They think it's been looking shabby for some time.
- Is there any new construction planned for expanding or changing our academic facilities?

Time is of the essence, so I really need all of this information very soon. Getting it quickly will make my job so much easier!

Thank you for your attention and consideration.

Robert Holinshed

Robert Holinshed

Revising the Request Memo

Formatting revisions

- *Headings.* The headings can be improved in two areas:
  Subject line. The subject of this memo could be more precise. It is the status of the master plan's construction and renovation projects.
  Signature line. When a memo is signed the printed name block is usually omitted.
- *Single topic:* The memo does deal with a single topic, namely, the various construction projects underway and already completed. However, the topic doesn't appear in the opening paragraph as an expansion of the subject.
- *Graphics.* The elements of the construction projects are grouped in a numbered list. The third section of the list would be clearer if divided into recreational and academic facilities.

Language and expression revisions

- *Reader-based with shared goals.* The writer of this memo is clearly focused only on his own problems and pressures. He has forgotten his reader and the goals they share for the university.
- *Conversational tone.* This type of information request memo might call for a less conversational tone than usual in memos because it covers a somewhat formal subject, a university master plan. Still it could do without legalese words and phrases such as forthright and expeditious in paragraph 2 and acronyms such as *ASAP* in paragraph 3. A more objective, less petulant tone throughout is recommended.
- *Concise style.* Some sentences contain redundancies and wordy writing such as "I have initiated and developed for your perusal a listing of some of these questions that need to be addressed."
- *Parallelism and variety.* Parallelism, or beginning each entry of a bulleted or numbered list with the same part of speech, could be

improved. The entries shift between first person and third, between questions and declarative statements.

- *Internal barriers to successful communication.* The memo is free of any direct barriers such as ethnocentrism, sexist or gender biased expression, and age bias.

Organization revisions:

- Introduction. This memo did not open effectively because it was writer-based instead of reader-based. In addition to using all *Is* and no *yous*, it took three paragraphs to expand its subject line into a clearly stated central idea. Instead of its freewheeling narrative opening it needs to be frontloaded. This means it will state its central-request idea directly and in no more than two paragraphs.
- *Development.* There is a logical pattern of development based on campus space and location. There are also chronological elements implicit in the phases of construction that could be more effectively organized.
- *Conclusion.* The last paragraph refers back to the subject of the memo but only through the writer's frame of reference. The conclusion would have more impact if a mutual or shared time frame were suggested with a polite request. This would replace the insincere cliché ending "Thank you for your attention and consideration."

Here is how this request memo would read if all the suggested revisions were followed. It contains 278 words instead of the original 403 words. The revised memo is not simply shorter; it is more concise, more specific, and more effective.

Following is a revised version of this request memo:

MADISON UNIVERSITY

TO: Cecilia York
Chief Operating Officer

FROM: Robert Holinshed
Director of Media Relations

DATE: June 14, 2000

SUBJECT: STATUS OF MASTER PLAN CONSTRUCTION AND RENOVATION PROJECTS

Can you find a moment in your busy schedule to give me a status report on the many projects underway on the Madison campus? I have provided four areas of construction and renovation that I wish to update for press releases and alumni association fund-raising events.

1. Buildings
- What is the scheduled opening date for the two nearly completed residence halls on Woodland Road?
- Is there a projected opening date for the residence halls on Summit Avenue? Since the groundbreaking occurred only last month, I realize this opening is far off. However, your best guess at this point would be welcome.
- Is the groundbreaking for the new University Center still planned for October?

2. Parking lots and garages
- What is the status of the main campus lots? Will there be temporary lots created when access to th main lots is hindered by construction equipment?
- What is the scheduled opening date of the new garage? How many spaces will it offer?

3. Academic facilities
- Is there any new construction planned for expanding or changing our academic facilities?

4. Recreational facilities
- Will Alumni Hall undergo any renovation or expansion?
- Will the tennis "bubble" be improved or replaced?

Can I look forward to your update in time for my meetings with our top area fund-raisers on July 7th? Perhaps we could go together to some of these events.

Robert Holinshed

P.S. Yesterday, I had a call from Matt Barton '87, Chair of the Chicago Alumni Association. His people have been great fund-raisers for Madison. He is anxious to work with us on spreading the exciting news of the Master Plan's progress!

Reply memo situation: Cecilia York, Chief Operating Officer of Madison University, has received Robert Holinshed's request for an update on the status of the University's Master Plan of construction and renovation.

Thinking stage.

1. I already issued some memos and the university published a letter about progress on the Master Plan construction and renovation projects just two months ago. I'll just refer him to that April letter.

2. Bob only joined us in March; the memos and update letter probably arrived while he was still settling in to his new office. I'll just take his memo—it's well organized and easy to respond to—and reply point by point.

Central idea. The purpose of my memo is to reply to Bob Holinshed's request for a status update on the Master Plan. I'll do this in a direct, frontloaded memo.

My central idea is: "Here is the update you requested June 14 on the status of the Master Plan construction and renovation projects."

The informal list. With my central idea clearly in mind I'll make a list of the key points of my memo. I already decided that Robert's memo was well organized, so I'll key in my replies to his requests. I've already got a narrowed down list to work with.

Closing. The final paragraph will refer Robert back to my central idea and respond to his action information requests.

Following is the first draft of a frontloaded, direct reply memo:

Madison University

TO: Robert Holinshed
Director of Media Relations

FROM: Cecilia York
Chief Operating Officer

DATE: June 15, 2000

SUBJECT: YOUR REQUEST FOR A STATUS UPDATE

I have received your request for additional information about the University's Master Plan of construction and renovation. I've had similar requests recently, so yours comes as no surprise. Many people are unaware of the magnitude of the Master Plan. It has been ten years in the making. I assure you it has been well thought-out and scrupulously planned every step of the way!

Here is an overview of the plan with reference to the points you raised in your June 14 memo.

1. Buildings

- The scheduled opening date for the two nearly completed residence halls on Woodland Road is Labor Day of this year. They were designed in postmodern style to blend in with the library annex also on Woodland Road, completed last year.

- The projected opening date for the residence halls on Summit Avenue is Labor Day 2001. They will also be postmodern in design but with a darker shade of brick.
- The groundbreaking for the new University Center is still planned for October. The design will also be postmodern in concept but will have some Norman decorative flourishes in deference to the earliest campus buildings of the late 19th century.

2. Parking lots and garages

- The status of the main campus lots is that they will remain open. However, there will be temporary lots created when and if access to the main lots is hindered by construction equipment.
- The scheduled opening date of the new multitiered garage is really twofold. It will offer 250 spaces for day and evening students in October with an additional 300 spaces to follow.

3. Academic facilities

- No new construction is planned at this time for expanding or changing the University's academic facilities. You might recall that the University expanded both the library and computer lab hours only this past January. And last year the University completely refurbished some of the older classroom buildings that had gotten somewhat shabby.

4. Recreational facilities

- Alumni Hall will not be expanded but it will undergo renovation. We haven't reached a time framework on this one as of now. But at some point in time, and sooner rather than later, we hope to have some more concrete information for the community.
- The tennis "bubble" seems to have been troubling people for the past year or so. We first thought about trying to spruce it up a bit, but upon additional reflection thought it best to replace the entire thing.

I hope this response has been helpful to you and that it will also help with your fund-raisers on July 7th? As far as attending some with you, that was a very kind thought. I'll have to get back to you on that.

Revising the Reply Memo

Formatting revisions:

- *Headings.* The subject line of this memo could be more precise. Its subject is actually a reply to a June 14 request for the status of the construction and renovation projects of the Master Plan. If memo is unsigned, the sender's name should be initialed.

- *Single topic.* Cecilia's memo does deal with a single topic, namely, the various construction projects underway and already completed. But the opening paragraph doesn't contain a frontloaded expansion of the subject line, namely, that she is complying with Robert's request.
  The memo digresses into architectural design details that appear to interest the writer but are not part of the information update that Robert Holinshed requested.
- *Graphics.* The reply is based on a point-by-point answer to a well-organized numbered list.

Language and expression revisions

- *Reader-based with shared goals.* Cecilia begins her memo focused on her reader but quickly reverts to her own frame of reference with a somewhat defensive tone. In responding to item 4, academic facilities, she forgets that Robert joined the University after the academic projects she mentions.
- *Conversational tone.* This type of reply memo would normally be more straightforward in expression. Cecilia might be this conversational in deference to a new team member.
- *Concise style.* Some sentences contain redundancies and wordy writing such as "with reference to the points" in paragraph 2 and "But at some point in time, and sooner rather than later" in item 4.
- *Parallelism and variety.* Parallelism, or beginning each entry of a bulleted or numbered list with the same part of speech, has been followed in almost every case. Cecilia starts each numbered entry with a direct answer to the questions Robert raised except for the question about the tennis bubble in 4.
- *Internal barriers to successful communication.* The memo is free of any direct barriers such as ethnocentrism, sexist or gender-biased expression, and age bias.

Organization revisions

- *Introduction.* This memo would have been more effective if it extended its opening and made a more precise frontloaded reply statement.
- *Development.* There is a logical pattern of development based on campus space and location, which follows Robert Holinshed's original request memo.
- *Conclusion* The last paragraph refers back to only one part of the action information closing of the request memo.

Below is how this request memo would read if all the suggested revisions were followed. It contains 268 words instead of the original

454 words. The revised memo is not simply shorter; it is more concise yet more specific. In addition, it is more effective because it is reader-based and emphasizes shared goals.

Below is the revised direct reply memo:

MADISON UNIVERSITY

TO: Robert Holinshed
Director of Media Relations

FROM: Cecilia York *CY*
Chief Operating Officer

DATE: June 15, 2000

SUBJECT: UPDATE ON MASTER PLAN CONSTRUCTION AND RENOVATION

In response to your request yesterday here is a status report on our university's Master Plan of construction and renovation. Your request comes at a good time, because the trustees have just signed off on the final parts of this $250 million plan.

1. Buildings
- The scheduled opening date for the two residence halls on Woodland Road is Labor Day of this year.
- The projected opening date for the residence halls on Summit Avenue is Labor Day 2001.
- The groundbreaking for the new University Center is planned for this October.

2. Parking lots and garages
- The main campus lots will remain open. Temporary lots will be created if access to the main lots is hindered by construction equipment.
- The new garage will offer 250 spaces in October and an additional 300 spaces in December.

3. Academic facilities
- Library and computer labs will enjoy extended hours beginning Labor Day. Renovation of academic facilities was completed last year.

4. Recreational facilities
- Alumni Hall will undergo renovation. Facilities will be enhanced, hours will be extended, the building made more accessible.
- The tennis "bubble" will be replaced with a large one to handle indoor basketball and volleyball.

I hope this response has been complete and that it will also help you speak with pride of our new facilities at the fund-raisers in July. They are so important to all of us at Madison.

I will be happy to attend some of these vital events with you. Let's meet in my office on Monday at 2:00 P.M. to agree on a schedule of my participation.

CREATING FRONTLOADED CONFIRMATION MEMOS

We would all like to think that careful preparation, writing, and revision will cancel any need for head-scratching, brow-furrowing confusion and questioning. Unfortunately, not true. Clear thinking and effective writing can greatly reduce the need for clarification and restatement but not remove it totally.

We have always understood the wisdom of following up oral discussions and decisions with written confirmations so that there are no uncertainties or misunderstandings. Today, however, we recognize something else. The same technology that has speeded up the pace of business exponentially has created problems in another area. Today many recognize that dashed-off memos, form letters, and e-mails eat up the time saved in their creation by the need for restatements and confirmations.

Whether desired for creating a permanent record of important oral discussions or necessitated by hasty, careless e-mails or by poorly adapted form letters, confirmation memos serve a valuable purpose. They are created by following the same steps as procedure, information, and request-reply memos.

Think. The thinking stage of writing successful confirmation memos is especially important. It is the "yesterday" of people and issues that we are bringing back to life today. Reliving "yesterday" is the primary purpose of today's memo you're about to write. The thinking stage of each confirmation memo reflects upon the four phases of purpose, information, persuasion, changes or results, and good will or public relations and moves forward with the following four questions:

1. *Information from the reader's perspective:* What are the facts or issues, as my reader will recall them?
2. *Persuasion:* Could our memories differ? Precisely how?
3. *Changes or results:* How do I bring my reader's recollection to agree with mine?
4. *Good will or public relations:* What do we do together now to reach our shared goal?

Write. Correct formatting, logical organization, and effective expression are always required in business writing to answer these questions effectively. Confirmation memos in particular need attention to formatting. Always use either a bulleted or numbered list for the points that are being confirmed. This will focus you and your reader on the points you want agreement on.

Revise. Revising or seeing a document again means stepping back from it and rereading it as if someone else wrote it. When revising a confirmation memo special attention should be paid to word choice and the connotation of words. Often we think there is a disagreement because each side attaches a different connotation to a word. Did we agree yesterday to "review" a particular decision or to "reconsider" it? The word *reconsider* suggests change, the word *review* does not.

Confirmation memo situation: Mark David Oxton and his district manager, Catherine C. Frank, discussed Mark's promotion to Status III Marketing Track at length on Thursday, April 4. Catherine has decided to send a memo to Mark confirming the key points they discussed about his new status at Augustus International, an executive services company headquartered in Boston.

Thinking stage.

1. The discussions and decision-making process were unusually long with Mark.
2. Mark joined us in November 1996. He was very disappointed that he didn't get this promotion in 1999. There were reports that he was looking elsewhere for new opportunities.

Central idea. The primary purpose of this memo is to confirm the oral discussion of the preceding day. But Catherine will also seek to reassure Mark about his value to their company. She will do this in a direct, frontloaded memo.

My central idea is: "This is a confirmation of our discussion of your new status and privileges at Augustus International."

The informal list. With the central idea as her focal point, Catherine makes a list of the key points of the planned memo. Then she narrows the list down to the reasons and examples that will *most* clearly convey her central idea to Mark, her primary audience.

1. Sorry this took so long. ✕
2. Mark's Stage III status will continue for one year. ✓

3. He will be enrolled in the Proxy Delivery Program. ✓
4. He will be re-evaluated after one year—company policy. ✓
5. He will partake in Executive Services lead generation. ✓
6. He will be assigned leads according to the *Program Procedural Guide.* ✓
7. Augustus will assist him whenever he needs it. ✓
8. He may use his new title on his business cards. ✓
9. Enclose the *Proxy Delivery Procedural Guide.* ✓

Organizing the list into paragraphs or graphically highlighted units. The narrowed down informal list should be rearranged according to one of the logical patterns: chronological, spatial, logical, problem–analysis–solution, order of importance. A *chronological* pattern could have been used starting with the background or past history of Mark's relations with the company, moving on to the present promotion, and ending with the evaluation he will face in one year. However, this would suggest a trial period and put Mark on the defensive. Catherine does not want to start their new relationship on such a negative note.

Instead, for this memo the more positive logical pattern would be *order of importance.* This logical pattern would highlight the best part of their oral discussion being confirmed first, then go down a list of the remaining points discussed in descending order of importance.

1. Mark has achieved Stage III status.
2. He will partake in Executive Services lead generation.
3. He will be assigned leads according to the *Program Procedural Guide.*
4. He will be enrolled in the Proxy Delivery Program for his exclusive lead assignments.
5. Enclose the *Proxy Delivery Procedural Guide.*
6. He may use his new title on his business cards and stationery.
7. Mark's Stage III status will continue for one year.
8. He will be re-evaluated after one year—company policy.

Closing. The final paragraph will refer Mark back to the central idea of his new status and include the offer of assistance whenever he needs it.

INTRODUCTION {
My purpose is to confirm. Picks up the subject line preview
Our oral discussion. Expands subject line into a central idea

DEVELOPMENT {
Of these specific points. Expands the direction of central idea
In a numbered list. Confirms specific points discussed

CONCLUSION {
Please note your agreement. Refers back to the central idea
And let's look to the future. Cues desired action as needed

Below is the first draft of this confirmation memo:

AUGUSTUS INTERNATIONAL

TO: Mark David Oxton

FROM: Catherine Frank
District Manager

DATE: April 5, 2000

SUBJECT: CONFIRMATION OF APRIL 4TH DISCUSSION

Often in fast-growing operations like ours we have to stop and take stock of our direction and progress. So, with those types of goals in mind I am writing to you today to remind you of the matters that we discussed previous to the present memo.

1. The first thing we discussed was your achievement of a new and higher status in our company, namely, that of Stage III of the Executive Services Marketing Track as evidenced by your **1999 Executive Services Progress Report.** I wish to take this opportunity to congratulate you at this time for this achievement and the new title that goes with it.
2. Finally, you are entitled to partake in the Executive Services Exclusive Lead Generation Program. I know how you have anxiously awaited this opportunity.
3. I am happy to say that as a result of this new status we will assign you leads as set forth in the **Program Procedural Guide.**
4. I am equally pleased to advise that we will be enrolling you in the Proxy Delivery Program for your exclusive lead assignments.
5. Enclosed herewith you will find the **Proxy Delivery Procedural Guide.**
6. You may use your new title on all your business cards and stationery.
7. Your Stage III status will continue for one year.
8. At the termination of said period of time you will be re-evaluated based upon the criteria as set forth in the **Executive Series Marketing Track,** which is in keeping with company policy.

I am delighted to be the bearer of this good news to you. I also wish to extend an offer of any assistance whatsoever in your new role. I am sure we will have a profitable future together. Please sign and return a copy of this memo to make a statement that everything I have included in it is an accurate summary of the matters we discussed yesterday.

If there are any questions don't hesitate to call.

Catherine

Revising the Confirmation Memo

Formatting revisions

- *Headings.* The subject line of this memo should specify the topic of their April 4th discussion, namely, Mark's new Stage III status. The memo should note at the end that there are enclosures.
- *Single topic.* Catherine's memo does deal with a single topic, namely, Mark's promotion and what goes along with it. However, the undirected opening paragraph doesn't contain a frontloaded development of the subject line. This would expand on the improved subject line and congratulate Mark on his achievement in a more forceful way.
- *Graphics.* The memo is developed with a numbered list, but distracts the reader by placing titles of guides in bold. Doing this makes it appear that these publications are the most important news being conveyed.

Language and expression revisions

- *Reader-based with shared goals.* Catherine begins her memo focused on herself instead of her reader. A rewrite of this could bring Mark, the primary audience of the memo, into her opening statement.
- *Conversational tone.* A confirmation memo of its very nature should be less informal and conversational than most routine memos. Catherine's conversational tone in #2 backfires. In trying to "feel his pain" she has dredged up unhappy memories.
- *Concise style.* Some sentences contain redundancies and wordy writing such as "At the termination of which time" and legalese such as "enclosed herewith" and "at the termination of said period of time."
- *Parallelism and variety.* Parallelism or beginning each entry of a bulleted or numbered list with the same part of speech, could have been followed in a reader-based manner by starting each entry with *you* or *your.*

- *Internal barriers to successful communication.* The memo is free of any direct barriers such as ethnocentrism, sexist or gender biased expression, and age bias.

Organization revisions

- *Introduction.* This memo will open more effectively if it builds on the subject line and makes a more precise frontloaded reply statement.
- *Development.* The intended pattern of development based on order of importance would be clearer and easier to follow if the entries in the numbered list were reduced and regrouped.
- *Conclusion.* The last paragraph should refer back to a good-news opening. A more personal, less clichéd conclusion would have ended the memo on a firmer, more vigorous note of shared goals. Instead of the typed name, the memo writer should close with a signature or simply initial her name on the "FROM" line.

Here is how this request memo would read if all the suggested revisions were followed. It contains 191 words instead of the original 324 words. The revised memo is not simply shorter; it is more concise yet more specific. In addition, it is more effective because it is reader-based and emphasizes shared goals.

Below is the revised confirmation memo.

AUGUSTUS INTERNATIONAL

TO: Mark David Oxton
Executive Services Consultant

FROM: Catherine Frank *CF*
District Manager

DATE: April 5, 2000

SUBJECT: CONFIRMATION OF APRIL 4TH DISCUSSION OF STAGE III STATUS

Congratulations, Mark, on achieving Stage III status of the Executive Services Marketing Track! This memo will confirm the specific points we discussed yesterday about your new position.

1. Your new status, based on your 1999 Executive Services Progress Report, carries with it the title of Executive Services Consultant. You may use your new title on all your business cards and stationery.
2. You are entitled to take part in the Executive Services Exclusive Lead Generation Program.

3. You will, as a result of this new status, be assigned leads as stated in the *Program Procedural Guide.*
4. You will be enrolled in the Proxy Delivery Program for your exclusive lead assignments. A copy of the *Proxy Delivery Procedural Guide* is enclosed.
5. You will automatially enjoy Stage III status for one year. Then the standard company evaluation process will take place. This process is based upon the criteria in the Executive Series Marketing Track.

Executive Services is ready to assist you in your new role. We look forward to a profitable future together.

If you agree that this memo summarizes our discussion yesterday, please initial a copy and return it to me.

Enclosures

13

Writing and Revising Negative News Memos

In the good old days a king would order the messenger who brought bad news killed. Such drastic action, of course, didn't change the message. It was still bad news. Today we don't kill the messengers, but we do resent the senders of hostile, ill-phrased, and insensitive messages.

Communicating bad news is one of the most difficult tasks in business writing. A subordinate asks for a raise, that you cannot approve. An unqualified job seeker requests an appointment to discuss a position with your company, a community organization asks for a contribution which you do not wish to grant. You decide you must let a good worker go because intense competition demands cutbacks.

Even in good times bad news sometimes has to be delivered. But it doesn't have to be delivered badly. Here are three guidelines we can all follow whenever we have to be the messengers of bad news.

1. Be even more reader-based than you seek to be when delivering neutral or positive news. Look at the request through the eyes of the sender. From the sender's standpoint no request is foolish. All effective communicators are audience- or reader-based, but successful managers are especially sensitive to the needs and feelings of their audience-staffs.
2. It may not be the easiest way, but the best way to deliver bad news is face to face. People receiving bad news are going to have some strong needs. They want the chance to express their negative

feelings. They will want the opportunity to press their case or appeal the decision. They will want reassurance that there are no hidden messages. These needs can best be met in a face to face discussion.

So if you have bad news to give to an employee or a valued client, confer with the individual, give the bad news in person, then follow up with a written statement for the record.

3. Finally, the natural and understandable desire to soften the blow can often backfire and cloud the message, resulting in more not fewer problems. Everyone appreciates honesty of feelings and clarity of thought, especially when being disappointed. We are often more angered by the timing and confusion surrounding bad news than by the news itself. Not getting a promotion is bad news. Not getting a decision for months and being left to wonder why is even worse.

With these guidelines in mind, the type of bad news message that will work best for each situation can be chosen: the indirect bad news message that defers or backloads the bad news or the direct bad news message that frontloads the bad news. What will also help your decision is stopping to reflect on the ages and stages of all successful communication.

APPLYING THE AGES OF SUCCESSFUL COMMUNICATION TO BAD NEWS MESSAGES

Yesterday. Writers of negative news memos must be particularly aware of the background of people and issues. How have matters reached this state? What was said in the past on this matter? Who said it? What was decided? Why was the decision a mistake?

Today. When writing a bad news memo it is especially important to understand that while *yesterday's* mistakes may have brought about today's difficult task, there is nothing to be gained from finger pointing and assigning blame. Our awareness of yesterday should have a positive result—a clearer focus on what must be done today. The keener our focus is today the more likely we are to achieve the changes that we seek.

Tomorrow. One thing all writers of bad news memos want is a better tomorrow. They realize that what they write "today" will have results tomorrow on both parties, the sender as well as the receiver, of the bad news. The last thing they want is a continuation of yesterday's problems. Therefore, they consider very carefully the possibility of unintended results of their messages on both the primary and secondary audiences. They write *today* to prevent those possible outcomes.

APPLYING THE PHASES OF SUCCESSFUL COMMUNICATION TO BAD NEWS MESSAGES

Purpose. Before writing a bad news message review the four main purposes of all business communication studied in Chapter 3

1. *Information.* The facts or issues as my reader sees them.
2. *Persuasion.* What they mean as I see them and precisely how our views differ.
3. *Results or changes.* How I change my reader's perception to work together with mine.
4. *Good will or public relations.* What we now do together to reach our shared goals.

Organization. Bad news memos like all forms of business writing can have their ideas arranged in a reader-based structure by selecting one of the following patterns of development. The ones checked are usually the best patterns for delivering negative news.

- Chronological ✓
- Spatial
- Logical
  1. Cause and effect ✓
  2. Comparison-contrast
  3. Classification and division
  4. Illustration
  5. Problem–analysis–solution ✓
  6. Order of importance

Expression. Even the most purposeful and logically organized bad news memo, if written in a negative way, can lose much of its persuasive force. Whenever this happens another opportunity for positive change will have been lost. More than that, a residue of additional bad news remains.

THE INDIRECT BAD NEWS MESSAGE

This is the method of deferring or backloading the bad news. It seeks to soften the blow by burying the bad news in the middle or latter part of the memo and surrounding it with positive statements about people and issues. This method is often a good choice whenever we seek to achieve one or more of the following results: an ongoing relationship with the receiver of the bad news or a continuing projection of the writer as a caring individual. The key element in the indirect pattern is placing the central idea at a latter stage in the memo. This doesn't mean that we leave our readers completely in the dark at the beginning of such a document. It means that we get to the bad news gradually and objectively.

Five degrees or methods of embedding the bad news:

1. By deferring it until a later paragraph of the document
2. By placing it toward the end of that chosen paragraph
3. By putting it in the subordinate clause of a complex sentence
4. By expressing it in the passive voice of the verb
5. By not stating it at all, but simply implying it.

INTRODUCTION	**Thanks**. Picks up the subject line preview of the coming news in an appreciative manner.
DEVELOPMENT	**Because**. Gives the reasons for the coming bad news. **Sorry**. Gives the bad news central idea as positively as possible.
CONCLUSION	**Thanks**. Cues receiver's mental and physical action elsewhere in the near term but back to the sender in the long term.

Subject line. State the general area of the main idea with neutral, objective, unemotional language in the subject line.

Emotional, combative subject line: DRESS CODE VIOLATIONS
Indirect, deferred load subject line: PROPOSALS FOR NEW DRESS CODE

Emotional, negative subject line: DISAPPOINTING REPORT ON CHAPTER 11
Indirect, deferred load subject line: YEAR END COMPANY STATUS

Expand the subject line gradually, while following the principles of writing a reader-based document. The writer can do this by showing that he or she is aware of and value the reader's opinion, even when each party has come to a different conclusion about its merits.

Four steps to follow when composing an indirect, negative news message:

1. Express appreciation for the suggestion offered, the request received, the interest expressed. Adopt a personal tone in the opening paragraph and refer only indirectly to the problem issue. Mention shared goals and other understandings that the sender of the message and the receiver have in common.
2. Give reasons for the change or decision you are about to reveal. Stating the reasons first cushions the blow, preparing the receiver gradually for the bad news to come. Do this in a reader-based way by using reasons that will make sense to the receiver.
3. Present the bad news itself in as positive a way as possible. Use objective language avoiding any words that connote personal rejection.
4. Treat the change as something that involves and affects you, the sender, and the receiver.

Direct, combative opening paragraph:

Last week you submitted to me some ideas for changing the company dress code, which just won't work. I wish to point out to you now why your flextime proposals will cause problems for everybody.

Indirect, deferred-load opening paragraph:

Thanks very much for forwarding your proposal for a dress code change for your department. I appreciate the creative input.

Direct, sour opening paragraph:

Last year we had some really disappointing results in several areas that are important if we are going to avoid being also-rans in our industry.

Indirect, deferred-load opening paragraph:

Last year our industry was faced with many challenges. Thanks to our continuing spirit of dedication and teamwork we rose to those challenges and improved our position in many areas.

Closing a deferred-load bad news memo. The same care taken in delivering negative news indirectly should extend to the conclusion. Even negative news should be presented with reader benefits and shared goals in mind. If nothing else the shared goal is to move on.

End on an upbeat, pleasant note that leaves the door open for a continuing relationship. It is wise to end this way for the simple common sense reason that you might need the person or the person's business in the future.

Four guidelines for concluding indirect, bad news messages:

1. Express appreciation again for the sender's interest or request. Depending on the situation, suggest other avenues that your reader might pursue.

2. Remain confident that your decision was correct. Don't refer back to the bad news or apologize. Apologizing suggests doubt in the wisdom of your decision.
3. Avoid clichéd endings that may only prolong the unpleasantness. Closing with expressions such as, "If there are any further questions, please do not hesitate to call me" will probably appear insincere anyway.
4. Suggest alternatives or some other face-saving proposals. Thank your reader again for the past idea or contact. Point to possible shared goals in the future.

THE DIRECT BAD NEWS MESSAGE

This pattern frontloads the bad news. It gets right to the point and does not attempt to buffer the unpleasant news. It makes a tough, no-nonsense, yet courteous statement. This approach is used when we seek one or more of the following outcomes:

1. No further requests or discussions from the receiver of the bad news.
2. A reputation as being tough and resolute in such situations.

INTRODUCTION	**Thanks.** Picks up the subject line preview of the bad news. **Sorry**. Expands the subject line into a fully stated central idea.
DEVELOPMENT	**Because**. Gives the reasons for the bad news
CONCLUSION	**Thanks**. Cues receiver's mental and physical action elsewhere.

Subject line. Use the subject line to introduce the main point of the memo with language that is calm, objective, and neutral. The expression or word choice may be more forceful than in an indirect bad news message, but it shouldn't cross the line into confrontation or accusations. This will only make a difficult situation worse.

Expand the subject line quickly. The reader strongly believes that he or she is correct or justified in seeking what either asked for. This is another reason why bad news messages should be especially careful to follow the principles of reader-based writing. One important way we can achieve this goal is by showing the reader that his or her opinion has been recognized and considered, even though we may disagree about its merits.

Four steps for delivering a direct, bad news message in a positive manner:

1. Begin with a courteous expression of appreciation. Courtesy is expected no matter how direct the message is. Adopt a personal tone. Refer directly to the problem/issue in your opening paragraph.
2. Move directly to the bad news. Use clear but courteous language, avoiding words that suggest any personal distaste for the idea, request, and most of all, the sender.
3. Give reasons for the change or bad news you have just delivered.
4. End courteously, expressing appreciation for the receiver's interest or proposal. Do not suggest any alternatives that might invite future discussion. The door is closed.

Closing a direct, frontloaded bad news memo. The more unwelcome the news we sometimes have to give our readers, the more important it is to end on a firm yet pleasant note. Most of all when we have to deliver such news it's just as well we make it clear that the matter is concluded. The door is not slammed shut, but it is definitely closed.

The four stages of a direct, frontloaded negative news memo:

1. Extend best wishes or, depending on the situation, suggest other avenues that your reader might pursue.
2. Your decision was correct. Don't refer back to it or apologize. Apologizing suggests doubt in the wisdom of your decision.
3. Avoid clichéd endings that may only drag out the unpleasantness. The decision has been made. Closing with expressions such as, "If there are any further questions, please do not hesitate to call me" will probably appear insincere anyway.
4. Even the most negative news can be presented without overlooking reader benefits and shared goals. If nothing else the shared goal is to move on.

CREATING A DEFERRED OR BACKLOADED BAD NEWS MEMO

Situation: A group of warehouse employees at Global Bonded Couriers has sent a request to Beverly Lyndon in Human Resources requesting that they be exempt from company dress policy. Beverly has been with Global for nearly eight years and relations with all departments have been very amicable. This is the first request she or any senior manager has received to exempt warehouse employees from the company dress code.

Below is Beverly's deferred or indirect negative news memo as first written.

MEMORANDUM

TO: All warehouse employees

FROM: Beverly Lyndon *BL*
Human Resources

DATE: April 30, 2000

SUBJECT: WAREHOUSE EMPLOYEES' MANDATED DRESS CODE

I am in receipt of the suggestions for changes in our company's dress code that you forwarded to me recently. The company dress code that I helped formulate nearly five years ago is something that I have always been particularly proud of. The code was arrived at after many meetings and consultations with knowledgeable persons in the field.

Here are some of my thoughts and conclusions on this subject. They were reached at a special meeting yesterday that I asked your representatives to attend. I regret to say that not all accepted my invitation. Here are the reasons that we decided to maintain the aforementioned dress code as it presently exists.

1. The company issued uniforms to you that were designed for the positive appearance they make. Don't forget that some of your own officers were on the committee that approved them.
2. We have many visitors and customers who tour all parts of our facility including the front office, shipping, and also including our warehouse. As you are aware, they come from many parts of our city and country. Some even visit from overseas from counties such as Germany, Ireland, and Jordan.
3. A few of these same visitors have commented favorably on the appearance of company personnel. I'm sure the dress code was the reason for this.
4. Remember that a dress code is enforced to make certain that employees maintain an image that is a reflection of the professional statement we make as a company.

I would like to take this opportunity to remind you that the specific details of our company's policy are stated in the employee handbook. Please study your handbook again.

Thank you for your cooperation in this matter.

Revising the Deferred, Backloaded Bad News Memo

Formatting revisions

- *Headings.* The subject line of a deferred load memo, as this was intended to be, could be more neutral. The word *mandated* tips the reader at this opening stage that the news is bad. Entries should be in a straight line vertically.
- *Single topic.* Beverly's memo does deal with a single topic, namely, the warehouse employees' dress code.
- *Graphics.* The memo is developed with a numbered list. Since there is no chronological order in the list it just comes across as authoritarian. A bulleted list would work better in such a backloaded situation.

Language and expression revisions

- *Reader-based with shared goals.* Beverly begins her memo focused completely on herself instead of her readers, who have petitioned her. A more effective opening would have offered thanks to her readers for their request.
- *Conversational tone.* The tone could be less stiff and formal toward someone who has been part of the Global team for six years.
- *Concise style.* Some sentences contain redundancies and wordy writing such as "I am in receipt of" and legalese such as "aforementioned."
- *Parallelism and variety.* Parallelism could have been followed in a reader-based manner by starting each entry with *you* or *your.* Variety of sentence length and structure could be improved.
- *Internal barriers to successful communication.* The memo is free of any direct barriers such as ethnocentrism, sexist or gender-biased expression, and age bias.

Organization revisions

- *Introduction.* Open the memo with an expression of appreciation following a more neutral subject line.
- *Development.* The intended pattern of development, cause and effect, would be clearer and easier to follow if the entries in the numbered list were shortened and rearranged.
- *Conclusion.* The last paragraph would be more likely to achieve the memo's goals if it expressed appreciation for the warehouse group's request and made note of shared goals.

Below is how this request memo would read if all the suggested revisions were followed. It contains 189 words instead of the original 285 words. The revised memo is not simply shorter; it is clearer and easier to read. Also it is more focused on the shared workplace relationship of sender and receiver.

Below is the revised, indirect bad news memo:

MEMORANDUM

TO: All warehouse employees

FROM: Beverly Lyndon *BL*
Human Resources

DATE: April 30, 2000

SUBJECT: DRESS CODE FOR WAREHOUSE EMPLOYEES

Thanks very much for forwarding your suggestions for changes in our company's dress code. Our company values employees' participation and proposals.

Here are our thoughts and conclusions on this subject. They were reached at a special meeting yesterday.

- We have many visitors and customers who tour all parts of our facility, including our warehouse. As you are aware, they come from many parts of our city and country. Some even visit from overseas.
- Your image is a reflection of the professional statement we make as a company. Many visitors have commented favorably on the appearance of company personnel.
- Your company-issued uniforms were designed with your comfort in mind and by a committee in which two of your officers participated.

For all of these reasons it was decided at our meeting yesterday to continue the dress code as it currently exists. The specific details of our company's policy are stated in the Employee Handbook, which you have all received.

Thank you again for bringing your proposal to my attention. Global Bonded Couriers remains open and interested in your suggestions for improving the workplace of our company.

CREATING A DIRECT OR FRONTLOADED BAD NEWS MEMO

Situation: Six months after sending her indirect negative news memo things have changed. After an acrimonious power struggle the warehouse employees at Global Bonded Couriers have chosen new leadership, which has revived the dress code issue. They have frequently violated the code themselves. Recently, when Global scheduled a tour for major clients, Beverly noticed employees with see-through tops, baseball caps, and otherwise out of uniform.

Below is Beverly's direct bad news memo in its first draft.

MEMORANDUM

TO: All warehouse employees

FROM: Beverly Lyndon BL
Human Resources

DATE: October 22, 2000

SUBJECT: Dress Code

I would like to remind all employees of Global Bonded Couriers' dress code. It remains in effect as of this writing, as it has for the past five years since I was instrumental in its conception and implementation. Prior to recent developments it has been observed as intended.

Please review your handbook regarding personal appearance. You are expected to dress in accordance with business standards common in our industry and elsewhere. Please do not *under any circumstances* come to work in peek-a-boo tops or very short skirts. Do not wear baseball caps inside the building at any time or season. We have many visitors and customers who tour our facility on an ongoing basis and your image is a reflection of the professional statement we make as a company.

All drivers and workers who have been issued uniforms are expected to be in uniform and properly attired during business hours."

Thank you for your cooperation.

Revising the Frontloaded, Direct Bad News Memo

Formatting revisions

- *Headings.* The subject line of a direct, frontloaded memo should be more specific and capitalized.
- *Single topic.* The memo does deal with a single topic, namely the warehouse employees' dress code.
- *Graphics.* The memo lacks graphic highlighting and appears squeezed into the upper half of the page. A bulleted or numbered

list is needed. In addition, underlining the already strong phrase *under any circumstances* is the equivalent of shouting. Unnecessary.

Language and expression revisions

- *Reader-based with shared goals.* The memo's opening paragraph is sender focused. It gives no indication that the receivers' opinions have been considered at all. It refers to the readers in a negative light.
- *Conversational tone.* The tone is by turns combative, sarcastic, and condescending. Even the most negative news can be delivered courteously.
- *Concise style.* Some sentences contain redundancies and wordy writing such as "as of this writing."
- *Parallelism and variety.* Parallelism would be used when a numbered list is introduced.
- *Internal barriers to successful communication.* Except for the unfortunate phrase *peek-a-boo tops,* the memo avoids internal barriers.

Organization revisions

- *Introduction.* Beginning the memo on a note of appreciation for the employees' suggestions coupled with a more specific but diplomatic subject line would earn the writer a more receptive audience.
- Development. A general-to-specific pattern of development would be effective in conjunction with a numbered list.
- Conclusion. The last paragraph should express appreciation for the warehouse group's request and take note of shared goals.

Below is how this reply denial memo would read if all the suggested revisions were followed. It contains 111 words instead of the original 155 words. It is not simply shorter, it is clearer and more courteous. And it achieves this in a firm and direct manner.

MEMORANDUM

TO: All warehouse employees

FROM: Beverly Lyndon *BL*
Human Resources

DATE: October 22, 2000

SUBJECT: DRESS CODE FOR ALL WAREHOUSE EMPLOYEES

Thank you for forwarding your most recent suggestions for changes in our company's dress code. Their merits were given careful consideration. Global Bonded Couriers' dress code, however, remains in effect.

1. "All employees are expected to dress in accordance with business standards."
2. "Tops must be opaque and the skirts no more than four inches above the knees."
3. "Baseball caps are to be worn only outside the building."
4. "All drivers and workers who have been issued uniforms are expected to be in uniform and properly attired during business hours."

Please review your handbook for additional particulars of this code.

Thank you for maintaining the standards of Global Bonded Couriers.

14

Writing and Revising Neutral or Positive News Letters

In many ways letters tell even more about us personally and professionally than do memos. By their very nature they travel far outside our workplace and reveal much about our temperament and expertise. The form and expression we use in our letters can often predict their success or failure in reaching the goals we set for them.

Like memos, letters are sent through three channels: hard copy, fax, and e-mail. They are almost always external, horizontal communications sent out to customers, suppliers, government agencies, and the general public.

Like memos, letters must sometimes convey neutral or good news and other times negative or bad news. This chapter will demonstrate how to write and revise a variety of neutral to positive letters. These will include typical request/reply as well as persuasive letters for the following needs:

1. Information and action
2. Orders
3. Claims and adjustments
4. Special situations

Unlike memos, letters are more formal in style and tone. Like all effective communication, however, their goal is always to be courteous and positive in tone.

Business and government agency letters that follow the writing principles analyzed in Part II, especially the triple plays of Chapter 6 for reader-based communication, are more likely to achieve their goals.

THE ORGANIZATION, FORMATTING, AND WRITING OF SUCCESSFUL LETTERS

Three Ages	**Three Phases**	**Three Stages**
Yesterday	Purpose	Think
Today	Organization	Write
Tomorrow	Expression	Revise

FORMATTING BUSINESS LETTERS

Options. The writer of a professional looking business letter follows correct formatting in two areas listed in Chapter 11:

1. *The page layout:*
- Full block style
- Partial block style
- Simplified style
- Indented style

2. *The headings:* "salutation or greeting" and "complimentary close" are omitted if one is using the simplified style. A "subject line" is optional in all letter formats except the simplified style, where a subject line stands alone in all capital letters without the word "subject" as a heading.

- *Letterhead or return address:* most companies' stationery includes the company name, optional logo, full address, phone, fax, and e-mail information. If not using a complete letterhead, any of this information is usually added.
- *Date line:* the date of the mailing of the letter, not its writing, is typed two lines above the inside address.
- *Inside address:* this will be the same as the address on the envelope. Include the professional name of the person to whom you are writing (even if you will use a less formal name on the salutation or greeting line), title, company, street address, city, state (using the two capital letters without periods assigned by the U.S. Postal Service), and zip code.

Ms. Mary Beth Farrell
Senior Vice President
ACA Client Solutions
345 Maple Avenue
Dayton, OH 45320

A letter addressed only to a title without naming the individual person is not off to a reader-based start. Check previous mail, the company's Internet site, or call the company for the correct name.

The following titles are customarily abbreviated: Mr., Ms., and Dr. Categories whose titles are not customarily abbreviated include:

Academic: Professor Emeritus, Professor, Associate Professor
Religious: Reverend, Archbishop, Sister
Military: Major General, Sergeant, Colonel
Civic: Representative, Senator, Member of Congress, Council person

- *Salutation or greeting:* Use *Dear* followed by the person's last name. Americans, known around the world for informality, tend to use first names very freely. In foreign correspondence always use full and honorific titles where appropriate. In letters at home only use the first name if you truly share a very friendly relationship.
  Use a colon after the person's name to whom you are writing. If you do not know the person's name, or if you are uncertain about the gender of persons with names such as Marion, Courtney, and Robin, use the person's job title alone. "To whom it may concern" shows a lack of effort and courtesy. *Ladies and Gentlemen* is outdated.
- *Optional subject line:* this is the equivalent of the subject line of a memo. It can either take the form of a verbal preview-summary of the letter or a combination of words and numbers such as referral numbers and order numbers. The subject line does not have to be a complete sentence; it takes the form of a grammatical fragment, for example, *Confirmation of Vacation Schedule Changes.* Since it is not a complete sentence it does not end with a period. Articles *the, a, an* are usually omitted.
  In the full and partial block letter styles, the subject line, in upper- and lowercase letters following the capitalized word *SUBJECT,* is printed two lines below the salutation.
  In the simplified letter style the subject line, competely capitalized and without the word *SUBJECT,* is printed two lines after the address.
- *Body or paragraphs:* whether full, partial block, simplified, or indented in style the paragraphs of the body or development are single-spaced with double spacing between paragraphs. Center the body of the letter on the page or, in the case of very brief letters, raise it slightly above center.
- *Complimentary close:* most business letters today close with the single word *Sincerely*. However, if a warmer, more personal closing

is desired use either *Cordially, With warm regards,* or *Best wishes.* Such closings should be part of a friendlier and more personalized business letter. If appended and out of context they will appear artificial and phony.

- *Signature:* Sign your name as it appears in the printed line, unless the letter is very friendly in tone. In that case sign your first name only, but make sure that you have also used the receiver's first name in the salutation.
- *Writer's printed name:* should appear four spaces below the complimentary closing.
- *Reference initials:* two lines after the printed name your initials in capital letters followed by a slash or colon appear first. These are followed by the keyboarder's initials in lowercase. If you type your own letter, no initials are necessary.
- *Enclosure line:* this line, two lines after the reference initials line, advises the reader that there are additional materials included with your letter. Several styles are used:

  Enclosure
  Enclosures (3)
  Enclosure: 1999 Annual Report

- *Copy line:* the abbreviation *cc*: is used followed by the names of any persons to whom a copy of your letter is being given. Copies of letters called blind copies are sent without acknowledgment on the copy line. This is at best a lapse of professional courtesy.

WRITING THE BODY OF THE LETTER

Purpose. The content of each letter is determined by our purpose in writing. Each time we write we should ask ourselves some key questions. For example,"Why am I writing *this* letter? Why *now*?" For direct, frontloaded letters the answer to such questions will be mainly information, the first of the four purposes of all business communication studied in Chapter 3. This does not mean that the remaining three purposes are overlooked, but that we are primarily focused on giving information. Persuasion, change, and good will are always part of any successful business document.

If the purpose of each letter is clear before writing starts, it can be expressed in one central idea. Writing a concise yet specific subject line is a good idea even if it is not used in the finished form of a letter as in the simplified format.

Writing a central idea/subject line is a good first step in limiting letters to a single topic. This does not mean a letter cannot cover a number of different points. It means that the main idea is clear from the start and that the remaining ideas are subordinated to it. Chapter 6 contains an outlining method that is useful for separating the main and subordinate ideas.

Organization. Like all expository writing, letters are organized in three parts: introduction, development, and conclusion. Since the majority of such letters will be routine and we will want to get right to the point, they are frontloaded or direct in organization and expression. They place the central idea up front in the introduction. Then they follow one of the standard patterns of development. The ones checked will usually work best for routine frontloaded letters.

- Chronological ✓
- Spatial
- Logical
  1. Cause and effect ✓
  2. Comparison-contrast ✓
  3. Classification and division
  4. Illustration ✓
  5. Problem–analysis–solution
  6. Order of importance ✓

Which patterns of development work best in business writing? Here are some suggestions for choosing a pattern to suit a specific type of letter:

- The chronological pattern: for orders, information, action, and procedure letters
- The cause and effect pattern: for claim and adjustment letters
- The comparison and contrast pattern: for persuasive and sales letters
- The illustration pattern: for claim and adjustment letters
- The order of importance pattern: for persuasive and sales letters

Expression. Purpose and organization alone do not guarantee a successful letter. A purposeful and logically organized letter must be written in a reader-based style. If not the document will probably lose much of its persuasive force and the writer will have missed an opportunity for positive change.

Revision. No matter how clearly it is thought out and how carefully it is written, letters always need to be revised. This can be done in either of two ways:

1. As you write, by changing and improving the content and expression sentence by sentence or paragraph by paragraph.

2. After you write, by changing and improving the content and expression of a complete first draft.

WRITING FRONTLOADED ACTION REQUEST LETTERS

Like all expository writing, information and action letters have three parts: introduction, development, and conclusion. Since the majority of such letters are routine in nature, we will want to get right to the point. Such letters are frontloaded or direct in organization and expression, that is, they place the central idea up front in the introduction in the form of a request.

The Information Request Letter

INTRODUCTION	**Please tell me this.** Picks up the subject or purpose **In this way.** Expands the subject into a fully stated central idea
DEVELOPMENT	**Tell me this.** Gives the specific points of information desired **By answering these questions.** In a numbered list
CONCLUSION	**Please do this.** Refers back to the central idea **By this date.** Cues desired mental and physical action

Now let's consider a specific situation requiring an information request letter.

Situation: Paul Sullivan wishes to purchase a Victorian era house in a historic preservation district on Cape Cod. Not only will the house need extensive renovations, but Paul would also like to create a studio for his glasswork hobby. He needs to know what rules govern the district before he signs a contract to purchase. This is the first draft of his letter in the full block style.

Paul Sullivan
30 Benning Road
Fairfield, CT 12045

Bunky Marsden
Chairperson, Historic Preservation Committee

Town of Leeds
30 Main Street
Leeds, MA 02661

Dear Mr. Marsden:

I have looked at a number of houses in Leeds with the intent of purchasing one. The one I most would like to purchase is an early Victorian house on Eaton's Lane. The house has been quite neglected for many years and will need extensive renovation. Nevertheless, I think it will be an impressive property when I'm finished with it. I've enclosed a photo of the house so that you'll know the property.

However, before I enter into a contract to purchase on March 15 I need to know if there are rules governing what one may or may not do to antique properties in Leeds. I understand that you, as head of the Historic Preservation Committee, could enlighten me about this. I've heard you Yankees run a tight ship up there.

Some of the things I need to know include policies about exterior alterations. How extensive can changes be to the exterior of the house? I am thinking of adding a glass works studio wing for my hobby. I also sell my glass artifacts. What about trees? Can I remove any that might be in the way of my proposed renovations?

I need this information very quickly.

Thank you for your cooperation.

Sincerely,

Paul Sullivan

Revising the Information Request Letter

Formatting

A letter's physical appearance should send a positive signal even before the receiver reads a word of it. The following list of the components of letters from Chapter 11 provides guidelines for revision. Items needing revision have Xs to their right.

1. Letterhead or return address
2. Date line ✕
3. Inside address
4. Salutation or greeting ✕
5. Optional subject line
6. Body or paragraphs ✕
7. Complimentary close
8. Signature

9. Writer's printed name
10. Reference initials
11. Enclosure line ✕
12. Copy line

- *Date line.* Missing
- *Salutation or greeting.* The name *Bunky* is of indeterminate gender. It would be safer to write *Dear Bunky.*
- *Body or paragraphs.* The body paragraphs of letters should follow one style. This letter combines block and indented style. We'll use a partial block for the revised letter.
- *Enclosure line.* Missing
- *Graphic highlighting.* In this letter, graphic highlighting is needed to focus the reader immediately on the key points of the document. A numbered list of questions would help the receiver navigate easily and quickly through the letter.

Language and expression

- *Diplomatic or political savvy.* The offhand remark, "I've heard you run a tight ship up there," may have been intended as a bit of humor. But when you are not physically present to see the reaction, humor in writing is risky. The remark could also be taken as challenging or implying "I'm pretty tough too!"
- *Conversational tone.* Every letter is a personal contact. Even a routine letter can be made more personal and conversational with personal pronouns such as "you" and "yours" used frequently. This letter uses "I" almost exclusively.
- *Concise style.* The opening paragraph is a longwinded, background filled narrative.It needs to get to the point in a reader-based way.
- *Freedom from internal barriers.* The epithet "Yankees" could have been used in jest, but such expressions are not advisable unless the reader is well known and not likely to be offended.

Below is the revised information request letter using the semi-block format. Instead of 203 words there are only 138. The revised letter is also more courteous, more clear, and much more reader based.

Paul Sullivan
30 Benning Road
Fairfield, CT 12045

February 26, 2000

Bunky Marsden
Chairperson, Historic Preservation Committee

Town of Leeds
30 Main Street
Leeds, MA 02661

Dear Chairperson:

Please provide building and renovations guidelines for the Leeds Historic Preservation District. I plan to purchase an early Victorian home at 10 Eaton's Lane in your beautiful village. The house has been quite neglected for many years and will need extensive renovation. I've enclosed a photo of the house so that you'll know the property.

Your answers to the following questions will help me become a welcome addition to your community.

1. What rules govern alterations to the exterior of the house?
2. Would I be allowed to erect a studio building for my glasswork?
3. May trees be removed to make room for such a studio?
4. Would the sale of artifacts be permitted at the studio?

Because a contract signing is scheduled for March 20, I would appreciate your answers to these questions by March 15.

Sincerely,

Paul Sullivan

Paul Sullivan

Enclosure

THE ORDER LETTER

Today, orders are usually placed by phone. Increasingly, however, websites are used. For these, a clear, unambiguous form and expression will help avoid time wasting delays and confusion.

- In the opening paragraph, use a direct but polite frontloaded opening to make it clear that you are ordering, not merely inquiring.
- In the body, list in columns the quantities, the catalog numbers, the item descriptions, and the cost. Subtotal these followed by tax and shipping as applicable, and then include the total cost.
- In the closing tell the form of payment and the expected delivery date. Express appreciation to the receiver for handling your order.

Situation: Melanie De Havilland, purchasing manager of Torres, Smith, and Co., needs a number of items for their new office very quickly because they want to be in business before the holidays. This is their first office in the region and they do not have credit agreements in place yet with local suppliers.

INTRODUCTION	**Please send this order.** Picks up the subject or purpose **In this way.** Expands the subject into a fully stated central idea
DEVELOPMENT	**Send these things.** Gives the specific order list **At these prices.** In a numbered list
CONCLUSION	**Please do this.** Refers back to the central idea **By this date.** Cues desired mental and physical action

Below is a first draft of Melanie's order letter.

Torres, Smith, and Co.
280 Tremont Boulevard
Chicago, IL 63014

May 23, 2000

Total Supplies
35 Wrigley Road
Chicago, IL 63015

To whom it may concern:

I need supplies as soon as possible for our new office in Chicago. You may not have heard of us, but Torres, Smith, and Co. is the fastest growing executive search firm in the entire Midwestern area. I saw many of the items we need in your weekly newspaper circular.

20	No. 56255 Keep Tight 73 qt. Storage containers	$139.80
15	No. 53789 Steelcabs 5-Drawer lockable steel file cabinets	449.25
10	No. 50244 Wipe-right 12 roll paper towels	79.90
	Subtotal	$668.95
	Tax @ 5%	33.44
	Shipping	40.00
	Total	$742.39

I need these items STAT. Therefore, I have enclosed a check for the full amount. If there are any shipping charges or other fees involved in shipping this order, just bill Torres, Smith, and Co.

Thank you for your attention.

Sincerely,

Melanie De Havilland
Purchasing

ag

Revising the Order Letter

Formatting
Elements of the format needing change are noted with ×s.

1. Letterhead or return address
2. Date line
3. Inside address
4. Salutation or greeting ×
5. Optional subject line
6. Body or paragraphs
7. Complimentary close ×
8. Signature ×
9. Writer's printed name ×
10. Reference initials ×
11. Enclosure line ×
12. Copy line

Salutation or greeting. "To whom it may concern" is cold, outdated, and bypasses the reader. Call and find out the name of the person in shipping or use a title such as *Shipping Manager.*

Complimentary close. Should be flush left since the return address and date are already flush left in the full block style.

Signature. Place flush left.

Writer's printed name. Position flush left.

Reference initials. Melanie De Havilland's upper case initials should precede the lower case keyboarder's initials.

Enclosure line. Should be added since there is a check enclosed.

Language and expression

This order letter could be more clear, more concise, and more courteous.

More clear: by naming the newspaper and date of the advertisement mentioned in the opening paragraph and by avoiding acronyms such as *STAT*. Even if the receiver of such a letter understands the acronym shipping it *immediately* is an unreasonable request.

More concise: by omitting the background narrative about the company in the opening.

More courteous: by using a polite request in the opening and expressing a note of appreciation in the ending.

The writer of the letter might have given more thought to the *tomorrow* of all business communication. She has told Total Supplies to bill her company for any additional fees. It's better in such a situation to ask the shipper to call first about any additional fees.

Below is a revised example of an order letter in full block style. Not only are there 101 words instead of 140, but the revised letter is clearer and more courteous.

Torres, Smith, and Co.
280 Tremont Boulevard
Chicago, IL 63014

May 23, 2000

Mr. Andrew Johnson
Total Supplies
35 Wrigley Road
Chicago, IL 63015

Dear Mr. Johnson:

Please send by Express Mail the following supplies from your May 22 *Chicago Register* advertisement.

20	No. 56255 Keep Tight 73 qt. storage containers	$139.80
15	No. 53789 Steelcabs 5-drawer lockable steel file cabinets	449.25
10	No. 50244 Wipe-right 12-roll paper towels	79.90
	Subtotal	$668.95
	Tax @ 5%	33.44
	Shipping	40.00
	Total	$742.39

Your shipping this order as quickly as possible will help us open our new office by June 1st. Our check for $742.39 is enclosed. If there are any additional charges please call me at the above number.

Sincerely,

Melanie De Havilland

Melanie De Havilland

Purchasing

MDH:ag

Enclosure

THE CLAIM AND ADJUSTMENT LETTER

Sometimes, despite our best efforts at researching and double-checking, things just go wrong. A widely admired company ships a defective product, an order gets damaged in transit, a service is performed poorly. There's negative news all around. No one is happy; not the person who has to write the bad news letter, not the receiver.

Even though they are bad news situations, most claim and adjustment letters should follow the direct, frontloaded pattern. Stalling, double-talking, and evasion do little good—threats even less. When done in a reader-based manner, direct claim letters are easier for both writer and receiver to handle.

An easy three-stage pattern for writing direct claim and adjustment letters:

1. State the problem in a clear subject line using identifying information for the reader
2. Explain the extent of the problem or any subproblems that have resulted
3. State the solution that you see for this problem

Situation: Astral Technologies booked a three-day marketing forum for 335 people at the Golden Palmetto Resort and Conference Center in Orlando, Florida. From day one, when the first arrivals had to wait two hours before occupying their rooms, to checkout four days later, problems with rooms, menus, and equipment continued. Jack W. Gostin, Astral's Forum Coordinator, wants an explanation and substantial refunds.

INTRODUCTION {
Here is the problem. Picks up the subject or purpose
I have. Expands the subject into a fully stated central idea

DEVELOPMENT {
I can prove my case. Gives the specific evidence
In this way. Uses a numbered list

CONCLUSION {
Please correct this problem. Refers to the central idea
In this way. Cues desired mental and physical action

Below is the first draft of the claim letter using the simplified letter format.

ASTRAL TECHNOLOGIES
2100 Astral Avenue
Austin, TX 78710

March 24, 2000
Ms. Debra Janoway, Manager
Conventions and Meetings
Golden Palmetto Resort and Conference Center
15 Lakefront Boulevard
Orlando, FL 02199

ASTRAL TECHNOLOGIES MARKETING FORUM MARCH16-20, 2000.

Dear Ms. Janoway:

The three-day marketing forum that we recently concluded at the Golden Palmetto Resort and Conference Center was an unqualified fiasco. From the problems with the early arrivals on March 16th, who were kept waiting interminably for their rooms to be readied, to the delays with checkouts on March 20th, nothing went as planned.

You and I met in January and supposedly finalized all the arrangements for our marketing forum as set forth in the enclosed copy of contract. You assured me that the renovations, which were going on that time, would be completely finished before my group arrived. You also guaranteed that the finished rooms and conference center would be "finer and more beautiful than anywhere I had ever been in America."

The closing night banquet was very disappointing due to unauthorized, last minute menu changes, shortage of staff, and problems with air-conditioning.

Your people assigned many rooms to my people that could only be described as Third World in condition. Rugs were soiled, bathrooms were not properly cleaned, and the furniture outside on the balconies was dirty. To show you that this is not the product of an "overly refined sensitivity," as one of your assistants had the temerity to suggest, I have enclosed photographs documenting the truth of what I said. One last thing - the promised amenities were nowhere to be found in many of the bathroom accommodations. Subsequent to my remonstrances some of these were provided.

Finally, the installation of the carpeting in the conference center could only be described as a "work in progress" when we arrived, which can be seen in the enclosed photographs.

Because you failed to provide the level of comfort and convenience that was agreed to in January, as evidenced by the aforementioned failures, I am herewith demanding a refund in full.

This refund is expected immediately.

Sincerely yours,

Jack W. Gostin
Forum Coordinator

JWG: cl
Enclosures (five photographs)

Revising the Claim and Adjustment Letter

Formatting

1. Letterhead or return address
2. Date line
3. Inside address
4. Salutation or greeting ×
5. Optional subject line
6. Body or paragraphs ×
7. Complimentary close ×
8. Signature ×
9. Writer's printed name ×
10. Reference initials
11. Enclosure line ×
12. Copy line

Salutation or greeting. The simplified letter format does away with the traditional greeting line.

Body or paragraphs. The development of the letter would be more effectively organized using the chronological pattern with illustration or examples. This will make the sequence and seriousness of the problems encountered by Astral Technology clearer and easier to follow.

Complimentary close. Omitted in the simplified letter format.
Signature. Reposition flush left.
Writer's printed name. Place flush left under the signature.
Enclosure line. This is needed to bring attention to the contract copy referred to in the second paragraph.

Language and expression
This order letter could be more clear and concise, and less emotional and combative. Offensive remarks such as "Third World" are out of order in professional writing.
More clear: by using *graphic highlighting* in a chronologically arranged, numbered list of the problems encountered.
More concise: by omitting wordy phrases such as "the furniture that was outside on the balconies" and legalese wording such as "subsequent to," "aforementioned," and "herewith." Plain English words such as complaints should be used instead of "remonstrances."
More courteous: by using a less combative writing style without such expressions as "your people" and "my people." A more polite, objectively stated request should be used in the ending.

Despite his clear disappointment, the writer could be more focused on the *today* of this business communication, namely, what can be done at this point about the resort's mishandling of the forum.

Below is a revised example of this claim letter in simplified block style. There are 280 words instead of 327. Yet it is more specific, clearer, and more courteous. In the end it should be more effective in achieving a resolution.

ASTRAL TECHNOLOGIES
2100 Astral Avenue
Austin, TX 78710

March 24, 2000

Ms. Debra Janoway, Manager
Conventions and Meetings
Golden Palmetto Resort and Conference Center
15 Lakefront Boulevard
Orlando, FL 02199

ASTRAL TECHNOLOGIES MARKETING FORUM MARCH 16–20, 2000: CONTRACT 5455

The three-day marketing forum that we recently concluded at the Golden Palmetto Resort and Conference Center met neither our expectations nor the requirements of our contract signed January 18, 2000. Please note the problems experienced from the March 16th early arrivals to the March 20th checkouts.

1. The 70 guests who arrived March 16th at 4:00 PM as scheduled were kept waiting two hours while their rooms were readied.
2. The poolside reception did not open at 4:00 PM as scheduled, but at 6:00 PM.
3. Forty-seven guests experienced soiled carpeting in their rooms and unclean furniture on their balconies.
4. Thirty-eight guest bathrooms were not supplied with the agreed amenities until I complained personally to the Concierge Desk.
5. The conference center, far from being "one of the most beautiful business facilities in America" as promised in the forum brochure, was still being carpeted the morning of our opening meeting.
6. The closing night banquet was very disappointing due to unauthorized, last-minute menu changes such as substituting flounder for Florida Pompano and round steak for Chateaubriand. There were also many complaints of poor service and inadequate air conditioning.

The Golden Palmetto Resort and Conference Center clearly failed to fulfill the terms of the enclosed contract. I personally brought items one, two, and six to your attention as they happened. The enclosed photographs clearly demonstrate the problems listed above in items three, four, and five.

For these reasons I am submitting this claim to you for a partial refund of $21,750. This amount is expected by April 10.

Jack W. Gostin
Jack W. Gostin
Forum Coordinator

JWG: cl
Enclosures (five photographs, one contract)

THE INFORMATION AND ACTION-GRANTED REPLY LETTER

When one is able and ready to grant any of the information and action requests received, there is no reason to hide the good news. An action-granted reply letter should tell the reader what he or she wants to hear in the opening paragraph. Using the direct, frontloaded pattern the writer can create an information and action granted letter with the following steps:

1. Use a subject line to help your reader focus quickly on your central idea.

2. State the good news positive reply in the opening sentence of the introductory paragraph.
3. Give the specifics answers, point by point, to your reader's requests for information or action in the development or body of the letter.
4. Conclude in a friendly and personal manner. Refer back to the good news of the opening paragraph. Extend an offer of additional information, if the reader needs or desires it.

Now let's consider a specific situation requiring an information reply letter. George Byron wrote to Hellespont Health Insurance requesting information about substance abuse and mental health coverage in his policy. He asked for a list of network providers, including individual professionals and facilities, whether he had to call in advance for approval before going to one of the professionals in the network, and whether he could get help in choosing a provider.

INTRODUCTION	**Yes, I'll be happy to.** Picks up the subject or purpose **Do what you asked.** Expands purpose into a full central idea
DEVELOPMENT	**Here's the information.** Gives the specific information desired **And here is more.** In a numbered list
CONCLUSION	**If you need more.** Refers back to the central idea **Just ask us.** Cues desired mental and physical action

Below is the first draft of the information reply letter using the full block format.

Hellespont Health Insurance
200 Elm Street
Houston, TX 33776
727-144-2400

November 22, 1999

Dear Mr. Byron:

Enclosed is a copy of Hellespont Health's new Behavioral Health Care Provider Network directory. This directory lists many items of interest to subscribers such as you including but not limited to participating network providers who specialize in mental health and substance abuse. The network includes not only individual practitioners, but also facilities such as hospitals, and specialized programs, which might be of special interest.

When selecting a provider from the directory, please call the toll-free Mental Health and Substance Abuse number listed on the back of your Hellespont ID card to get precertification. (Precertification means that the mental health and/or substance abuse service was approved in advance by Hellespont's Behavioral Health Care Management Program.) Except in the case of an emergency condition, members must obtain precertification. When you call the toll-free number, you will speak with a trained mental health counselor who will precertify the necessary services and refer you to an appropriate provider.

Remember that under the terms of your contract, any and all mental health and substance abuse services must be received from Hellespont network providers. If you have any questions about mental health and substance abuse services, please call the number on the back of your ID card.

Sincerely,

Linda Hamilton, M.D.
Vice President
Senior Medical Director

Revising the Claim Letter

Formatting

In the following revision checklist, items that need improvement are marked with an ✕.

1. Letterhead or return address
2. Date line
3. Inside address
4. Salutation or greeting
5. Optional subject line ✕
6. Body or paragraphs ✕
7. Complimentary close
8. Signature
9. Writer's printed name
10. Reference initials ✕
11. Enclosure line ✕
12. Copy line

Subject line. A subject line is optional but recommended in reply letters to focus the reader immediately on the favorable reply you have ready.

Body or paragraphs. The development of the letter would be more effectively organized using chronological order. This will make it easier for the reader to understand the procedures explained in the reply letter. The concluding paragraph would be helped by adding more precise information such as a phone number to call, rather than referring the reader to a membership card which may not be handy.

Enclosure line. Needed to refer to the directory mentioned in the first paragraph.

Language and expression

This reply letter could be more clear, concise, and personal:

More clear: by using *graphic highlighting* in a chronologically arranged, numbered list of the precertification procedures mentioned.

More concise: by omitting wordy phrases such as "including but not limited to"

More courteous: by beginning paragraph three with the simple *please.*

Below is a revised example of this direct, frontloaded reply letter. It has 194 words instead of the original 213. Yet it is more reader-based and easier to follow.

Hellespont Health Insurance
200 Elm Street
Houston, TX 33776
727-144-2400

November 22, 1999

Dear Mr. Byron:

SUBJECT: YOUR NOVEMBER 10 INQUIRY ABOUT BEHAVIORAL HEALTH CARE

Enclosed is a your copy of *Hellespont's Behavioral Health Care Providers* directory. This directory lists individual practitioners, facilities such as hospitals, and specialized programs.

To select a provider from the directory, please use the following procedure.

1. Call the toll-free Mental Health and Substance Abuse number, 1-888-444-9000, listed on the back of your Hellespont ID card to get precertification. (Precertification means that the mental health and/or

substance abuse service was approved in advance by Hellespont's Behavioral Health Care Management Program.)

2. Except in the case of an emergency condition, members *must* obtain precertification.
3. When you call the toll-free number, you will speak with a trained mental health counselor who will precertify the necessary services and refer you to an appropriate provider.

Please remember that under the terms of your contract, all mental health and substance abuse services must be received from Hellespont network providers. If you have any other questions, please call the same toll-free number, 1-888-444-9000. Our trained professionals are ready to help you 24 hours a day, every day.

Sincerely,

Linda Hamilton

Linda Hamilton, M.D.
Vice President
Senior Medical Director

Enclosure

THE ADJUSTMENT GRANTED REPLY LETTER

Few types of business communication need pay as much attention to the three writing ages of yesterday, today, and tomorrow as adjustment letters. These are letters written in response to customer claim letters.

Customers are disappointed and often angry when they write claim letters. The result is that although such letters are not always calm or diplomatic, the writer of the response must be. When faced with the responsibility of answering letters like these, the writer needs to stop and ask some questions.

1. *Yesterday:* What caused the problem?
2. *Today:* How do I correct the problem?
3. *Tomorrow:* Will my action today keep the customer tomorrow?

Since it is easier to retain customers than find new ones and since we live in such a litigious age, most businesses grant adjustments whenever possible. In granting adjustments the writer follows reader-based guidelines such as the following in the form and content of the letter:

- Use the direct, frontloaded pattern, that is, give the good news immediately in the opening sentence.
- Avoid negative thought and language. Don't apologize and express regret about the situation. Nothing is achieved by rehashing old news and reopening old wounds. Don't fix blame or question customers' motives in seeking adjustments. You have decided to right the wrong, probably at some immediate expense to your business. If you do it begrudgingly, you might end up losing the customer as well.
- Close on a forward looking note, namely, future business.

Situation: John Petersen, proprietor of a wholesale flooring company, has received a claim letter for the replacement of wood floors his company installed four months earlier. The job was done in a prime building in which he had wanted to do business for some time.

The letter states that the prefabricated parquet squares have begun to buckle in 3 of the 12 rooms where they were laid, because they were of "inferior quality." It also states that the workers sent on this job were inexperienced and "obviously rushed" by the foreman to complete the job quickly. Mr. Petersen decides to swallow the loss now and replace the flooring, even though the customer did not take his spoken advice about its suitability for the humid climate.

INTRODUCTION	**Yes, I'll happily.** Picks up the subject or purpose **Approve your claim.** Expands purpose into a full central idea
DEVELOPMENT	**Here's what I'll do.** Gives the specific information desired **For you, my valued customer.** In a numbered list
CONCLUSION	**If our company can do more for you.** Suggest possibilities **We're always here.** Cues desired mental and physical action

Below is the first version of John Petersen's adjustment grant letter using the indented format.

Petersen Estate Flooring
Via Mizner
Palm Beach, FL 32665

January 5, 2000

Russell Pine, Managing Agent
Chatsworth Towers
10 Ocean Drive
Palm Beach, FL 32550

Dear Mr. Pine:

You have been a valued customer of Petersen Estate Flooring, and we will be happy to replace the flooring in the solariums and breakfast rooms on the eleventh through the twentieth floor apartments of Chatsworth Towers.

The flooring that was installed was of the highest quality oak available today. It was assembled and installed completely by hand in the finest tradition of old-world craftsmanship. I personally assigned my most experienced workers to your job cite to guarantee your total satisfaction and that of your discriminating shareholders at Chatsworth Towers.

However, as I warned you prior to the commencement of the project even the finest oak flooring is not suitable for the conditions of high humidity that are typical of this area especially in the summer months. Have you thought of having the air-conditioning and de-humidification systems checked? You will recall that I advised you to go with the marble flooring in the breakfast rooms and the hand painted tiles that I import from Majorca for the solariums. Solariums are especially subject to high humidity, which is most certainly the cause of the buckling you complained about. I have enclosed brochures on the marble and tile floorings. Perhaps you would like to reconsider your choices at this time.

I would like to send in my men as soon as possible to get the job done correctly. I will be in touch with you shortly to advise you of the starting date. I regret any inconvenience this may cause.

Sincerely,

John Petersen
President

JP: rh

Revising the Adjustment Granted Letter

Formatting

The areas that need improvement are followed by Xs.

1. Letterhead or return address

2. Date line
3. Inside address
4. Salutation or greeting
5. Optional subject line ×
6. Body or paragraphs ×
7. Complimentary close
8. Signature
9. Writer's printed name
10. Reference initials
11. Enclosure line ×
12. Copy line

Subject line: A subject line is optional but needed in a case like this when both parties deal with many projects each day. It could also be used to focus the reader immediately on the favorable reply the writer has ready.

Body or paragraphs: A positive reply adjustment letter such as this would be more effectively organized using a combination of chronological and cause–effect order to help the reader focus on the sequence of events that caused the problems to occur. The concluding paragraph would be more effective with a more positive and specific action information closing.

Enclosure line. This is needed for the two brochures mentioned in the third paragraph.

Language and expression

This adjustment letter could be much more positive and less accusatory. Assigning blame to the managing agent lessens the good will to be gained by agreeing to replace the flooring. Some ways to improve the language and expression of the letter are as follows:

More correct: the word *cite* in the second paragraph is correctly spelled. However, the spell-check does not alert the writer that it is the wrong word. The word *site,* or location, is needed here.

More clear: by using *graphic highlighting* in a chronologically arranged, numbered list of what will be done to change and improve the situation.

More concise: by omitting lengthy background narratives.

More reader-based and courteous: by suggesting early starting dates to demonstrate sincere determination to correct the situation and asking the receiver if those dates would be convenient.

Below is a more effective version of this adjustment letter using 240 instead of 284 words.

Petersen Estate Flooring
Via Mizner
Palm Beach, FL 32665

January 5, 2000

Russell Pine, Managing Agent
Chatsworth Towers
10 Ocean Drive
Palm Beach, FL 32550

SUBJECT: REPLACEMENT OF FLOORING AT CHATSWORTH TOWERS

Dear Mr. Pine:

You have been a valued customer of Petersen Estate Flooring for many years, and we will be happy to replace the flooring in the solariums and breakfast rooms on the eleventh through the twentieth floor apartments of Chatsworth Towers at no expense to you.

The materials were of the highest quality oak available today. The installation was done by the most experienced craftsmen using time-honored traditions of old-world craftsmanship.

I am ready to start the flooring replacement project immediately. Will the following schedule be convenient for you and the affected shareholders at Chatsworth Towers?

1. The week of January 20th: remove and replace flooring on the eleventh through the fifteenth floors.
2. The week of January 30th: remove and replace flooring on the sixteenth through the twentieth floors.

For the new building being constructed on Lake Avenue you may wish to consider the marble and tile flooring that we import from Europe. It is shown in the enclosed brochures. Or you may wish to view samples at our Via Mizner showroom.

Please let me know if the schedule proposed above is convenient. I will be happy to schedule the flooring replacement differently, if you so request.

Sincerely,

John Petersen

John Petersen
President

THE PERSONNEL REPLY LETTER

The direct or frontloaded pattern is used for replying to inquiries about personnel. The reason for this is that the sender is giving the receiver what he or she requested and in that sense it is a good news message. Of course you may not always have good things to say about the person you have received the inquiry about, but a clear and unambiguous direct reply is still preferred.

The stages of a direct, frontloaded personnel reply letter:

1. Use a subject line to establish an immediate link to the requested information.
2. If you have received a personnel inquiry listing specific points of information, respond in kind with a numbered list.
3. Close in a positive manner, emphasizing good will and continuing relations with the inquiring party. When you do not have completely favorable news about the subject of the inquiry, close without leaving an opening for future discussion. Your company or agency may be cautious about doing personnel evaluation letters in the first place. Going into detail in a somewhat unfavorable reply might set off alarms in the legal department.

Situation: Robert Shaw, the Principal of the Oak Hill School for Children with Special Needs has received an evaluation request for Marilyn Giglia from William Colon of The Independent School in San Jose, California. Ms. Giglia, who worked with Mr. Shaw for seven years, has applied for a position at The Independent School.

INTRODUCTION	**Yes, I'll be happy to.** Picks up the purpose or subject line **Do what you asked.** Expands purpose into a full central idea
DEVELOPMENT	**Here's the information.** Gives the specific information desired **As you requested it.** In a comparable numbered list
CONCLUSION	**I was happy to help you.** Refers back to the central idea **With this letter.** Cues desired mental and physical action

Below is the first draft of a direct personnel reply letter using the simplified letter format.

The Oak Hill School
26 Sycamore Lane
Tarrytown, NY 12580

May 4, 2000

Mr. William Colon, Principal
The Independent School
42 Hamilton Avenue
San Jose, CA 95760

PERSONNEL EVALUATION ON MARILYN P. GIGLIA

Since joining the staff seven years ago, Marilyn Giglia has proven herself to be a teacher of exceptional quality and competence. Although concentrating in the area of English at all levels, she has also taught a variety of subjects including science, history, and health. All these were taught with advanced preparation, motivation and an understanding of the components necessary to present the information to a heterogeneous grouping of emotionally disturbed students.

Ms. Giglia attends to everything she does in a warm, open, supportive and compassionate way. The youngsters with whom she deals recognize this and not only tend to perform well for her, but seek her out as an adult who they can trust, confide in and seek advice from. At the same time Ms. Giglia runs her room in this manner, she is also able to set very clear limits as to what is acceptable and what is not, and will seek out help from a supervisor when she feels that a situation has gone far enough and a youngster needs to leave the classroom. I have noted and expressed with amazement and pleasure that almost every time I have entered her room, despite the "hectic chaos" which might be going on all around Oak Hill on a "normal" day, Ms. Giglia's class is present, quiet, books open and a productive class session is under way. In addition, Ms. Giglia will not let a youngster "slip by" but will follow them up, be it school work or behavior and see to it that they know that she cares enough to "stay on their case" about the issue.

Ms. Giglia has always been an enthusiastic, caring and supportive member of the staff. She has always done more than her share on staff functions, with school Special Event activities and in general, it is comforting to know that one can always count on her for help and support on any activity or situation. An example at the moment, is her current support for graduating seniors, in the absence of Mr. Harrison, by helping them fill out college applications and doing some of the follow-up work necessary to complete plans after graduation. She also recently set up two substitute teachers in preparation for their teaching two English classes while the regular teacher was out on sick leave.

To summarize, Marilyn Giglia has performed at Oak Hill like a dedicated professional. She approaches her daily task with enthusiasm, as a solid individual with a sensitivity and caring and receptiveness to dealing with anything that comes her way. She is there for the staff, she is there for the students and she is held in esteem by both groups, quite evidently. Her contribution to Oak Hill is an enormous one.

Marilyn P. Giglia will be a significant asset to your school. I know that I speak for my entire professional staff and myself when I say that we will miss her here at Oak Hill.

I appreciate the value you place on my opinion and judgement.

WILLIAM COLON, PRINCIPAL. THE OAK HILL SCHOOL

WC: nb

Revising the Personnel Reply Letter

Formatting

In the following list, areas that can be improved are highlighted with ✕s.

1. Letterhead or return address
2. Date line
3. Inside address
4. Salutation or greeting
5. Optional subject line ✕
6. Body or paragraphs ✕
7. Complimentary close
8. Signature
9. Writer's printed name
10. Reference initials ✕
11. Enclosure line
12. Copy line

Subject line. The writer of an information reply letter should include the date of the original request letter. This helps focus the reader immediately on the specific request that is being answered.

Body or paragraphs. Mr. Colon's positive reply letter could be more effectively organized using a combination of spatial and illustration logical patterns of development. The spatial pattern could guide the reader, for example, from campus to building to classroom. While the illustration pattern would provide examples of Ms. Giglia's performance in each area.

Reference initials. In the simplified form only the keyboarders initials in lowercase are printed.

Language and expression

This letter, while very complimentary, is very long and rambling. Making it much more concise would help the reader grasp the key points of the subject more quickly. *Graphic highlighting* in the form of a numbered list of the responses to the specific questions asked would also make the letter more reader-based.

One way the writer of the letter could achieve the goal of being *clear and concise* is by using shorter sentences. In the second paragraph there are two sentences over 50 words long. That is about double the maximum length recommended for effective business and professional writing.

Below is a revised frontloaded information reply letter in the simplified letter format. It is 275 words instead of the original 508 words. It is more reader-based because it refers directly to the specific points of information requested and does it more concisely.

The Oak Hill School
26 Sycamore Lane
Tarrytown, NY 12580

May 4, 2000

Mr. William Colon, Principal
The Independent School
42 Hamilton Avenue
San Jose, CA 95760

PERSONNEL EVALUATION ON MARILYN P. GIGLIA REQUESTED APRIL 25

Here are my responses to your inquiries about Marilyn Giglia. For your convenience, they are listed in the same order as your letter.

1. Academic strength and classroom performance. Since joining Oak Hill eight years ago Marilyn Giglia has excelled at teaching our emotionally challenged student body. In addition to her primary subject, English, she has successfully taught science, history, and health. She has done all these with a very high level of preparation, motivation, and professionalism.

2. Personal and classroom interaction. Ms. Giglia is warm and supportive at all times, which encourages her students to trust her as an adult from whom they can seek advice. However, she sets clear limits on acceptable classroom behavior. As a result, no matter how hectic the outside may be, her room is always quiet and productive.
3. Team player. Ms. Giglia has always been an enthusiastic and supportive staff member. In fact, she has always done more than her share on staff functions and special events. Currently she is filling in during a teacher's absence by helping graduating seniors complete their college applications. She has also just prepared two substitute teachers to fill in during a regular teacher's leave of absence.

To summarize, Marilyn P. Giglia has performed at Oak Hill like a dedicated professional. She is held in the highest esteem by staff and students. Ms. Giglia will be a significant asset to your school. My entire staff and I will miss her here at Oak Hill.

I appreciate the value you place on my opinion and judgment.

William Colon

WILLIAM COLON, PRINCIPAL. THE OAK HILL SCHOOL

nb

15

Writing and Revising Indirect or Deferred-Load Letters For Negative News, Persuasion, and Sales

Just as there are situations within corporations and government agencies that may be the subject of internal, negative-news memos, there are situations requiring external, negative-news letters. An unsubstantiated claim about a product must be denied. A request for sensitive information must be turned down. Requests for donations to charitable events cannot always be granted. Requests to attend and address meetings cannot always be accepted.

While most people realize that they cannot agree to every request, they still are disappointed when someone turns down *their* request. Some people give a shrug, adapt, and find someone else or some other way to get their need fulfilled. But others get annoyed, even hostile, when turned down.

Learning how to write a sensitive, empathetic negative-news letter is a very important skill. It might not make the bad news pretty, but it can prevent hard feelings of rejection and a nasty trip down the slippery slope of ill will.

Persuasive and sales letters, while not explicitly carrying bad news, can face a similarly unwelcome reception. For this reason, writers of such letters should use the same indirect pattern that negative-news writers employ, namely, the indirect or deferred load method.

The most important aspect of the indirect pattern is placing the central idea at a later stage in the letter. This is not to suggest that we leave our readers guessing or in the dark at the beginning of negative-news or persuasive and sales letters. It does mean that we get to the central idea of the letter gradually but deliberately.

Purpose and Development

Whenever sitting down to compose an indirect or deferred load letter the writer adheres to the same four main purposes that writers of direct, frontloaded letters follow: information, persuasion, results or changes, and good will or public relations. While these purposes exist to a greater or lesser degree in every business document, the area of emphasis will vary. As a result, the method of development will change.

As we saw in the preceding chapters, when the primary purpose of a memo or letter is to give information that the reader will be happy about, or at least neutral to receive, the central idea goes up front in the introductory paragraph.

However, when the information or persuasion is being delivered to an unreceptive audience, the central idea will be deferred to a later paragraph in the body of the document. When this happens, the purposes of information and persuasion are not primary but are being used to lead up the primary purpose, which is the result or change being announced.

When this indirect or deferred presentation of the central idea is done effectively the writer will get the desired results. The receiver, while not exactly getting what he or she sought, is left with a feeling of good will toward the writer and the organization.

Conclusion

Bad news letters and persuasive letters both use the indirect method of presentation and development but differ in the function of their concluding paragraphs. The negative-news letter ends with a statement of feeling; the persuasive or sales letter ends with a call to action.

CREATING EFFECTIVE, DEFERRED-LOAD NEGATIVE-NEWS LETTERS

Before writing even the first draft of a negative-news letter the writer always pauses to recall the three ages of successful business communication.

1. *Yesterday.* Try to determine as precisely as possible what has occurred in the past to cause the present problem. Who has sent the request you have decided must be denied? Do you have any

personal feelings at all toward that person? If so, has it been a pleasant or unpleasant relationship?

2. *Today.* How can I avoid delivering the bad news badly? How can I do it in a positive way?
3. *Tomorrow.* By delivering my bad news in a positive way I can avoid damaging a good relationship with the person or group. Or I can at least avoid worsening an already strained relationship.

Purpose

The primary purposes of negative-news letters are similar to those of indirect memos:

- *Information:* To tell people about problems involving situations and issues
- *Damage control:* To prevent or change people's negative reception of ideas and issues

How successfully we achieve these purposes will affect not only our primary audience, the targeted receiver of the message, but also our secondary audience. These are the unknown numbers of people who will learn of the news and how we delivered it to our primary audience.

The relative degree of bad news will determine just how indirectly we craft our message. There are five degrees or methods of embedding the bad news. The following list is in increasing order of indirectness, from least to most indirect. While you will always use the first method, deferring the bad news to a later paragraph, you may not always feel it necessary to go to the higher levels of indirectness. Whether you do will be a factor of your review of the *yesterday, today,* and *tomorrow* of each situation. Whichever level you choose, always use *positive language* to convey negative news.

Five Ways to backload or soften negative news:

1. By deferring the bad news until a later paragraph of the document. As a general rule, place it in the next to the last paragraph.
2. By placing the unwelcome news toward the end of that chosen paragraph; hold off until the last sentence, almost as a throwaway or afterthought.
3. By putting the negative news in the subordinate clause of a complex sentence:
   Negative expression: "We only give cash refunds within 30 days of purchase, after that *we do not give cash refunds.*"
   Positive expression: "We gladly give cash refunds within 30 days of purchase, after that *we give store credits.*"

4. By expressing it in the passive voice of the verb:
   Negative expression: "We only give cash refunds within 30 days of purchase, although cash refunds *are not given* after that."
   Positive expression: We gladly give cash refunds within 30 days of purchase, although store credits *are given* after that."
5. By not stating it at all, but simply implying it: "We have a very generous cash refund policy for all returns made within 30 days." This expression implies, but never directly states, that no cash refunds are given after 30 days.

The four stages of unfolding bad news successfully:

1. Adopt an objective yet personal tone. Avoid any direct mention of the problem or issue in your opening paragraph. Instead, mention shared goals and other understandings that you have in common.
2. Give clear, simple reasons for the unhappy change or decision you are about to reveal. These should be reasons in plain English, readily understood by your reader, not couched in jargon or legalese.
3. Disclose the news as something that involves and affects you, the sender, and the receiver. Place it in a brief subordinate clause with the verb in the passive voice.
4. Gently close the door. Offer alternatives or face-saving damage control proposals wherever feasible. You've done nothing wrong, so there isn't any reason to apologize.

Subject line and central idea. Write the purpose or central idea in one clear sentence. Even when it will not be used explicitly in the optional subject line, it is the first step in limiting the message to a single topic and organizing the message.

Development or body. Ease into the subject line gradually. Follow the principles of writing a reader-based document. Writers of bad news letters need to show that they are aware of and have considered their readers' opinions, even as they lead the reader to a different conclusion that writer and reader can both share.

Conclusion. The care you have taken in delivering the negative news indirectly should carry over into the conclusion. The more unwelcome the news you have given your reader, the more important it is to end on a pleasant, courteous note. Most of all avoid any suggestion that the matter is still open for discussion.

- Extend best wishes or, depending on the situation, suggest other avenues that your reader might pursue.

- Remain confident that your decision was correct. Don't refer back to the bad news or apologize. Apologizing suggests doubt in the wisdom of your decision.
- Avoid clichéd endings that may only prolong the unpleasantness. The decision has been made. Closing with expressions such as, "If there are any further questions, please do not hesitate to call me," will probably appear formulaic and hollow at this point.
- Remember that even negative news can be presented with reader benefits and shared goals in mind. If nothing else, the shared goal is to leave the bad news behind and move on.

WRITING AN EFFECTIVE CLAIM DENIAL LETTER

Everyone thinks his or her claim is justified. Even perhaps someone demanding $10 million for spilling hot coffee on himself. The real problem at work is emotional. The claimant thinks he or she was wronged, and not in some abstract, theoretical way. When a product fails to deliver as promised, perhaps the advertisement's to blame for raising unreasonable expectations. Nevertheless, the claimant feels wronged or betrayed in some deeply personal, intangible way.

Claimants don't want to hear excuses, they want remedies. And they tell their friends and anyone who'll listen just how upset they are with the product and the company. Does this mean you grant every claim? Sometimes, when they are unjustified or unreasonable, you decide you must say "no." Can you refuse the claim without losing the customer?

Tone

What causes the loss of customers is often not the denial of the claim but the way it was handled. The respondent got as emotionally involved as the claimant did, causing the worst case scenario short of litigation—an ugly shouting match in public.

The calm, logical thought process outlined above for creating a bad news letter must be accompanied by similarly cool, dispassionate language. Assessing blame, finger pointing, and accusations are neither wise nor productive. The bad news letter situation is the one case where writing a reader-based document observes the "you view" by hardly ever using the *you* word.

Situation: Liya Krikheli and Gloria Coppola purchased tickets for "The Battle of the Baritones." The event was billed as "an evening of vocal splendor with the three greatest baritones in the world: Megalo Stoma, Gromkiy Golos, and Duze Usta." The sold-out performance was scheduled to take place on Saturday evening at the Bernheimer Arena in Denver under the control of the impressario, Boca Grandita. Thursday evening Stoma's manager said he could not perform in the excessive heat. Golos's agent called to say that the singer was suffering from a severe case of laryngitis. Usta said he would not go on alone for a solo recital unless his portion of the gate was tripled.

The arena decided to mount a concert with three different performers: Pe Katan, Micri Voce, and Patara Piri. The arena changed their Internet website and their radio advertisements, and posted signs at the entrance to the parking lot and arena announcing the change and the policy regarding refunds.

Liya and Gloria traveled such a long distance for the concert that they decided to enter the arena and listen to the substitute performers. They left after the first encore arias and asked for their money back. When refused at the box office, they wrote a letter demanding a refund. Management has decided to deny the refunds.

INTRODUCTION	**Our Arena is proud.** Picks up the purpose or subject line **Of its concert offerings.** Expands purpose into a full central idea
DEVELOPMENT	**Because of these facts.** Presents reasons leading up to central idea **The arena only does this.** Without mentioning refund denial
CONCLUSION	**Please enjoy these passes.** Ends on a positive note **At a future event.** Cues receiver to the future

Below is the first version of the claim denial letter:

The Bernheimer Arena for the Performing Arts
Boulder Freeway Denver, CO 77600 612-777-7800

July 26, 2000

Liya Krikheli
Gloria Coppola
Seven Border Boulevard
Denver, CO 77625

Dear Liya and Gloria:

SUBJECT: BERNHEIMER ARENA OFFICIAL REFUND POLICY

I received your letter explaining your displeasure with the events that took place during last week's concert at the Bernheimer Arena. I am unhappy that you believe I and my organization deliberately deceived you, when I believe that we tried our best to rectify a rather unpleasant situation. When the impressario, who scheduled The Battle of the Baritones, informed me of the inability of his world class stars to perform I investigated the matter. It turned out that there were many issues of a personal nature as well as medical ones.

The Bernheimer Arena was never responsible for the singers who were going to perform at the concert; we just provided the facility and the advertising of the event.

In order to clean up the mess left, that Thursday we decided to go on with a modified version of the originally promised concert. At that time I took many steps to guarantee that the public were made aware of the changes. I did all of the following. I changed our web site and radio advertising to say that for reasons beyond our control Megalo Stoma, Gromkiy Golos, and Duze Usta would not be appearing. I described the very high level of the replacement baritones Pe Katan, Micri Voce, and Patara Piri. In addition to the aforementioned actions I furthermore set up signs at the entrances and parking lots of the Arena.

Somehow upon entering the premises you must have missed all of the signs. I did not as you claim in your letter have any newspaper advertising featuring the originally scheduled baritones published the day of the concert. I was not trying to deceive anyone into believing that the original concert was going to take place. I was only trying to salvage a bad situation, and I feel that I made a very genuine, documented effort to communicate the changed program.

Ticket refunds were available prior to the commencement of the event. You only had to go to the box office and turn in your tickets. But as you told me you stayed until the encores I cannot grant you a $120.00 refund of the two tickets. I understand that you claim that you didn't know anything about the talent change until the event was well underway, so I am enclosing two complimentary passes for a future event. I am sorry for the unhappy experience you suffered but I hope you come back in the future.

Sincerely,

Debra Simidian
Manager, Advertising and Special Events

DS: ag

Revising the Claim Denial Letter

Formatting

Areas that can be improved are marked with Xs.

1. Letterhead or return address
2. Date line
3. Inside address
4. Salutation or greeting
5. Optional subject line X
6. Body or paragraphs X
7. Complimentary close
8. Signature
9. Writer's printed name
10. Reference initials
11. Enclosure line X
12. Copy line

Letterhead or return address. Should include the Internet site referred to in the third paragraph.

Subject line. A subject line is optional but might not be wise in a claim denial letter. Unless it is so vague as to be meaningless, it will tip off the reader too early that the news is bad.

Body or paragraphs. This claim denial letter is effectively organized using a combination of chronological and cause–effect order. However, the *graphic highlighting* of the disclaimer in the second paragraph is not a good idea. It only underscores the combative tone of the first paragraph. As used it's the graphic equivalent of shouting. The conclusion needs some major changes. The writer is offering the two passes in such a begrudging, negative way that the hoped-for results will never occur.

Enclosure line. Required for the two complimentary passes offered in the last paragraph.

Language and expression

Claim denial letters need to be as positive as possible, never combative and accusatory. Questioning motives and sincerity will not bring about good will. A calm, objective statement of reasons and policies is needed. Similarly, rehashing and expressing sorrow over what went wrong only serves to reopen the wounds. In addition, the language and expression in the letter can be improved by making it:

More concise: by omitting lengthy background narratives and wordy phrases such as "prior to the commencement of the event."

More reader based and courteous: the combative *I* versus *you* wording should be replaced with *we* and *you.*

Below is a more effective version of the claim denial letter using 246 instead of 426 words.

The Bernheimer Arena for the Performing Arts

July 26, 2000
Liya Krikheli
Gloria Coppola
Seven Border Boulevard
Denver, CO 77625

Dear Liya and Gloria:

The Bernheimer Arena has been presenting a variety of cultural events for our community for more than twenty-five years. More than half a million people have enjoyed many of the great orchestras, folk and classical dance groups, and vocal artists of the world here in Denver. We have always been proud of our reputation for accommodating our customers' wishes and needs.

Sometimes things occur that are beyond our control. Late last Thursday, after learning of the sudden indisposition of the three baritones scheduled to perform on Sunday, we took many steps to advise the public of the changes.

- We changed our website and radio advertising to say that Megalo Stoma, Gromkiy Golos, and Duze Usta would not be appearing.
- We described the very high level of the new baritones Pe Katan, Micri Voce, and Patara Piri
- We set up signs at the entrances and parking lots of the arena announcing the revised program.

In keeping with our long-standing policy, refunds are available, and freely given, until an event begins.

I am enclosing two complimentary passes for a future event. They are valid for a full year.

We hope to see you enjoying one of the many upcoming events scheduled at The Bernheimer Arena.

Sincerely,

Debra Simidian

Debra Simidian
Manager, Advertising and Special Events

DS: ag

Enclosures (2)

Boulder Freeway ✱ Denver, CO 77600
WWW.BERNHEIMER.ARENA.COM ✱ 612-777-780

LETTERS DECLINING INVITATIONS

The hectic pace of business often forces us to choose between equally important demands on our time. We face daily conflicts between our business and personal lives. Sometimes it is not just a scheduling conflict. There can be diplomatic and political reasons for not attending or speaking at an event.

We have business trips to make right in the middle of a family medical crisis. Invitations to attend seminars and address meetings cannot always be accepted. You get an invitation to dinner from an important British client, who wants to discuss a new project. He's only in New York overnight before flying on to Los Angeles, but you are already scheduled to address a major trade show.

Faced with such conflicts, we determine our priorities and decide which responsibility is paramount. This means, of course, that some company, agency, or charitable organization is going to be turned down. More to the point, some individual is going to be disappointed. And perhaps that individual is going to take the rejection personally.

Writing a diplomatic, empathic invitation refusal letter is a very necessary skill to acquire. It will not change the fact of the turndown, but a well-written letter *today* can prevent negative fallout in the form of lost good will *tomorrow.*

The four stages of unfolding bad news in the invitation refusal letter

1. Adopt a personal tone of good will in the opening paragraph. Avoid any direct mention of the scheduling conflict or other possible reason for the turndown in your opening paragraph. Instead, mention shared goals, offer praise for the activities of the group or individual that extended the invitation, and express appreciation for the interest shown in you.
2. Give clear, simple reasons for the unwelcome news you are about to reveal. These should be expressed in plain English without clichés or jargon.
3. Disclose the news in a positive way as something that involves and affects you, the sender, and the receiver. Place it in a brief subordinate clause with the verb in the passive voice. Or, if possible, do not state the bad news at all, but imply it.

4. Close on a friendly, forward-looking note. Don't refer back to, or express regret about, the invitation you have just declined. Offer alternatives wherever possible or desirable. Once again, if you've done nothing wrong there's no need to apologize.

Situation: Virginia Thompson, vice president of marketing at International Textiles, has received an invitation to dinner in New York from Piero Visconti, head of the fashion house of Visconti. While not a major buyer of International's in terms of quantity, the House of Visconti is highly valued as a prestigious account. Ms. Thompson is scheduled to testify at a congressional subcommittee hearing in Washington, D.C. the next morning before flying on to a trade show in Milan later in the day. She needs time to prepare for this testimony and cannot squeeze in the time-consuming formal dinner Mr. Visconti has in mind.

INTRODUCTION	**Thanks for your kind invitation.** Establishes a positive setting **Your dinners are a pleasure.** Reinforces positive relationship
DEVELOPMENT	**Because of these facts.** Presents reasons leading up to central idea **Could we do this?** Suggests alternative to the formal dinner
CONCLUSION	**Please consider my idea.** Ends on a positive note **For the future event.** Cues receiver to the future shared event

Below is the draft of Ms. Tompson's full block style decining the invitation.

International Textiles Corporation

February 7, 2000

Mr. Piero Visconti
House of Visconti
15 East 57th Street
New York, NY 10001

SUBJECT: FEBRUARY 20TH DINNER PARTY SCHEDULING CONFLICT

Dear Piero:

I received your invitation today to attend your dinner party on February 20th. I wish I could. I hear that invitations to your evenings are still in great demand. I hadn't even been aware that you were going to be in New York at this time of the year.

Business pressures on me have been huge. Please don't get me wrong. I'm not complaining. The orders for our new materials have just been flooding in! I can't wait to show you the new samples.

I have been called to testify at congressional sub-committee hearings on the day after your dinner. Furthermore, I must catch a flight later that same day from Dulles to Milan to speak at the trade show and show more of our superior Tasmanian 140's patterned fabrics. You'll want to see and buy these magnificent fabrics for your own line!

I truly regret not being able to attend on February 20th. Please forgive me and let me know when we can meet. Would Milan be good for you after the trade show is over?

Cordially,

Virginia Thompson
Vice-president, Marketing

VT: tr

400 Park Avenue New York, NY 10029
212-445-3000 www.InternationaTextiles.com

Revising the Letter Declining an Invitation

Formatting
Areas of suggested change are highlighted with Xs.

1. Letterhead or return address
2. Date line ✕
3. Inside address
4. Salutation or greeting
5. Optional subject line ✕
6. Body or paragraphs ✕
7. Complimentary close ✕
8. Signature ✕
9. Writer's printed name ✕
10. Reference initials

11. Enclosure line
12. Copy line

Date line. Moving this entry to the right side in the partial block style will give the letter a less formal and rigid appearance.

Subject line. Using a subject line is too cold and hard-nosed for turning down a personal invitation such as this. Its very presence unnecessarily signals a tone of business formality, instead of the personal relationship that has existed.

Body or paragraphs. The letter gets off to a bad start by declining the invitation in the opening line, instead of deferring it to a later paragraph. The conclusion reopens the wound instead of looking forward to a shared future event.

Complimentary close. Movetotheright in keeping with the partial block style of the opening.

Signature. Since she addressed Mr. Visconti by his first name in the greeting line, Ms. Thompson should sign off with just her first name. Move to the right under the complimentary close.

Writer's printed name. Also moved to the right in the partial block style.

Language and expression

Invitation-declining letters need to be as positive and diplomatic as possible. This letter implies in the opening paragraph that Mr. Visconti's dinner invitations aren't quite the golden bait they used to be.

Achieving the goal of being more *reader-based and courteous:* each paragraph opens with I, setting an unpleasant "It's all about me" tone to the letter. Using the pronoun you more often will improve the tone of the letter.

Below is a more sensitive and diplomatic version of the letter using 148 instead of 186 words. The partial block style has been chosen instead of the rigid full block style. This along with the changes in tone and expression make it more personal, more sincere, and more reader-based. In the end it is bound to be more effective.

International Textiles Corporation

February 7, 2000

Mr. Piero Visconti
House of Visconti
15 East 57th Street
New York, NY 10001

Dear Piero:

What a pleasure to receive your invitation today to your dinner party on February 20th. Its arrival immediately brought back memories of other magical and treasured evenings shared with you and your celebrated friends.

Early the next morning on February 21st I must be in Washington. I have been called to testify at congressional subcommittee hearings on trade issues that affect both of our businesses. Since trade issues also call me to a conference in Paris on February 16th through the 18th the evening of your dinner will be the only time remaining to prepare for the congressional hearings.

On March 10th I will be in Milan for the Spring showings. Please let me know if you can join me at the Principe di Savoia on March 11th for dinner.

Cordially,

Virginia

Virginia Thompson

VT: tr

400 Park Avenue New York, NY 10029
212-445-3000 www.InternationalTextiles. com

INDIRECT OR DEFERRED MESSAGES IN PERSUASIVE AND SALES LETTERS

What possible connection can there be between declining an invitation to a dinner party in New York City with an international guest list and selling lawn care in Virginia? Both at their heart will depend on persuasion to be successful. In the first case a writer must persuade her reader that she would truly like to attend his event but that she cannot. The writer of a letter about lawn care must persuade his readers that his product and service are worth the cost.

Looked at this way every letter can be seen as having the purpose of selling something—goods, services, ideas, or thoughts. Sales ability is basically the power of one person to move goods by persuading other people that they need them, or by winning other people's support or approval of a plan or idea.

There are also noncommercial sales letters, for example, those that champion good causes, such as charities, healthcare issues, or volunteerism.

No sales or persuasive letter is easy. Each requires a careful balance of frontloaded psychology and a backloaded writing style.

Writers of persuasive and sales letters stop to consider the three ages of all productive business communication and writing:

1. *Yesterday.* What has my reader's experience been on this subject in the past? This applies as much when the reader is a specific known individual as when the reader is an unknown entity. The *yesterday* of persuasion and sales also considers the product you're selling, whether it be material or spiritual. Know your product. You will gain and keep the attention of your reader by what you say about that product. How will it be useful to your reader? How will it fulfill their desires?
2. *Today.* How can I craft my message in a letter today that will bring about the change I desire in this individual or group? How can I make my reader buy my product, my idea, my feelings? It's important to make your letter friendly and human. Put your personality on paper. Your letter is you speaking. Show by your letter that you are friendly, knowledgeable, and trustworthy. Connect with your reader through shared goals. "These things are good for you and for me. We both need them."
3. *Tomorrow.* How can I predict and prevent unintended negative fallout from my message?

Sales and persuasive letters of their very nature need to be reader-based. Business and government writers should always think of their readers, but now more than ever before. The reason for this is that the reader is thinking "What's in this for me? Can you prove it? Okay, I'm open. Show me!"

People will buy goods, services, and ideas if they believe these will benefit them. The benefits must be concrete and accessible. There's not much point in selling ice to an Eskimo. Self-interest is a major factor in successful sales and persuasion. Even writers of letters for charitable causes know that there aren't many absolutely pure altruists around. Such writers realize that they also must appeal to reader benefits. Call it selfish or self-interest, but it works.

Three ways of conceiving and constructing letters that sell:

1. *Psychological.* Get attention, provoke interest, arouse desire, obtain decision. Attention is natural curiosity focused on something specific. Interest is understanding what is new and how it relates to what is old. Desire is the wish to take advantage of the benefits being offered. Decision is based on confidence in the writer's action information closing of the letter.
2. *Logical.* The second is a more logic-based, deductive formula: general, specific, conclusion. The writer opens with a statement so broad and authoritative that no sensible person would dare dis-

pute it. Next, he or she shows that this general statement includes a specific idea. The inevitable conclusion is that what has been said about the general is also true about the specific.

3. *Emotional.* The last formula is more earthy: picture, promise, prove, push. The persuasive writer opens with an attractive, sexy description of what he or she is selling. Next comes the promise that it will do wonders for the reader or at least benefit the reader in some specific way. Then come examples of the product or idea in real-life use, proving that it has worth. Finally, the persuasive writer makes the tactical move and urges the reader to take advantage of the promised and proven value.

Each of these three methods for creating an effective persuasive letter begins with a similar purpose, that is, getting the reader's attention. Here are some ways to achieve this objective.

- Open with an unusual fact or startling statistic: A kangaroo can cover 30 feet with each jump!
- Begin with a rhetorical or thought provoking question such as: "Do ostriches really bury their heads in the sand?"
- Start with an anecdote: "Centuries ago in Ireland many couples were having marital troubles. The elders came up with a solution: The couple that didn't quarrel for one year would win a prize—a side of bacon. Ever since then when one neighbor saw another bringing home the bacon he knew that all was going very well at home next door.
- Give the reader a challenge: "You can get a suntan in the shade!"
- Offer a compliment: "Because we value your patience and diplomacy, we'd like you to handle this project."
- Reader benefit: "You can double your reading speed in only ten days."

The Soft Sell or Deferring the Persuasive Moment

Most people do not want to be told how to run their affairs. The heart wants what it wants. The tone of such letters, whether selling products or ideas, should be persuasive rather than insistent and "pushy." It should be indirect or backloaded, that is, the central persuasive idea should be deferred until later in the letter.

In the days of the old American West there was a bit of folkloric wisdom shared by the cavalry. They said you could push and pull all you wanted and an old Missouri mule wouldn't budge. All it took to get him working for you was to recognize that "he was an individualist who hated nagging and needed a chance to make up his own mind about things."

Below is a plan for organizing a persuasive sales letter based on the first method above.

INTRODUCTION	**Did you know that?** Captures the reader's attention **You need .** Provokes reader's interest
DEVELOPMENT	**It's a proven fact that.** Rouses desire for central idea **When you buy this.** Pushes direct sales objective
CONCLUSION	**You will get this.** Obtains reader's decision **If you do this.** Directs reader's action

Situation: Sarah Goodspeed has recently taken over a tree and garden care company. As a professional arborist she especially wants to increase sales of her company's tree services. Coincidentally, there has been an increase in a blight affecting linden trees in her area. She has a new treatment that she is sure will work.

Below is the first draft of her sales letter in the full block style.

Trees, Bees, and Thee . . . .
Old Willow Lane
Albemarle, VA 33711 714-889-8890 Fax: 714-889-8891 Goodspeed @ Trees.com

April 20, 2000

Mr. Thomas Hamilton
24 Prince George Way
Albemarle, VA 33709

Dear Mr. Hamilton:

Fed up with that brown linden tree? Get it green again for only $49.!!!

I'm sure that you will agree with everyone else in our area that linden trees are beautiful specimen trees that can play a prominent part in the landscape. Unfortunately, as you are no doubt also aware, linden trees are particularly and increasingly susceptible to a very nasty and potentially deadly pest called Linden Leafwrecker. This notorious blight can cause under certain adverse conditions unattractive and unsightly browning early in the summer and, sad to say but true, early dropping leaves.

I can help you avoid this problem by sending out my specialists to your property to protect and restore your potentially beautiful trees. Yes, believe me my **Linden Leafwrecker Preventative** treatment will absolutely cure this blight. Guaranteed! The treatment will only cost you $49.00 and must be done by May 20th.

I want to make it easy for you to do this. Call my toll free number 1-888-650-4050 so that I can schedule your timely application of my product. Thank you for your business.

Sincerely,

Sarah Goodspeed
Proprietor

Revising the Persuasive Sales Letter

Formatting
Items on the following list that can be improved are marked with *X*s.

1. Letterhead or return address
2. Date line
3. Inside address
4. Salutation or greeting
5. Optional subject line ×
6. Body or paragraphs ×
7. Complimentary close
8. Signature
9. Writer's printed name
10. Reference initials
11. Enclosure line
12. Copy line

Subject line. In a persuasive or sales letter a subject line can be used to get the reader's attention. However, when writing in the indirect pattern, the idea is to defer the sales pitch. Don't hit the reader with it in the subject line before you've had a chance to build interest and arouse desire for the idea or product.

Body or paragraphs. The opening paragraph of a persuasive sales letter should continue gaining the reader's interest. This letter will lose the reader with its longwinded narrative opening. The conclusion should focus more clearly on the decision-making process. A postscript with an incentive would give a final push to the decision.

Graphic highlighting. This sales letter would benefit from additional graphic highlighting. In the second paragraph, **bold** type could be used effectively on the name of the blight preventative treatment and the low cost to the customer. This would emphasize the push.

Language and expression

More *yous* and fewer *Is* would give this letter more reader-based language. Words such as *absolutely* and *guaranteed* in the second paragraph are dangerous. Can Sarah really guarantee the success of the treatment? What about weather or other factors over which she has no control? By putting her signature to this guarantee she is possibly making this letter the equivalent of a binding contract. Sarah might be exposing herself to costly litigation.

If all of the above suggestions are adopted Sarah's revised letter will read as follows. Using the partial block style for a more informal, friendly format, it contains only 165 words instead of the original 185 words. Yet it is more vigorous and includes the incentive-giving postscript.

Trees, Bees, and Thee . . . .
Old Willow Lane
Albemarle, VA 33711 714-889-8890 Fax: 714-889-8891 Goodspeed @ Trees.com

April 20, 2000

Mr. Thomas Hamilton
24 Prince George Way
Albemarle, VA 33709

Dear Mr. Hamilton:

Fed up with that brown linden tree you bought?

Linden trees are beautiful specimen trees that usually play a prominent part in the landscape. Unfortunately, linden trees are vulnerable to a nasty pest called Linden Leafwrecker. This blight causes unsightly early summer browning and premature leaf dropping.

You can avoid this problem by having our tree specialists protect your beautiful tress from this pest with our **Linden Leafwrecker Preventative** treatment. On average this treatment is only **$49.00**. For best results this treatment should be done before May 20th.

To take advantage of this great offer, please call our toll free number, 1-888-650-4050, today and we will schedule a timely application for your trees. Thank you for your business.

Sincerely,

Sarah Goodspeed

Sarah Goodspeed
Proprietor

PS Here's another great idea for you. If we haven't already done so, we will gladly give you a free evaluation of all the ornamental trees and shrubs on your property when we come out to do this treatment.

IV

Writing Reports for Business and Government

16

Report Writers, Managers, and Audiences

Reports are a pervasive fact of life on all levels of corporate and governmental life. They are the essential, informational glue that holds large organizations together. They serve many purposes and take many forms. Some reports are purely informational, giving managers and other employees many different types of information about company or agency operations. Others are primarily analytical or persuasive. Their aim is to study problems and offer solutions, in other words, to bring about additions or changes in thought and action.

Some reports are internal forms of communication aimed at adding to or changing policies within an organization. Others are external forms of communication, for example documents seeking grants or funding.

Reports vary in their complexity or structure. Some are relatively simple and are presented in the format of interoffice memos using preprinted forms. Others take the form of letters to clients and government agencies, while still others are lengthy reports created by teams or groups.

In many ways, the skills needed to write a successful business report are no different from those required for writing effective memos and letters. Whatever their length or type, reports follow the triple foundations of all successful business writing.

The Three Ages of Successful Business Reports

1. **Yesterday.** Business and government writing does not exist in some black hole of time and place. Like all communication, reports

have a "before" or a "yesterday". Before beginning to write, they ask themselves such questions as, "Who has assigned me to compile this report? Or was it my idea, a voluntary project? What has been said or written to date on this situation or issue? What new information—what new facts—have come to light since then?"
2. **Today.** Report writers next ask such questions as, "What should I write and do today in relation to this new information and insight into people and issues? Who is my reader or primary audience? My secondary audience? Are they laypeople? Executives? Experts? Technicians? A combination of these?"
3. **Tomorrow**. Finally, the report writer questions, "How will what I do today affect 'tomorrow'? Will it improve or will it backfire and worsen the situation? Will it create a stream of useful information and thereby facilitate decision making, or just muddy the waters?"

The Three Phases of Successful Business Reports

1. **Purpose.** Reports share with memos and letters the four principal purposes of all workplace communication: information, persuasion, change or results, and public relations or good will. The report writer has to stop and ask such questions as, "Is my primary goal to inform my readers about a subject? Or is it to respond to a request for proposals? Is it to persuade? To analyze? To sell?"
2. **Organization.** "Will I use the direct pattern and frontload my central idea? Or should I use the backloaded method and defer my main idea until later in the document?"
3. **Expression.** "Should my choice of language be easy and colloquial as in a routine memo, or technical and formal as in a third-person narrative-analysis?"

The Three Stages of Successful Business Reports

1. **Thinking.** When the preceding three ages and three phases have been carefully considered, the thinking stage of the writing process is almost complete. Further thought will be needed on the best way to present the material in the body of the report.
2. **Writing.** One or more of the patterns of logical development will serve to present all of the information and ideas contained in a report: chronological, logical, problem–analysis–solution, or order of importance.
3. **Revising.** It is almost always necessary to rewrite and revise either sentence by sentence while writing, in totality when the documented is completed, or by a combination of the two methods. Successful rewriting is not just an extended spell check. It some-

times requires rethinking of the purpose, ideas, and manner of expression of the whole document. The principles and procedures for revising reports follow the guidelines laid out in Part III for revising memos and letters.

CREATING READER-BASED REPORTS

There is another major way in which the skills needed to write successful business reports are no different from those learned for writing effective memos and letters. Whatever their length or type, reports must follow the principles of reader-based communications. When they achieve this goal, reports are characterized by four qualities:

1. **Reports should focus on reader benefits and shared goals.** In this context the reader may be understood as the corporate unit or government agency as a whole. Like any communication, the report is created by a writer but it is not about the writer. It's about an objective situation or issue. Once the writer has defined the purpose in creating a report, he or she has a goal in mind. Adapting this goal to the report audiences is the act of creating a shared goal. The reason for writing and the receiver's reason for reading must become one. Some ways that report writers can do this include the following:

    - By learning as much as possible about the needs of the reader-audience.
    - By thinking of needs that the reader may not even be clearly aware of.
    - By evaluating how the report writer can best meet or fulfill those needs.
    - By suggesting how the writer can help the readers reach these goals.

2. **Reports must be organized in an audience-based structure.** This means not only using the kind of reader-based language discussed in Chapters 4 and 6, but organizing the document around the shared goals you have already established. This is done by grouping or prioritizing the report's ideas, that is, separating the major and secondary topics in an outline and making the relationship between them clear to the reader. The alphanumeric outline form, which is very useful for achieving this objective, is shown in Chapter 6.
3. **Reports should provide a cue-based navigation system.** There are many verbal and visual ways to give the audience direction in the journey through the report's ideas. Some of these include:

- *Signposts that predict the major points and subpoints:* Title, Table of Contents, Letter of Transmittal, Executive Summary or abstract, and other headings and subheadings.
- *Signposts that summarize or introduce the sections and paragraphs within sections:* thesis statements beginning sections, topic sentences at the start and sentence summaries at the ends of paragraphs, and finally conclusion or summary sections.
- *Signposts that guide the reader visually:* varying fonts; using bullets and numbering; varying formatting with indentation, spacing, rows, and columns; inserting pictures, graphs, and tables.
- *Signposts that guide the reader verbally:* transition words and phrases, and conjunctions such as "in addition," "nevertheless," "moreover," "however," and "finally"; repetitions, pronouns, and summary nouns.

4. **Reports should develop a persuasive argument.** Reports may be long or short, informal or formal, periodic or situational, informational or analytical. But there will always be an underlying element of persuasion. Business writing, with very few exceptions such as social situations requiring thank-you or sympathy notes, is based on the desire for change. We want to make something happen or be known. It is never altruistic. We want results. Simply expressing our point of view is hardly ever enough, because it may conflict with the way our reader already sees things. The report writer and the report reader must share results as well as goals. As a result, there can be three possible outcomes of a report just as there can be of memos, letters, discussions, and other forms of communication:

   - The report will completely change its readers' minds or attitudes so that they see the situation or issue exactly as the writer does. Even if the writer is the universally recognized, leading authority on the planet, this is an unrealistic expectation.
   - The report will change no one's opinion. Unfortunately, this outcome is all too common and regrettable. But it is often not the writer's fault alone; and it is avoidable.
   - The report will modify or change the readers' viewpoint. This is a realistic and achievable outcome that the reporter can achieve this by providing new information or a different way of looking at a situation or issue. The reader-audiences are responsible for deciding whether that new information, in fact, makes the different way a better way.

CREATING REPORTS BASED ON READER PROFILES

Reports share with memos and letters the fact that they are all forms of communication that have three basic components: a writer, a message, and an audience. To succeed they must be reader- or audience-based, not writer-based. Report writers often get into trouble by beginning to write before they have carefully analyzed the "yesterday" and the "today" of their audience. To steer clear of this problem report writers don't begin writing or even outlining before clearly defining their audience and having the answers to the following questions.

1. Can I be certain in advance of exactly who and where my readers will be?
2. Will my reader-audiences be familiar with the reasons for the report and the person(s) who authorized it?
3. Are the members of my audience knowledgeable about the report's subject?
4. Does my audience know anything about my credentials?
5. Is your audience likely to read the entire report?

The answer to each and every one of these questions may very well be "No!" How then can report writers get a better fix on an audience before beginning to write? They have to do more than identify names, titles, and roles. Report writers must determine who their audience(s) are in relation to the purpose and content of the report. This means learning the specific operational profiles of the persons who will read the report, as well as their personal and professional profiles.

Audiences for reports parallel the directions in which all business communication flows: horizontal and vertical, internal and external. However, the report writer is usually a separate entity from any of these potential audiences. This is because very few reports are written for audiences within the same unit, for example, one corporate vice president of marketing for an audience of other marketing vice presidents.

However, the differences between these audiences and writers go well beyond differences in training. In addition to different areas of expertise and education, the audiences will have different concerns, such as production, budget, or purchasing. Personality differences as well as organizational politics and competition may also distance writer and audience.

Reports Intended for External Audiences

Report writers addressing audiences in a different organizational unit usually address a person in an organizational role. When this happens, the writer is really addressing a department or group rather than an individual. As a result, the report will have audiences beyond the individual addressed. It may be read mainly by staff personnel, or it may be sent to other people, for example, lawyers, controllers, and consultants.

As a result, even when a report writer and audience share the same organizational level, they may have little in common except their rank and employer. The report writer may recommend a piece of equipment on the basis of cost-effectiveness. The writer's audience, however, may be concerned with long-term business relationships, client preferences, and budgets.

Reports Intended for Internal Audiences

When the communication flow is vertical, the differences between author and audience increase. Reports aimed at different levels of an organization have complex problems of communication for that reason; and they must also face communications problems when the report is distributed laterally on the different vertical levels. The report writer must define and focus on the primary audience, because that audience will have to act or make decisions for change based on the report. However, the writer must organize and write the report with the goal of delivering not mere information, but useful knowledge to the secondary audiences as well.

Combination Internal and External Report Audiences

Many reports, while they are assigned and created for internal audiences, also end up being read by external audiences—those outside the corporation or agency that have commissioned them. These audiences have the same problems of differing levels as the vertical, internal audience of a company or agency. Perhaps most significantly for the writer, this one report may give the external audience and the public at large a favorable or unfavorable prism through which to view the entire corporation or governmental agency.

Using Profiling to Bond with Report Audiences

In the thinking stage of writing a report, an author might consider using a standard organizational chart. However, such charts are like form letters—sometimes useful, generic places to begin but not ends in themselves. A unit on the organization chart looks like any other unit, but in fact each has different human beings with varied roles, backgrounds, and personalities. In other words each has a different frame

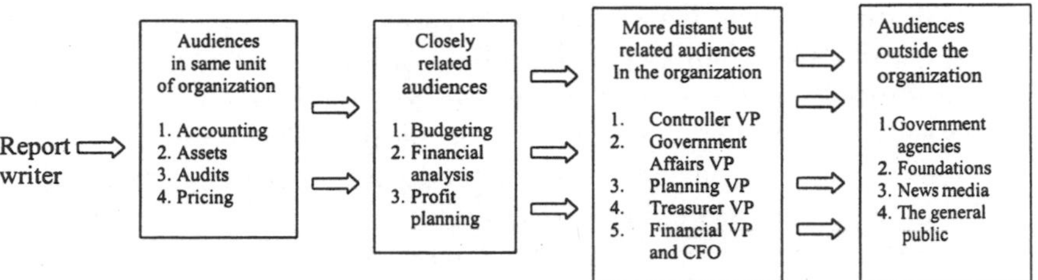

Organizational Profile Diagram

of reference. Instead of a formal organizational chart, the report writer might use one based on close and distant audiences for the report findings.

Studying such a chart the report writer will realize that even the audiences in his own unit and those in neighboring units will vary in backgrounds and organizational concerns. The writer can also see that as the scope of the chart widens, fewer and fewer specifics are known about the audiences. Finally, in the process of studying the audience situation with an audience proximity chart such as this, the writer finds not only the fact that there are functional differences, but the nature of those differences.

Using an Audience's Frame of Reference to Create Personal Profiles

When preparing an audience proximity chart like the one above, we tend to think of our audience as individuals: their status in the organization, their temperaments, their degree of knowledge and sophistication. To go beyond this level of audience analysis, report writers should consider the functional as well as the individual qualities of their audiences.

1. Learning the functional characteristics of the writer's audiences means identifying any meaningful differences between their organizational role and the writer's. The writer has to ask what kind of knowledge is important and useful for them. Will their corporate or agency functions and points of view make it easier or more difficult to understand the report's contents? What do they know about the writer's role? Are they group-oriented, that is, do they consult immediately with their staff or people in other parts of the organization or are they mostly solitary thinkers?

   Considering the "tomorrow" of the report, the writer has to think the report will affect the roles of the people in the report audience.

Will the report uncover facts or suggest courses of action that will reflect badly or embarrass members of the report audience?

2. Individual qualities refer to the frame of reference of the audience member, including such things as culture, socioeconomic status, religion, race, ethnicity, and level of education. The writer should try to be as specific as possible in this assessment. Just because they come from the same cultural or ethnic background, the report writer and audience may not share the same values and attitudes. Similarly, two people may have attended the same university, but in different eras. Even 10 years can alter the educational landscape so greatly that the two fellow graduates really do not have that much in common. Whether in the humanities or the technical fields, language and viewpoints often change greatly over time. Two people, who on the surface seem to have much in common including the *same* education, find that they hardly speak the same language.

   The flip side of this is that people who do not seem to have much in common on the surface may actually share the same individual or personal qualities. As we saw in Chapter 4, dealing with the individual, as an individual, is always a key factor in true communication.

The Functional Profiles of a Report's Audiences

Creating and analyzing an audience profile diagram will get every report off to a good start. An inexperienced report writer will have to spend more time on this thinking stage of writing. To a seasoned writer this comes more quickly, as does the awareness of primary, secondary, and intermediate audiences and the overall impact on an organization of each report.

This stage focuses on the "tomorrow" or consequences of a report. One of the most important of these is how the report will be used. Most readers will have little interest in the technical aspects of a report. Instead, they will want to know such things as why the report was commissioned, what are the results, what will it cost, how will it impact sales, budgets, or unions. Readers will also want to know what happens next and who the real decision makers will be.

After considering these questions the report writer must decide an order of priority for his or her different audiences. Which are the primary and secondary audiences? What is the intermediate audience?

1. The *primary audience* for a report is the person or persons whose viewpoint the report writer seeks to modify or change in some way, either by providing new information or a different way of looking at a situation or issue. The primary audience in turn will act or create changes in the corporation or agency based on the information provided by the reporter. Whether the decision maker

is close or distant, on a higher or lower level of the organization, he or she is the primary and most important audience of the report.

In an ideal world the primary audiences will always act purely on the basis of their functional roles in the corporation or agency. However, individual qualities of their frames of reference, such as their values and attitudes, will likely enter into the mix. Part of analyzing an audience is determining when such personal factors are likely to affect decision making. Another thing to consider is the degree to which the decision-making primary audience bases decisions on staff input and recommendations. In this common occurrence the report's primary audience includes the decision maker's staff as well.

Each report eventually enters into an organization or agency's system, where personnel is always changing. As a result, every report has to be self-sustaining, that is, usable by succeeding primary audiences whether they are in close proximity or distant.

2. *Secondary audiences* of reports include people who may not be primary decision makers yet are affected by recommendations or conclusions in the report. This audience will include all that must adapt to the changes management enacts as a result of the report. Careful analysis of secondary audiences in the "thinking" stage of report writing will suggest what additional information should be included in the report.
3. The third or *intermediate audience* includes the people who forward the information the report contains to the primary audience rather than use it themselves. An intermediate audience such as a report writer's supervisor does not use the report's information to make decisions for change. While a report is often addressed to the writer's supervisor, the supervisor merely moves the information through the organization.

The three steps of determining the organizational, personal, and professional profiles of a report's audiences will help the report writer clarify the three ages (yesterday, today, and tomorrow), the three phases (purpose, organization, and expression), and the three stages (thinking, writing, and revising) of report communication. In turn, this understanding of the needs of the various audiences will help the writer design the report in a fully reader based and successful way.

HOW MANAGERS SERVE TO LINK REPORT WRITERS AND AUDIENCES

Locating report audiences is the first major step on a communication journey. The next step is to understand that from a manager's point of view reports are instruments for accomplishing tasks and achieving goals. The information they contain is not an end in itself but a means for achieving an end, namely, well-informed decision making. A report, therefore, will be a truly reader- based document if it fulfills the needs of the managers and audiences it has located.

How does a report writer find out what management needs to see in reports? In general, when a manager reads a report he or she looks either for information alone or for information and analysis that will assist decision making. Managers are busy people. They need to decide quickly whether reading a report is worth a little or a lot of their time. To speed-read or to study? That is the question. The answer depends on the responses to the questions raised in three areas:

1. *The subject of the report.* What is the subject of the report and what are the qualifications of the author?
2. *Its facts and ideas.* Does it contain useful knowledge or merely information? Are its conclusions valid, that is, based on research and facts?
3. *The changes to follow.* Are the changes it recommends realistic?

Some of the things managers may want to know more specifically can be seen in the following categories of probable questions:

1. *Problems in the field.* What trouble has developed? What, if any, history? Responsibility? Specific equipment involved? What action needed now? Product or program changes? Whose decision? Scheduling decisions? Workforce?
2. *Funding.* Budget changes? Self-funding? Government grants? Bonds issue? Taxes? Foundations?
3. *Materials.* Characteristics and limitations? Environmental impact? Extent and value of use? Cost factors? Availability and resources? What alternatives?
4. *Building and products.* Environmental risks? Zoning variances? Competition? Schedule? Workforce? Life expectancy? Durability? Completion date?
5. *Problems and responsibility.* Exact nature? Scale and importance? What has been done so far? By whom? Relative success or failure? Attempted solutions? Alternatives? What do we do now? Who does it? When?
6. *Evaluation and testing.* The subject of the study or test? What controls and safeguards were put in place? Were they observed? What were the results? What was concluded and recommended? What changes are required of the organization or agency?

Managers want this information direct and frontloaded in a brief, concise, and meaningful way. This can take the form of subject lines and introductions with clear central ideas in memos and letter-formatted reports or executive summaries in longer formal reports. For a summary or abstract to be useful it must give clear information on the three central points listed above: the subject of the report, its facts and ideas, and the changes to follow.

For a manager to get a clear idea of the subject of the report, the writer must define the problem or situation at hand, then present the needs to be satisfied or the goals to be achieved. Next the writer must explain the steps or stages of meeting those goals, the conclusions to be drawn from the facts and analysis, and finally the specific recommendations for change.

The information managers want is usually dictated by their role in the organization, but how they want it furnished or displayed is more often the result, not of what they read, but how they read. And managers' reading habits tend to follow a pattern based on common speed-reading techniques. All managers, no matter how busy, will read the executive summary or abstract. Most will read the introduction as well as the conclusions and recommendations section. Very few, if any, managers read the entire body of a lengthy report, much less the appendix, notes, or bibliography.

What all this means for the report writer is clear. If the reporter wants to achieve his or her goal of delivering meaningful facts and ideas in a reader-based way, the design and organization of the report must be adapted to the manager-audiences' practice of reading. Most readers, especially managers, are interested in zeroing in on the core issues and the ideas that grow directly from them. They usually leave the fine points of specialized knowledge for their staffs.

Report writers must also remember that managers' education and experience will usually be different from their own. Even more importantly, managers' knowledge and familiarity with the specific problem or issue being reported almost never equals the reporters. This is why the writer has to write at a technical level suitable to the reader, whether the subject is healthcare, asbestos removal, or higher education. Highly specialized, detailed material should be reserved for the appendix. In other words, all parts of the report should be written in a reader-based style adapted to the audience(s) located.

What is the Working Relationship the Writer-Reporter Needs to Maintain with Management?

The writer has needs and responsibilities beyond precisely locating audiences. There is also a crucial lateral relationship, which is the one between reporter and management in the report-writing process. Scheduling a series of conferences based on the three phases of writing is an effective and productive way to fulfill these responsibilities.

1. **Thinking conference.** Report writer and management must establish shared goals before the project begins. The first meeting between manager and reporter must clarify exactly what is needed and expected of the report writer in conceptual areas and in very practical matters. The writer will learn, for example, the number and type of management decisions that will depend on the report, as well as the time frame for completing the project. Such a conference will also clarify for the reporter exactly what is expected as the project continues. The reporter might want to request a follow-up confirmation memo from management to make sure that both parties clearly agree upon the requirements of the project.

   During the investigative stage the reporter should meet again with management to review the research conducted thus far. In addition to the information gathered they can discuss what conclusions have been drawn at this point as well as the evidence supporting these conclusions. Reporter and manager can also review the recommendations that are being considered and the changes these will require of the company or agency.

   The report writer should take advantage of the manager's larger point of view for the company or agency and its work. With this broadband perspective the reporter can understand and appreciate the importance of the project and gain much-needed insight into what information the managers will need for decision making. As a result, the writer can determine what parts of the report at this point can be cut and which may need further development.

   Manager and reporter will each gain other practical benefits from a meeting at this stage. The reporter, knowing the conference is coming, will probably take the time to be sharper and clearer about his or her opinions and presentations. The manager, likewise, will gain greater understanding of the report's progress and its discoveries. This will improve the level and effectiveness of managerial-level discussions of the project.
2. **Writing conference.** After this conference the reporter should be ready to write an outline of the proposed report. With the report outline in hand, the writer should meet with management to review it point by point. If the manager is satisfied, the reporter should get a clear authorization to expand the outline into a complete report. If the manager is not satisfied with the outline, however, he or she must make clear to the report writer what

organizational problems exist in the outline. It is much easier for the author to make structural changes at this stage of the project than after it is written. Criticism at a later stage may appear more personal and the productive bond of shared goals may be broken.

3. **Revision conference.** When the report is completed the writer should meet with management for review and approval of the finished report. The report writer will have already gone through the revision stage required of all writing. The manager, however, may indicate some parts that need additional revision from management's point of view. If these requests for change are lengthy and detailed it is a sign that the initial conference in the thinking stage failed to meet its goals. If the manager just prolongs what is perceived as mere nit picking he or she will appear hesitant and indecisive. If the report is clear and persuasive it will serve its intended purpose. The manager can move on to distribution matters. The shared goals of manager and reporter have been achieved.

17

Report Purposes, Formats, and Categories

Business and agency reports seem to have an unlimited variety of forms and purposes that defy categorization. There are short and long reports; informal and formal reports; memo and letter reports; periodic and situational reports; feasibility reports and proposals. However, it is possible to bring some order to the topic by classifying reports according to their purpose, their format, and their content.

The Three Major Purposes of Reports

Like all business writing, reports serve to inform, persuade, get results or change, and achieve good will or public relations. However, each report will have its own balance or percentage of these elements.

1. **To inform.** Information is the lifeblood of business and government. Without it no organization can function successfully. Whether short or long, informal or formal all reports communicate factual information geared to a specific end or purpose. Often, the information or facts are all that is requested.
2. **To analyze.** Sometimes reports, whether long or short, go beyond a mere statement of facts. When they go beyond the purely objective and offer an interpretation of those facts or an opinion about the significance of those facts, they become analytical in nature. Such reports tend to have a greater element of persuasion than primarily informational reports.

3. **To recommend.** Often the informational and the analytical functions are combined with a third goal or purpose, namely to recommend or propose a course of action. Here, the element of persuasion is much more pronounced.

The Four Main Formats of Reports

Although styles vary from company to company, following are the four forms they generally assume.

- 1. **Memo.** An informal report meant for internal corporate or agency circulation may be presented in the form of a memo. If so, it would use the traditional *To, From, Date,* and *Subject Headings* and be organized into the introduction, development, and conclusion sections, as shown in Chapter 11. Many organizations have preprinted forms for this type of short memo reporting.

2. **Letter.** Informal reports intended for external communications can be presented in any of the letter formats shown in Chapter 14. However, they will have sections specifically geared to their reporting purpose.
3. **Semi-formal report.** On the next level of complexity are informal reports that use a special report format with title page, introduction, body, and conclusion and/or recommendations as separate pages and sections.
4. **Formal report.** Finally, there are formal reports. These have the same sections as the preceding type but because they are so much more complex they have many additional parts. While varying from company to company, these include separate sections such as a table of contents, executive summary or abstract, memo or letter of transmittal, appendix, notes, and bibliography.

THE FOUR CATEGORIES OF REPORTS

The first three types of reports listed below are distinguished by their goals or purpose. The fourth category, the formal report, can have any of the three same goals. Its distinguishing characteristic is the length and complexity of its format.

- Informational
- Analytical
- Proposals
- Formal reports

Types of Informational Reports

Informational reports include two major groups: the periodic and the situational. Both primarily require facts rather than opinions or recom-

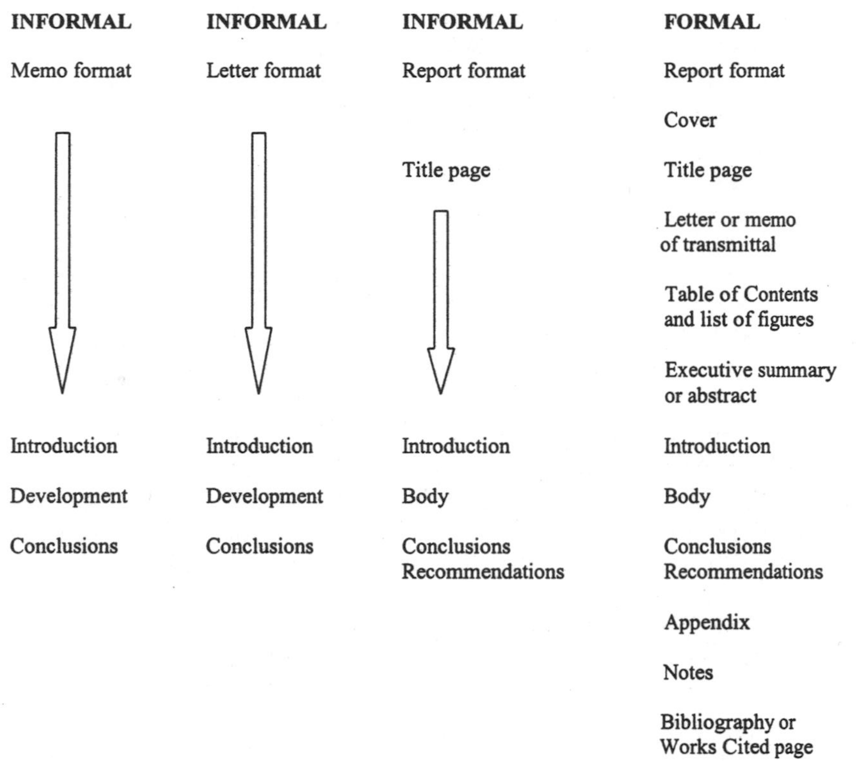

The Types and Structures of Reports

mendations. The names of the various types of reports indicate both the purpose and the general subject of the report.

1. **Periodic reports.** A major form of organizational record keeping, are routine reports issued on a regularly scheduled basis. Such reports are often submitted using preprinted forms because the activities they describe are so consistent that they need the same amount of space and headings each time.

   Preprinted forms are also a good management tool because they make certain that the required information will always be included and that the report will not digress or be needlessly long. For the report writer the major concern is simply getting the required information, not the skills of organization and expression. Using pre-printed forms or not, periodic reports include the following types:

- *Routine supervisory reports.* All companies and agencies need a steady flow of information on their operations to serve as a basis for management decision making. Managers require statistical and personnel information before they can decide what changes need to be made. Some, for example, need weekly, monthly, and yearly sales reports to monitor the success of products and personnel. Others need a steady stream of accounting and financial information, including capital expenditures and cash flow.

- *Progress reports.* These include any type of report on an ongoing project. As such they pay careful attention to the three ages of communication: *yesterday, today,* and *tomorrow.* Progress reports trace the inception, the current status of work, and the completion of a project or study. Reviewing past progress reports can help a manager make time and budgetary decisions for future projects.

  The construction of a harbor tunnel, the testing of a new drug, the conversion to decimalization in financial institutions—all require constant supervision. Such reports supply managers with information such as whether a project is staying on schedule and within budget or whether the assigned personnel are adequate and effective. As a result, report writers must supply their primary and secondary audiences with a concise background summary of the project to date, a very specific factual account of the present period, and a look to what will be done in the future or next phase of the project.

  Some organizations distinguish between *progress* and *status* reports: the former term being used for information about the change or advance in the endeavor, the latter term for information about the current condition or state of a project. The terms do not really define separate entities. Progress and status reports must both consider the background, present condition, and future direction of a project. The *status* report simply gives more weight to the present condition.

  Some progress reports go beyond the fact-based perimeter of strictly informational reporting. This is more likely to happen when problems arise on a project and recommendations are requested about future direction. Managers near and distant on the proximity chart need to know whether changes should be made in design, implementation, or personnel before beginning the next stage of the project. If these are the needs of the audience, the reporter must add analysis and an element of persuasion to the information gathered.

- *Compliance reports.* City, state, and federal agencies demand that companies doing business with them prove they are complying with government rules and regulations. The Equal Employment Opportunities Commission, the Occupational Safety and Health Administration, the Securities and Exchange Commission, and state banking commissions are some of the agencies that require reports intended to protect consumers, employees, and investors.

Federal agencies likewise require that state or municipal agencies receiving benefits or supervised by them comply with their regulations in areas such as workplace safety, grants, and funding.

One area of compliance reporting that has grown significantly concerns the environment. The National Environmental Policy Act requires that all federal agencies in considering grant requests evaluate the possibility of adverse effects on the environment such as land and water use, air quality, and noise levels. Reports include environmental information and environmental assessment papers, findings of no meaningful impact papers, and environmental impact reports.

2. **Situational reports.** One-time reports geared to specific, individual events. They are also used for special problems and issues that arise, sometimes unexpectedly, in large organizations. Because they are nonrecurring, there are usually no preprinted forms for such reports. Each must be an original creation in content and expression. However, some situational reports—for example, accident reports—may use preprinted forms. These are provided to make sure that all necessary information is included for insurance purposes and any legal eventualities. Some of the occasions that call for situational reports include the following:

   - *Trip reports.* Anything from a one-day trip to the suburbs to a three-week trip through the Pacific Rim will require a report. These keep management informed on activities and expenses when employees work outside the office.

     Corporate managers will use a site inspection report, for example, to learn how well a new plant or system is functioning. A sales meeting or convention report will tell management how cost-effective and professionally helpful these occasions are for improving business learning and earnings.

     Governmental agency and administration managers can use site inspection reports to find out how suitable a location is for a new correctional facility or halfway house. Similarly, they need reports from probation officers, social workers, and health care providers to judge the effectiveness of programs and whether they need to be supplemented or substantially changed.

A trip report should include the following information that primary and secondary audiences will need for decision making:

1. Where and when the employee traveled
2. The purpose of the trip
3. The people who were visited
4. What was learned from them
5. What the trip cost, with accompanying receipts

- *Special projects—test reports.* Sometimes managers need reports on situations that are unique and of a theoretical nature. Such reports may be purely informational. When recommendations are requested, they become analytical as well as informational reports. One type of special project is the test or research report. Producing such reports requires technical expertise as well as writing skills.

To be useful for management, test reports should include the following information:

1. The reasons and objectives in performing the experiment or conducting the research
2. What was done, including the methods procedures, equipment, and controls that were followed in performing the test
3. The results of the research or testing; what conclusions were reached
4. What recommendations will be made as a result of the research or test; what actions should be taken or not taken.

- *Incident and accident reports.* These cover unexpected events that occur in corporations and agencies, often with financial and legal ramifications. As a result reports must be submitted as soon as possible to managers, legal departments, and oversight agencies. Incidents requiring reporting include environmental situations such as asbestos findings, accidents resulting in damage to property or injury to people, and possible or actual criminal activity.

Such incident reports will be useful to managers when they include this necessary information in either or both of the following ways:

1. In chronological order: what was occurring immediately before the incident; what the reporter and other witnesses saw, heard, smelled, felt at the moment of the incident; what happened relevant to the incident immediately afterward. Omitted totally are subjective feelings and opinions. Names and times, on the other hand, should be as accurate and factual as possible.
2. In spatial order: the reporter describes the situation as his or her your eyes scanned the scene horizontally from left to right and vertically from top to bottom. Distances, colors, and speeds

are recorded as precisely as applicable. If injuries occurred, the report writer should be as specific as possible about the injuries witnessed, the machine that caused the injuries, the person that appeared to have committed the crime.

Types of Analytical Reports

Analyzing a subject, a situation, or a problem effectively usually requires a report writer to follow three steps based on the problem-analysis-solution pattern of development discussed in Chapter 9.

1. The report writer must identify and separate the subject or problem into its essential parts.
2. The writer has to next examine carefully the individual elements to determine their significance and relationship to the whole. Doing this will reveal the important fact that the whole is not merely the sum of equal parts. It is the sum of parts that must be put into a logical pattern, known as order of importance: descending from most important to least, or ascending in climactic order from least to most important.
3. Finally, the reporter will be able to understand the causes, the key features, and the possible solutions to a situation or problem.

Like informational reports, analytical reports supply managers with facts; but they move beyond this stage to recommend a course of action or persuade the different audiences that taking some course of action or thinking in a certain way is the right thing to do.

1. **Feasibility reports.** A feasibility study is ordered when managers need to determine whether a proposed idea for change can really be accomplished or will actually work. If so, should they proceed with a given course of action? Basically feasibility studies analyze the relative merits of a change that has been proposed in facilities, marketing, financial structuring, personnel, product line, or any other organizational responsibility. They consider the cost as well as the length of time needed to implement the proposed change. Feasibility studies help managers assess the pros and cons of a proposal for change because they analyze all the separate elements before recommending a course of action.

   Feasibility studies generally analyze one of three situations:

   - A change or action is proposed, but its effectiveness or likelihood of success is unknown. For example, a highway commission knows that a second level can be added to a bridge. It needs to know whether such an addition will actually improve traffic flow in the region.

- A problem exists, but the best actions to solve the problem are unclear. A great urban museum that attracts visitors from all over the globe faces growing community opposition to its expansion plans because they will attract even more visitors, as well as more traffic, litter, and noise. Should the museum cut back or stop the expansion entirely? Should it route all cars and pedestrians to the side and rear entrances, and limit the size of groups?
- Two or more solutions for a problem exist: a bridge and a tunnel. When this is the case, managers need information and recommendations to make the right choice. This type of feasibility report is sometimes called a *yardstick report*. It is called this because in it the report writer uses a *yardstick* or standard of measurement to determine which of the two alternatives would be the most effective in terms of cost, time, personnel, and even public relations.

2. **Justification reports.** Simply because something is feasible does not mean it should automatically be done. For example, after considering the feasibility of a proposal for a new program or additional personnel, managers need to determine whether it is justified, that is, warranted. Justification reports analyze a proposal and make recommendations to proceed or not. Managers count on such reports to determine whether the time and money required to achieve them represent a wise and reasonable commitment of the organization's resources.
3. **Research studies.** When corporations and governmental agencies need a scientific analysis of a problem, they authorize and fund a research report. Such reports follow the problem–analysis–solution pattern. They determine the essential elements of a problem, for example, the decline in reading scores of American high school students on standardized tests. Researchers collect data, analyze it, and draw conclusions. Making recommendations may or may not be part of the research project assigned.

Types of Proposals

Whether intended for business or government use, a proposal is a plan for solving a problem or performing an action. Proposals vary greatly in purpose, form, and length. They are used for internal and external communications, for vertical and horizontal audiences. They can be informal or formal in design. They can be solicited or unsolicited. They can be one page created by an individual or 100 pages created by a team or group.

Examples include proposals to change procedures in a company or agency, to convince a corporation to move a division to a certain city or county, to obtain funding for research, to win contracts, to build or alter facilities and installations. What all such proposals have in common is that they add a strong element of persuasion to the information and analysis they provide.

Proposals, whether written for business or governmental purposes, fall into either of two categories:

1. **Solicited.** When corporations or government agencies know exactly what they want they solicit proposals to fill that need. In a sense the organization does some high-level comparison shopping to find out who can best fill their needs. They announce or publish a request for proposals (RFP) or a request for bids (RFB). In the corporate setting, such requests are usually sent out after meetings to discuss and clarify the specific need of the company. A proposal written in response to such a formal request is a solicited proposal.
2. **Unsolicited.** Sometimes individuals, companies, or agencies see a need going unattended. Like nature, they "abhor a vacuum," especially when the vacuum represents an opportunity for gain. They send out something that parallels a sales letter in content but not in form. In such a case the individual or organization volunteers a proposal that says in effect "Look what we can do for you, if you just give us a chance!"

Proposals, whether solicited or unsolicited, may be informal or formal. The difference is more in structure than in content. Both have sales and persuasion as their principal goals; but they seek to achieve these goals with different formats:

1. **Informal.** Informal proposals are usually done in the form of a letter. They tend to run from two to five pages in length and include the following sections:

INTRODUCTION	**State the reasons** for making the proposal from the reader's point of view **Grab reader's attention** with financial and practical benefits to be gained

DEVELOPMENT
- **Present your qualifications** as the writer of this specific proposal
- **Identify** the problem
- Make the actual and specific proposal to solve this problem
- **Describe** the personnel you will offer and the cost or budget for the project

CONCLUSION
- **Summarize** the benefits your proposal will give your reader
- **Request** authorization or approval from your reader to begin the project

2. **Formal.** Formal proposals have the same elements of the informal ones just outlined, but they contain other sections, explained in the next chapter, which may expand the length of a typical proposal from five pages to hundreds of pages.

Because the objective of any proposal, solicited or unsolicited, is to gain approval, such reports must be particularly audience-based. And because the stakes are usually high in terms of finances and professional reputations, effective and skillful proposal writing is a highly valued art.

18

Report Research, Statistics, and Illustrations

RESEARCHING THE SUBJECT BY USING PRIMARY AND SECONDARY SOURCES

Research is the process of learning as much as possible about a specific subject. This is done using oral and written forms of communication to obtain information from primary and secondary sources.

Primary Sources

The primary sources of research are those that the report writer uses to obtain new and original information on the subject.

1. **Surveys.** This form of research is necessary for many types of informational reports such as special projects, analytical reports such as feasibility studies, justification reports, research studies, and proposals. Surveys typically collect information from primary sources through computer programs, in-person and telephone interviews, polls, and questionnaires.

   However, time and expense factors make it unrealistic to survey everyone involved. As a result, samples are taken to represent the entire group or population. A *random* sample means that everyone in the segment of the population being studied has an equal chance of being selected. The second type is the *stratified* sample, which works by dividing the general population into *strata,* or subgroups, based on factors such as social position and education. If the survey of the health care needs of professional women chooses an equal number of respondents from groups of women teachers, bankers, lawyers, and doctors, for example, the survey is nonproportional. However, if the number of women chosen from each stratum parallels the percentage of women in each of the professions in the society as a whole, the survey sample is proportional.

Two common methods of conducting surveys are through interviews and by questionnaires.

- **Interviews.** Whether conducted in person, by telephone, or by e-mail, survey interviews work better when they are the oral equivalent of reader based written documents. The interviewer may be looking for some type of objective truth about a product or service, however, the subject's frame of reference cannot be overlooked. Similarly, the interviewer may have his or her agenda, but, whether conducted in a "people on the street" style or with an expert in the field being studied, the interview should be done with the subject's convenience and comfort in mind.

  The research reporter has to prepare a set of questions very carefully, yet be ready to rephrase them if the subject's body language and facial cues reveal confusion or incomplete understanding. This ability to spot a problem and rephrase a question immediately is an advantage the interview format has over the written questionnaire.

  Recording the interview will be very helpful for the interviewer. However, before doing any recording, permission must be obtained. This should not be presumed; secret recordings can be a violation of law.

  An interview literally means a glimpse or picture *between* two people. It is not supposed to be an adversarial interrogation. It should be as relaxed, personal, and friendly as possible.

  An action-information closing should be used for the interview just as for a memo or letter. The subject of an interview deserves the courtesy of being informed about what to do at the end of the conversation; for example, ask questions about the use of the information gained or how to obtain a copy of the interview.
- **Questionnaires.** This type of survey can be conducted by mail or in person. There are advantages and disadvantages to both types. When surveying by mail, for example, there is no one to ask the quetions and guide the respondent. This necessitates differences in the design of the survey and questionnaire. While mail-in surveys are relatively inexpensive, they have a low response rate.

In-person questionnaires are much more costly but they have the highest response rate. Developing the survey "instrument" or package of specific questions requires great care and precision. In person the subject's body language and facial clues can tell the researcher if a question is unclear or troublesome in some personal way. When the questions are written, there are no second chances. The surveyor won't even be present. Whenever possible a list of questions should be tested on a sample group to gain immediate, spontaneous feedback on the clarity and tone of the questions.

Like interviews, questionnaires should be reader based. The surveyor who remembers his or her own typically annoyed skepticism every time a questionnaire is received will produce a more reader-based document. The researcher, for example, can motivate the audience for the questionnaire by answering the skeptic's question, "What's in it for me?" immediately. First, by appealing to the altruistic side of most people by showing how the information they supply will benefit the common good. Second, by appealing to the profit motive by offering an incentive: cash, something free, or something of value at a greatly reduced rate.

The number and the order of the questions should be reader- or subject-based. The questions should be well thought-out and very specific. A good questionnaire is not a fishing expedition. Each question should have a specific objective. The survey should begin with simple ones to let the participant ease into the experience, then build up to more important questions as the list advances.

Ethnocentrism and leading questions, which implicitly suggest the answers desired, for example, "Don't you agree that most politicians are crooks?" will not produce accurate results.

The questions should be listed in a purposeful way such as in a chronological, numeric, spatial, or alphabetical order.

The researcher has to decide whether a yes–no format, a check-off format, or an open-ended format will best suit the audience and subject. The yes–no question is the most elementary and basically yields factual information. Check-off responses are in effect multiple-choice questions. They are the easiest and quickest for respondents and large samplings. The open-ended style is more suited to small samplings of people. It requires more time but also provides more subtlety in responses. When a researcher has a subject with politically or morally sensitive issues, the Likert Scale is recommended. It offers a multiple-choice set of responses across a range from *strongly agree* to *strongly disagree.*

Preferences lists are useful for determining the degree of satisfaction with a product or service: from *low* to *high, inferior* to *superior, least important* to *most important.*

2. **Experiments.** A valuable way for businesses and government agencies to gather information about the probable success or failure of product and program changes. Experiments use deductive reasoning based on cause and effect. They change each variable one at a time, while leaving all other factors constant, to measure the effect or result. For example, if you wish to learn which, if any, vitamin supplements will alleviate a symptom or disease, you could perform either or both of the following experiments.
   - One test group remains constant while a series of vitamin supplements are administered over a period of time. All possible variables are controlled so that the members of the test group are as alike as possible in age, sex, economic and educational backgrounds, and so on.
   - Two identical test groups, one of which is the control group. The experimental factor is given only to the experimental group, not the control group. Any changes that occur are attributed to the element introduced by the experiment.
3. **Personal observation.** Another form of research using primary sources. It is scientific and deductive in nature, but does not introduce variables into what is being observed the way experiments do. Meaningful observations require set procedures and checklists to make sure that different observers, times, and places do not skew the results.

Secondary Sources

Secondary forms of research include sources of information already discovered by others. Published sources include books, journals, magazines, newspapers, periodicals, and technical reports. Unpublished sources include company records, diaries, legal documents, and medical and personal records. The library and the Internet are the two main sources of existing published information.

1. The **library** is no longer a source of printed books and magazines alone. Everyone is different, but a typical library contains many sources of information for report writing research, including the following:
   - Computer resources give the researcher access to information at a much greater speed than card catalogues. The three sources of information are databases, CD-ROMs, and online searches.

     Databases are electronic indexes containing files in every profession; for example, the *Business Periodicals Index* and *Trade Industry Index* for business research, the *Criminal Justice Period-*

ical Index for law enforcement, the *Cumulative Index to Nursing and Allied Health Literature* for health care.

CD-ROMS are compact disks that contain a thousand times more information than a floppy disk. They are "read-only memory" sources, meaning that they are closed systems limiting the researcher to what is placed on the disk. One such CD-ROM, Info-Trac, contains over 1 million articles on many fields, including law, health care, business and education, published in magazines such as *Forbes, Physician's Weekly,* and the *Harvard Business Review.*

Online searches provide researchers with lists of books and articles, including relevant information on authors, publishers, dates of publication, and so forth. They can also supply specific facts in many different fields including stocks, bonds, commodities, consumer products, and current events. Some of the most popular databases are CARL UnCover, DIALOG, and WILSONLINE.

- Government documents available to the public provide enormous sources of information for researchers. Everything from apple growing to zygogenesis is contained in government reports, with much in between on consumer safety, herbal supplements and prescription medications, government entitlement programs, and hundreds of other topics.

  These government reports can be found in publications such as *Environmental Health Perspectives, Journal of the National Cancer Institute, Military Review, Occupational Outlook Quarterly,* and *Program Manager* either in hard copy or on the Internet.

  Three ways to access the information published by the United States Government Printing Office (GPO) include the *U.S. Government Periodical Index, The Monthly Catalog of U.S. Government Publications,* and the *CIS Index to Publications of the United States Congress.*
- Newspapers and magazines contain much information for researchers not just in the daily reporting of the news in such papers as *The Los Angeles Times, The Boston Globe, The Washington Post,* and *The New York Times,* but in feature stories based on investigative reporting. Like government reports, the publications of the so-called popular press are available on the Internet as well as your library's shelves.
- The online catalog of a library lists not only books but also computer programs, CD-ROMS, encyclopedias and other reference works, and periodical indexes. Online catalogs link researchers to databases to obtain information on authors, titles, and specific subject areas.

- Reference books contain great quantities of fact-based information. Libraries have sections or rooms devoted to reference works such as encyclopedias, manuals, and dictionaries. Besides general encyclopedias such as the *New Encyclopedia Britannica,* there are also specialized ones such as the McGraw-Hill Encyclopedia of Environmental Science and Engineering and the *Encyclopedia of Banking and Finance.*

2. The **Internet** is an immense linkage of computers and computer networks whose purpose is to collect and exchange information. Its nearly limitless resources are available to everyone with access to America Online, MSN (Microsoft Network), or other servers.
   - The World Wide Web is the most well known product of the Internet. It makes vast amounts of information available in a mixed-media format of words, graphics, sound, and video. The Web enables researchers to access information from around the world with dizzying speed. Financial information from Hong Kong, medical news from Boston, trade information from Singapore, diamond news from Rotterdam—it's just a tap away.
   - Hypertext is the name of the system for creating web "pages." Unlike the pages in a traditional book, web pages may have animation and sound. Web pages are written in HyperText Markup Language (HTML). Formerly, Web addresses always began with http://www, which stands for hypertext transmission protocol://world wide web. Today, the *http* is built in or assumed. Having its Internet address or a universal resource locator (URL) enables a researcher to go directly to a website for information.
   - Search engines are powerful vehicles that locate and serve up information on the Web. They can search numerous databases simultaneously to find the information sources a researcher needs. Altavista, with its vast database of over 25 million web pages; Infoseek Guide, with its Infoseek Personal feature that updates a user's special interest list; and Lycos, which flashes a relevancy rating for each item of information found are just three search engines available to today's researcher.
   - A "directory" search is used by a report writer who is in the earliest stages of researching a subject and has not yet narrowed down the search for information. Moving among different suggested websites, the researcher will soon learn how the subject can be limited for more precise study, for example, by narrowing from government grants to obtaining government grants.
   - A "key word" search will yield results more quickly for the more focused report writer, that is, the writer who already has a specific topic to investigate. For example, the writer looking

for information on obtaining government grants for college programs would find that there are 290,562 pages on the Internet under *obtaining government grants.* Using opening and closing quotation marks as in "obtaining government grants" will narrow the search to 58 pages. A key word search under "college government grants" will focus the report writer on a mere 2 pages.

STATISTICS AND REPORT WRITING

Statistics, a branch of mathematics, is the science of collecting, analyzing, and interpreting numerical data. The term *statistics* is also used for the numbers or the data itself. Some equate statistics with what is presented in tables in a report. In any case, statistics are an integral part of reports for business and government agencies.

When the purpose of the report is purely informational, the job of the report writer is mainly to collect and present data. However, when a report is analytical in nature, such as a feasibility study, the report writer must show how the data that is presented in charts and tables suggests or dictates a course of action.

There are four basic terms necessary to understanding how numerical data is described or analyzed:

1. The *mean* refers to the arithmetical average of a group of numbers. The mean is calculated by adding a group of numbers and dividing the total by the number of entries. If a restaurant menu has five entrées priced $16.50, $17.00, $17.00, $19.50, and $23.00, the total is $93.00. The mean or average price of an entrée at that restaurant is $93.00 divided by 5, or $18.60.
2. The *median* is the midpoint in a list of figures going from lowest to highest or highest to lowest. Instead of dividing the five restaurant entrées by five as you would to arrive at the mean price, you would divide the five items into two groups, with the median price of an entrée being $17.00. The median is more informative and descriptive than the mean when there is an extreme or radically different number in a list. For example, if the last item in the list of entrées had been $55.00, the mean would have been $25.00 but the median still $17.00.
3. The *mode* is whatever number in a list appears most frequently, in other words, whatever is the most popular or repeated number. In the list of menu entrées the mode figure is $17.00 because it appears more frequently than any other entrée price.
4. The *range* is a measure of the difference or variability in a set of figures. It is arrived at by subtracting the lowest number in a list

from the highest number. The range in the list of entrées from $16.50 to $23.00, therefore, is $6.50. However, if the last item were priced at $55.00, the range would be $38.50. The *range* statistic is very useful when there is a significant disparity in a list. The far greater range of $38.50 would make someone wonder why or what has caused such a range of prices.

Sources of Statistical Information

Statistics can be obtained through such primary-source research vehicles as surveys, questionnaires, experiments, and personal observations. In addition to the secondary sources listed above, report writers can also obtain statistics from a variety of government and industry sources, including:

- The Gale Research Company and Predicasts, Inc., offer extensive sources of information and statistics. Predicasts publishes market information and forecasts arranged by company, country, and product under titles including *Expansion and Capacity Digest, Predicasts, Forecasts,* and *World-Regional Casts.*
- The *Handbook of Basic Economic Statistics,* the *Statistical Abstract of the United States,* and *Standard and Poor's Statistical Service.*
- The North American Industry Classification System (NAICS) was introduced in 1997. It provides economic and financial statistics in different areas such as health care and social services, information systems, and professional and scientific services. Statistics based on this hemispheric system are now available.
- On a global level, statistical information can be found in publications such as *Principal International Businesses, Major Companies of Europe and Japan,* the *Index to International Statistics,* and *The Statistical Yearbook.*
- There are also many guides that are helpful in locating the type of statistics needed for a particular report subject. One of these is the *Statistical Reference Index,* which provides statistical sources from professional and trade organizations. Another is the *American Statistics Index,* which offers government statistics arranged by categories and agencies. The *Encyclopedia of Business Information Sources* identifies basic statistical and informational sources. *Predicasts Forecasts* provides a geographical directory of statistical information with the codes of the North American Industry Classification System.

Presentation of Statistical Information

Whether in memos, letters, or reports, business and government agency writers have to make many decisions about recording numbers.

Basically the choice is between words (ten thousand dollars) and figures ($10,000).

The following list of rules and suggestions reflects current practice. There are so many choices and variables that the most important rule of all is to be consistent. Arbitrarily switching between words and figures will confuse the reader and the writer. If a numerical amount is presented in words in one place in a report, it should be expressed that way throughout.

1. Numbers one through nine are expressed in words; 10 and above in figures.
2. Regardless of the number involved, always use the words to begin a sentence: *Three dollars was deducted from the balance.*
3. Numbers are used for the following items: dates, measurements, money, page numbers, percentages, ratios, and temperatures. To avoid violating rule #2, rephrase any sentence beginning with one of these items. For example, *19 feet separated the first and second tiers* could be rewritten as: *The first and second tiers were separated by 19 feet.*
4. Very large numbers are expressed in a combination of words and figures as in: *The budget proposal was cut by 55 million dollars.*
5. If consecutive numbers appear in the same phrase, use a number for one (the smaller of the two) and a word for the next, as in: *The architect's plan called for 5 ten-foot steel beams.*
6. Decimals should be used instead of fractions, especially in technical writing or whenever precise measurements are needed.
7. Numbers are advised rather than words wherever possible in any documents with multi-cultural audiences. This is especially recommended to avoid confusion when the numbers are very large.

USING ILLUSTRATIONS TO PRESENT STATISTICS EFFECTIVELY

There are many words used to describe the various illustrations used in reports. Charts, graphs, tables, and figures are just a few of these terms. In this section, we will group these terms into two categories: *tables* and *figures*. Examples of each appear in Appendixes A and B.

- **Tables** are parallel rows or lists of statistical information arranged to show changes in variables quantities such as cost, personnel, time, age, and regions.
- **Figures** are all illustrations other than tables, such as line graphs, pie charts, bar graphs, and flow charts, and drawings.

Whether the report writer creates them alone or with graphics software such as Clip Art, Print Artist, and MS Paint, tables and figures function in a similar manner. They present information in a visual rather than a verbal way. Even though some words are used, the key to the value of figures lies in the proverb "a picture is worth a thousand words." This is why they are often referred to not simply as *visuals* but as *visual aids*. The value of their eye-appeal is only a means to an end.

The primary purpose of illustrations in a report is to summarize and communicate key ideas in a direct, unambiguous way. Illustrations of any type are never substitutes for ideas, but additions and aids to understanding ideas. To achieve this end, figures, like all real communication, must be reader-based. Keep them clear and simple.

The Function of Tables and Figures

Tables and figures give life and force to ideas for many audiences in multiple ways:

- They are the vital link between raw data and useful knowledge. They give us a specific way to look at statistics, enabling us to draw conclusions. Bar charts enable us to compare and contrast data; pie charts show the relation of the parts to the whole.
- They give report audiences concrete, vivid, and quick representations of ideas. To do this tables and figures must be designed effectively.
- They save space and words. Very complicated and detailed information can often be communicated more quickly by the report writer and grasped more easily by report audiences through carefully planned and well-designed figures. One table or bar chart can sum up pages of data covering many months or even years.
- They speak a universal language, just as music does. This is why they are especially valuable in simplifying and presenting complex material for cross-cultural audiences.
- They can be very persuasive. Figures can call attention to key ideas in a visual way that is hard to resist. For this reason figures are a very effective tool, especially for proposal writing.
- The Construction of Tables

Tables present data with little or no interpretation, leaving readers to draw their own conclusions. However, the way the table presents data, for example, the choice of categories and titles, can subtly influence audiences. The layout or arrangement of the table can invite or dissuade readers from comparing the statistics in the columns.

Presenting Tables in the Text

1. *Number and title:* all tables should be numbered consecutively corresponding to the list of illustrations that accompanies the Table of Contents. When there are many illustrations, tables may be listed separately from figures in this introductory list (Table 1, Table 2, Table 3 . . . Figure 1, Figure 2, Figure 3, Figure 4 . . .).

   The titles should be informative rather than descriptive. Supply the reader as needed with the *who, what, where, when,* and *why.*
2. *Table components.* The principal parts of tables are the headings, stub, and columns.
   - Headings are the titles of the vertical columns in the table. The terms *spanner head* or *column head* are sometimes used to cover a group of columns in the table, in which case subheadings are used for the individual columns.
   - The stub is the first vertical column on the left side of the table. It identifies the horizontal rows in the table.
   - The columns contain the actual statistical data being used to illustrate the particular point the report writer is making.
3. *Textual link:* the reader should be told about each table before it occurs. Every one should be previewed with expressions such as: "Table 4 illustrates the percentage of . . ." or "The progressive dilution of . . . is shown in Table 6."
4. *Location:* all tables should be placed as closely as possible to the textual link. This will make it easier for the reader to refer to them without interruption or searching back and forth in the text of the report. If necessary, rearrange the paragraphs of the report to accommodate the table on the same page with its textual link.
5. *Order of statistics:* list the data in logical order. Depending on the information involved this order could be alphabetical or descending numerical order from the highest to the lowest numbers.
6. *Page placement:* limit tables to one page whenever possible. If a second page is needed for a long table, write *continued* at the bottom of the first page and at the top of the second page. Repeat the column headings on the second page of the table.
7. *Source:* unless the entire table or the statistics in a table are the result of the reporters own research, the source must be recognized and given credit. This credit can be placed in parentheses under the table title but is usually done directly beneath the table, as in *Source: National Alliance on Caregiving* or Source: U.S. Department of Commerce, Bureau of the Census, *1998 Conference on Statistical Reporting,* June 1998, p. 320. If additional information is needed to read the table correctly, it is placed in footnotes directly under the source information, not at the bottom of the page.

The Choice of Figures

All figures provide information graphically. The choice of particular figures is determined by the type of idea the report writer seeks to convey to his or her audience.

Bar charts

The primary purpose of bar charts is to show comparative data at a specific time or over an extended period of time. Whether vertical, horizontal, grouped, or segmented, bar charts are like thermometers in appearance and function. They show similar elements rising, falling, or (rarely) remaining stationary over time. Bar charts can be thought of as tables converted into visual form. While they might not be as statistically precise as tables, bar charts make a greater and immediate visual statement.

The *stub* or vertical column on the left of the chart identifies the statistical information, for example, in percentages, dollars, or geographical regions. All vertical and horizontal columns must be labeled and the bars within them of equal width. The *grid* is the field on which the bars are displayed. Finally, three-dimensional bar charts are purely decorative. They do not seem to communicate statistical information in bar charts any more clearly or forcefully and, therefore, are unnecessary.

There are three common types of bar charts:

- *Simple* bar charts use solid individual bars, either horizontal or vertical, to compare items over a period of time. The varying length of the bars shows changes in one type of data, for example, magnitude or quantity over time or in different regions.
- *Multiple* bar charts compare several variables over a period of time. Multiple vertical bars can show component parts of several variables; multiple horizontal bars can portray several variables over a period of time. Limit the number of bars in a year's grouping to four. Beyond that the chart and its message for the reader gets cluttered.
- *Segmented* or stacked bar charts show at a glance the different parts of a measured whole by subdividing each bar.

Line graphs

The primary function of line graphs is to show quantitative changes over time. Line graphs do this by showing a continuous relationship between two variables, one of which is dependent, or subject to change, the other of which is independent, or not subject to change. Common dependent variables include money and weather. The most common independent variables are time and distance.

The dependent variable is depicted in the vertical stub, the independent variable in the horizontal time line. The background of vertical and horizontal lines against which the line graph is displayed is called the *grid*. Where the vertical and horizontal lines intersect is called the *data point*. For example, the dollar range of a share of stock, zero to $100 appears in the vertical stub. The increments of price, distance, or time on the vertical stub are called *ticks,* from which we get the term *up-ticks,* for increases in bond prices or yields. The hours of the trading day appear in the horizontal line. The price at which the stock traded over the course of a day's session of stock exchange trading is shown by the continuous line in the graph.

Like bar charts, line graphs are often based on tables of data. Unlike bar charts, however, line graphs show movement and change in a quickly visible way. As a result, report writers must be careful in their design and presentation. Just as the arrangement of a table can invite or discourage readers from comparing the statistics in the columns, the design of a line graph can affect the reader's perception of the data. The vertical and horizontal scale of a graph can distort the reality of the change in the variable. For example, reducing each unit of the horizontal axis of a line graph from 2 inches to 1 inch while increasing the vertical axis from 1 inch to 2 inches would make a change in the price of a stock appear much more precipitous than it may in fact have been.

Two commonly used line graphs include:

- *Single line* graphs show just the change that occurred in a single dependent variable over time or distance. Single line figures are useful for showing changes in variables such as sales, prices, and production.
- *Multiple-line* graphs depict how several dependent variables compare with one another over a period of time. When constructing multiple-line graphs it is important to make clear visual distinctions among the different lines, for example, with different colors or with dotted, dashed, or continuous lines. The different lines must also be labeled or identified with a *legend.* As with multiple-bar charts, limiting the number of lines in a multiple-line graph to four makes reader comprehension easier and quicker.

Map charts

Sometimes called *statistical maps,* map charts are useful for showing a combination of quantitative and geographical information in one picture. The most familiar statistical maps are the weather maps shown every day in newspapers and television weather stations. Maps showing distribution of income by states or regions are another common form of map chart.

Various graphic techniques including color and shading can be used to distinguish the geographic areas of a map chart. As with multiple bar and line figures, map charts need legends to tell the audience how to read or understand the chart

Pie charts or circle graphs

The main function of pie charts is to show the subdivision of the whole (the pie) unit into parts (the slices). In this it serves a similar purpose to the segmented bar chart. Pie charts are especially useful in financial documents and government reports. They give readers quick insight into budgets, the distribution of sales, earnings, and expenses. Pie charts allow the reader to see and compare two things simultaneously: the relationship of the parts to the whole and the relationship of the parts to each other.

Some things to remember when serving up a pie chart:

- The slices of the pie should be easy to distinguish by color, shading, or cross-hatching.
- Begin cutting the slices clockwise at the 12 o'clock mark with the biggest piece of the pie first.
- Work clockwise in descending order.
- Each slice should be identified with a horizontal legend.

The slices must add up to 100 percent.

Pictographs

These are analogous to bar charts in that pictographs or pictograms show comparative data at a specific time. Instead of showing the data in the form of bars, however, pictographs convert the statistics of a table into symbolic pictures or icons arranged vertically or horizontally. Each icon, for example, a house, a person, a car, or a coin, represents a unit of measurement. The icons should always be of equal size. It is the number of icons that carries the message. While they might not be as statistically precise as tables, pictographs make immediate visual statements with ready audience appeal.

Flow charts and organizational charts

What separates these figures from the previous visual aids is that flow charts and organizational charts are not based upon statistical information.

- *Organizational charts* show the levels of authority and responsibility in a corporation or agency. Rectangles are the most common figure used to represent the divisions and sub-divisions of an organization. How the rectangles are linked vertically and horizontally makes the chain of command immediately visible.

Organizational charts, because they often look like upside-down trees, are sometimes called *decision trees.* The "root" is the Chief Executive Officer, the "limbs" Vice Presidents, the "branches" Managers.

- *Flow charts* use graphics similar to the rectangles of an organizational chart to show how some physical process or decision-making procedure, for example, approving a loan application, is carried out. But where an organizational chart is static at the time of creation, the flow chart is dynamic.

  The interconnected elements of a flow chart are often depicted with different shapes, for example, ovals for the start and completion of a procedure, rectangles for the steps of the procedure, and diamonds to highlight decision-making steps in the process. Arrows are used in flow charts to emphasize the movement and direction involved in a process.

Deploying Figures in the Text

All figures used in a report should be self-sufficient. This means that whatever type of figure is used it should be able to stand on its own outside the text of the report. A person in the primary or secondary audience should be able to gain knowledge from the bar chart or line graph without the paragraphs of text that surrounded it in the report.

All figures should be identified and presented in the following way:

1. *Number and title:* all the figures in a report should be numbered consecutively corresponding to the List of Figures that accompanies the Table of Contents (*Figure 1, Figure 2, Figure 3...*). The titles should be informative rather than descriptive. Supply the reader with the *who, what, where, when,* and *why.*
2. *Subtitle:* if the information in a figure is very complicated, it may be necessary to use a subtitle, sometimes called a *legend,* to explain or identify elements of the figure. If a subtitle is needed, print it in smaller type below the title.
3. *Textual link:* the reader should not be surprised by a figure. Everyone should be introduced or prepared for it in the text with expressions such as: "Figure 3 illustrates the difference between . . ." or "The increase in . . . can be clearly seen in Figure 7."
4. *Location:* all figures in a report should be placed as close as possible to the textual link. This will make it easier for the reader to understand their significance without interruption or searching back and forth in the text of the report. If necessary, the writer can

rearrange the paragraphs to accommodate the figure on the same page with its textual link.

5. *Source:* unless the data on which a figure is based is the result of the report writer's own research, for example, a survey the writer conducted, credit must be given to the source. This can be done in parentheses under the table title but is usually supplied directly beneath the table, as in *Source: Bureau of Labor Statistics.*

19

The Content and Structure of the Formal Report

More than any other form of business writing, formal reports require attention to four promoters of successful communication, highlighted in Chapter 1.

1. *Preparation.* Getting ready for the specific task that is about to occur, whether a memo, letter, or a report, is a deliberate process. By definition, a formal report requires the greatest amount of planning and preparation.
2. *Precision.* Being "on the mark," or right on target with ideas and expression as opposed to "far afield" or "out in left field." Precision and clarity go hand in hand with preparation. The length of a formal report cannot be allowed to dilute the clarity of its message.
3. *Presence.* Having the ability to convey a sense of poise and self-assurance. This capacity results from being prepared internally and externally—mentally and physically. Being at once calm yet ready for action gives one what is called a compelling personality, one that inspires respect and confidence. Reports that are carefully planned, written, and visually striking inspire respect and confidence in the validity of their findings.
4. *Preference.* This quality of successful report communicators works in two ways. Because they have prepared themselves for the specific report subject at hand, they enjoy the ability to make choices jointly with managers. Because they deliver a report with

clarity and presence, they become part of a team that sets priorities. Report writers who gain this level of preference enjoy a very real, practical advantage over others.

DEFINING THE SUBJECT OF REPORTS

The first stage of preparing to write a formal report is determining the subject. The ideas that form the subject of a report are usually determined by managers and executives in the organization and explained to the report writer in the first of the three meetings described in Chapter 16 or at an earlier preliminary meeting. Finding the precise words to express that subject in written form is perhaps the defining moment for the report writer.

Defining the subject/problem of a report is an extension of the method demonstrated in Chapter 9 for developing a central idea. It is a process of narrowing and expansion: narrowing the initial idea down to specific cases while expanding the number of words used to describe it into a complete sentence. This is not the same thing as a thesis. A thesis goes beyond the subject or central idea to express an opinion.

Steps to Define the Subject of a Report

1. Start with the names of the various types of reports, for example, *trip report, feasibility study, compliance report, progress report.* These names indicate both the purpose and the general subject of the report.
2. Limit the subject area contained in the name of the report by expanding its specific elements into an informal list of possibilities, for example:
   - Converting Gonzaga Hall to central air conditioning.
   - Doing it in six months
   - For under $250,000
3. Construct a sentence using these elements: The subject of the report is the feasibility of converting Gonzaga Hall to central air conditioning within six months for under $250,000.

The generic topic *feasibility report* has become the specifically expanded subject *The feasibility of converting Gonzaga Hall to central air conditioning.*

FORMAL REPORT WRITING STYLE AND EXPRESSION

Formal reports, especially ones written for external audiences, use a formal writing style of "standard written English." Some of the reasons and qualities of this report writing style include the following:

- It uses the third person for singular and plural nouns and pronouns to convey an objective, dispassionate, scientific tone. For example, the *report writer* or *researcher* rather than *I* or *we*, the *subjects of the study* rather than *our subjects, the survey respondents* rather than *our respondents.*
- It avoids contractions such as *won't* or *didn't* in favor of the more formal *will not* or *did not.*
- It uses longer and more technical words than informal report writing. This is not to impress the reader with esoteric vocabulary, but because the subject matter requires it.
- It uses a variety of sentence length and structure to avoid monotony for the readers of long reports. For example, it uses compound sentences such as, "The agency has recently proposed sharp reductions in the allowable level of sulfur in diesel fuel and hopes to issue a final rule by the end of the year." In addition, it makes use of complex sentences such as, "Although one percentage point sounds small, government officials said the finding was important because of the huge number of people exposed to particulate pollution." (See Chapter 10 for additional information on sentence structure.)

The same principles of clear and concise writing listed in Chapter Seven that will help memos and letters communicate a writer's ideas more effectively will also make reports easier to read and more likely to achieve their purposes.

- Choose concrete words not abstractions. Concrete words refer to actual material things. Abstract words refer to ideas and generalities. Say "by June 2001," not "at some future date" or "in the not-too-distant future."
- Use plain everyday words not bookish words that suggest the writer creates messages with a thesaurus on the left side and a dictionary on the right. Use *learn* not *ascertain, review* not *recapitulate, end* not *termination.* Also use plain English instead of "legalese," for example, use the words *additional* not *appurtenant, later* not *hereinafter, for that reason* not *wherefore.*
- Use technical language when necessary, but sparingly. The members of the writer's immediate group may understand the highly technical language, but the secondary audiences, who may have decision-making power, may not. If they do not understand the report's language, it may just crash and burn.
- Avoid slang and buzzwords, clichés, acronyms, and Instant Messenger abbreviations. Expressions such as "I would like to take this opportunity" are not only clichés but are wordy wasters of space

and time. Words and phrases such as "a can of worms," "herding cats," and "policy wonks" might be understood by you and your circle but may be lost on your often unknown secondary audiences.

- Use action verbs not lengthy noun phrases. The action verb *investigate,* for example, is more vigorous than the noun phrase *conduct an investigation of.* The passive voice, while generally avoided in business writing, except for conveying negative news, is used in formal writing to convey a sense of objectivity: "The information that was gathered by the survey" suggests scientific, inductive reasoning at work. "I used a survey to gather information" implies personal factors may be in play. The passive voice helps to focus the reader on the action rather than the person performing the action.
- Remove redundancies and compound prepositions, which use several words instead of single ones. "Now" is more concise than "at this point in time." "Because" is clearer than "due to the fact that."

THE FINISHED STRUCTURE OF THE FORMAL REPORT

Cover

Formal reports are bound like a book's binding in some material to enhance their appearance and ability to withstand repeated use and being passed from reader to reader.

Title Fly

Originally called the "fly page" when it was a blank sheet meant to protect the printed title page, it now contains the title of the report. This title should be clearly informative for the reader by including the *who, what, where, when, why,* and *how* of the report. These refer to the organization's name, the subject matter, the location(s) involved, the date, the purpose, and the method as in this example: ANALYSIS OF THE GOTHAM CITY MAYOR'S EXECUTIVE BUDGET FOR 2000 BASED ON THE YEARS 1999–2003.

Title Page

In addition to the title, the title page provides the report audiences with the name and title of the recipient, the author(s) names, the corporation or agency that developed the report, the author(s) names and company name (if different from the receiving company), and the exact date it was presented.

Letter of Transmittal

The transmittal letter, or memo if the sender and receiver of the report are in the same organization, should be written in the frontloaded, direct pattern. It may be less formal in style than the report itself but should include the following information:

1. The name of the person and the organization to whom the report is being sent.
2. The title of the report and (where applicable) by whom it was authorized.
3. The key points of the report and their significance to the reader.
4. A note of appreciation for the confidence implied in the assignment.
5. An action-information closing, that is, what the receiver should do after reading the report, and what follow-up actions the writer is ready to do for the reader and organization.

Table of Contents

This page represents another step in the gradual unfolding of the contents of the report. It tells the reader the principal sections of the report and on what pages they can be found. Any table of contents is directly related to the outline that is created to organize all the information in the report. Depending on the length and complexity of the report, either the main headings or the main and subheadings in the outline become the elements of the table of contents.

List of Figures

This list of the various charts, diagrams, drawings, and graphs that appear in the report may be placed below the Table of Contents if there is room on the page. Figures are consecutively numbered with titles as well as the pages on which they appear.

Abstract or Executive Summary

Busy executives often do not have time to read entire reports. This brief summary expands the key sections of the Table of Contents, including the conclusions and recommendations, for their convenience and to assist in their decision-making processes. If an executive focuses on some information in the summary, he or she can locate it in the Table of Contents for additional information. To answer the question "How brief is brief?" the executive summary should be in proportion to the length of the entire report. A 10 percent ratio of summary to report has been suggested as a guideline.

Creating frontloaded executive summaries or abstracts

Some people will actually read the report writer's finished work from cover to cover. Others will speed-read the document by reading the opening and closing and only the first and last sentences of the paragraphs in between. The executive summary or abstract is the one section report writers can be guaranteed their audiences will read in full. This is why it is the most important part of most reports. In fact, the number of readers who go on after the abstract is probably in direct proportion to the skill with which it is written.

Some confusion is caused by the variety of terms used to describe this section of a report. Some report writers use the term *abstract* to describe a very brief 10- or 12-line statement of the key points of information a report will contain. In this sense, an abstract can be considered an expansion of the report's Table of Contents.

Others use the term *summary* or *executive summary.* Usually the term *summary* refers to a section at the end of a document that brings together the key points that have gone before. However, in report writing, the term is used for a longer statement of the most important information that will follow in a given report. While longer than an abstract, it does not go beyond two pages. The term *executive summary* usually connotes a fuller expression of conclusions, recommendations, and other decision-geared information.

Finally, there are terms such as *foreword, digest, descriptive abstract,* and *information abstract* to define this section of a report. This chapter will use the terms *abstract* and *executive summary* interchangeably for the section at the beginning of a report that presents its key elements in a short or condensed form.

The reason for this choice is that the term *abstract* denotes its brevity, while the term *executive summary* describes its useful purpose for managers. In fact, the abstract is often called an executive summary because it serves two functions. First, it provides the managers in the units served by the report enough information about the report's contents to decide whether to budget time for a full reading. Second, it provides related managers and higher level executives with sufficient understanding about the content and results of the study to fill their organizational and decision-making responsibilities.

The abstract is not only a key element for the report writer's internal audience and those in close proximity on the chart of readers, it is a key section for the report's secondary and external audiences. The people a company or agency most wants to impress are also going to head straight for the executive summary or abstract. With a good first impression they may sample some of the report's introduction, conclusions, and recommendations to see if they are equally tasty. The abstract is the crucial first impression a report makes and it must contain the central ideas of the report in a clear and direct frontloaded fashion.

While each report and abstract has its own set of needs and goals there are some general guidelines that should be followed to make your abstract more effective. These are very similar to the functions and characteristics of good subject lines and opening paragraphs in frontloaded memos and letters.

Form. Every abstract must be concise and clear. A lengthy abstract is a contradiction in terms. How brief is brief? Some have suggested that an abstract should be between 3 and 10 percent of the length of the entire report. However, this is an arbitrary figure. The idea that an abstract be no more than one full page might also seem arbitrary, but makes sense considering the busy schedules of most managers.

Report writers should not try to accomplish this objective by cutting essential information or by a type of shorthand that drops articles and transitional words and phrases needed for unity and coherence. If the abstract is kept brief, but in the process made less clear and more difficult to read, it is no longer a reader-based communication.

The executive summary or abstract must be consistent with the total report. While it does not have to have the same organization or wording, it should not have any data, information, or ideas that do not appear in the body of the report. Nor should it contain conclusions or recommendations, which go beyond those that appear in the body of the report. This would only confuse a reader of both.

Content. The abstract must include enough specific information about the subject of the project or study to fulfill the administrative needs of a busy manager. To accomplish this goal the report writer must include a clear statement of the problem or issue that is the subject of the report. In addition, the more important results, conclusions, and recommendations should be included in the abstract.

Although the abstract is a type of introduction, it should be able to stand on its own. Abstracts, in fact, are often reprinted all by themselves in publications that specialize in abstracts of reports covering particular fields. Such executive summaries should contain the principal points of information as well as the conclusions they support. The reason for this is not only to give managers a jump-start on the report but also to make sure that the abstract makes total sense even when separated from the complete report as it travels through different audiences. The abstract that cannot stand on its own must be rewritten, in all probability by someone other than the original report writer.

Style and expression. Report abstracts, in addition to being brief, should be written in formal, standard English, as described above.

The Report Itself	**Introduction**—purpose, procedures, and scope of the report **Development**—the findings of the report: information/analysis **Conclusion**—conclusions drawn and recommendations for action

Introduction

The introductory section of the report includes the following information:

1. The background *yesterday* of people, actions, and events: this information will help place the reader in the historical context necessary to understand the problem or subject of the report. The reader will learn how the problem that caused the report developed over time. In addition, the reader will find out who has done what up to this point and what the consequences of those actions were.
2. The problem and purpose of the report: this section will explain in detail for the reader what steps are being proposed to solve the problem and why.
3. The scope and limitations of the report, that is, the perimeters of what is included and what is not included. Some explanation of what is excluded may be necessary, for example, budget restrictions or the impossibility of gaining complete information because of insurmountable difficulties or forces beyond the control of the report writer.
4. The methodology used, meaning how the information in the report was gathered. It might have been through primary sources such as interviews or secondary sources such as library and Internet research.

Body

The body is the largest section, generally taking up at least two-thirds of the entire report. It contains the discussion of the central problem and includes the writer's analysis and interpretation of the data or statistical information gathered. The body should be carefully organized, using one or more of the following patterns of development:

- *Chronological:* by time order
- *Spatial:* by a pattern of place or location
- *Logical:* by one of the following patterns:
  Cause and effect
  Comparison-contrast
  Classification and division
  Illustration
- *Problem–analysis–solution:* what the problem is and why it exists; and what can be done to change or solve it.
- *Order of importance:* either ascending, climactic order from the least to the most important, or descending from the most significant to the least. This method works well in tandem with the preceding problem–analysis–solution pattern.

The report writer should choose a pattern that will best convey the research, analysis, and conclusions drawn. The logic of the pattern should be made visually clear for the report audiences by the use of appropriately designed and easy-to-follow headings and subheadings, as demonstrated in the following chapter.

In addition to choice of a logical pattern of development, the organization of the body should be made clear and thus easy to read by the use of:

- *Thesis statements for sections.* The thesis statement provides the reader with the central idea of the section to follow. A good thesis statement does not just state a fact, it has a controlling idea for the entire report or major section of a report, and it has a key word or phrase. For example, "The Bank of Utopia is ranked as the <u>most efficient</u> bank holding company in the nation, demonstrating management's ability to control operating expenses and enhance revenues, while successfully growing its core business."
- *Topic sentences for paragraphs.* The topic sentence gives the reader the central idea of each paragraph. Like a good thesis statement, it contains a controlling idea for the remainder of the paragraph and a key word. For example, "The objective of liquidity management is to <u>ensure the availability</u> of sufficient resources to meet all financial commitments and to capitalize on opportunities for business expansion."
- *Transitional words and phrases to connect sections, paragraphs, and sentences within paragraphs.* For example, "The <u>initial</u> allocation" . . . the <u>second</u> allocation . . . the <u>final</u> allocation."

Conclusion

The conclusion of a formal report has two components, both of which should be presented in a numbered or bulleted list to make it easier for the different audiences to grasp the various conclusions drawn. These lists should observe parallel structure, meaning that each entry in these lists should begin with the same part of speech. This technique for writing more effective reader-based sentences is explained in Chapter 10.

The Conclusions section pulls everything together for the reader with a summary of the findings drawn from an analysis of the information gained from primary and secondary sources. The following list demonstrates parallel structure. Each entry begins with an adjective, noun, and verb in the past tense.

Most employees stated . . .

Some back office personnel expressed the opinion . . .

Few employees believed . . .

The Recommendations section should relate directly to the conclusions, that is, they should be based on the findings just reported and summarized. The recommendations should also be realistic and reasonable and should not introduce or require any new information. The list that follows also demonstrates parallel structure. Each entry begins with a verb in the imperative voice, which is appropriate for a section that is telling the reader in a confident tone what should be done as a result of the conclusions that were just presented.

Expand the width of the aisles . . .

Use tiles instead of carpeting on the floors . . .

Change the wine display racks from metal to wooden shelves . . .

Appendix

This section contains material that isn't essential for understanding the body of the report but may still be of interest to some readers of the report. The plural form is either the Latin derived *appendices* used for more scholarly audiences or *appendixes,* which follows the more common way of making words plural in English.

This material may include questionnaires, case studies, charts, drawings, tables, parts lists, computer printouts, and other data too lengthy for insertion into the body of the report. Different types of information should be placed in separate appendixes each designated with its own letter and title as follows:

Appendix A: Personnel Services Costs

Appendix B: Full-Time Headcount

Appendix C: Revenue Detail

Appendix D: Five-Year Expenditure Analysis

Notes

The type of additional information provided in this section varies in different fields; however, it generally falls into one of the following categories:

1. When information or opinions in the report are obtained from outside sources such as books, articles, and websites, the source must be credited. When sources are given at the end of the report they are called *endnotes.* When this is done at the bottom of the page on which the source is quoted, it is called a *footnote.* The third way is to credit the source parenthetically within the paragraph where the quote appears. This last method seems the most reader-based, because it allows the reader to learn the source without looking elsewhere in the text of the report. All three methods of documentation can be found in the publication of the Modern Language Association titled *MLA Handbook for Writers of Research Papers.*[1]
2. The term *notes* is also used by some report writers for information, appearing at the end of a report in the manner of appendixes. They do this when there is a mix of visual and verbal information as in the following notes to a bank's annual report:

   Note 1-Summary of Significant Accounting Policies
   Note 2-Business Combinations
   Note 3-Securities
   Note 4-Loans
   Note 5-Allowance for Loan Losses
   Note 6-Premises and Equipment

Bibliography or Works Cited

These are parallel and somewhat overlapping terms. A Bibliography is literally a picture or list of books consulted for the report, although bibliographies in practice include books, articles, websites, and other sources. A Bibliography may include works only some of which are actually quoted in the report. A Works Cited page, on the other hand, includes only those works that are actually quoted in the report. Report writers should choose one of the terms only. It would confuse the reader to see a Bibliography *and* a Works Cited page.

Whichever term is used, the list of books and articles is arranged alphabetically according to the authors' last names. The entries are single spaced with a hanging indent after the first line, meaning that the second and succeeding lines are indented five spaces. This highlights the authors' names, making identification easier for the reader. Double spacing is used between the entries in the alphabetized list.

ORGANIZING, OUTLINING AND PRESENTING THE FORMAL REPORT

Organization is a key part of all effective writing. The simplest letter to a friend may have chronological structure; that is, it records events as they happened in time. Business memos and letters may be frontloaded or direct in organization, or endloaded and indirect in structure, as shown in Chapter 8. Even informal reports need to be clearly organized to transmit their information successfully to their readers.

Formal reports especially, because of their length and complexity, need strong and clear organization. In fact, they require an external and an internal structure to convey their ideas to their audiences. If such organization is lacking, the reader will get lost in a jungle of ideas and information and either misconstrue the report's message or give up reading the report altogether.

The external structure of a formal report is based on the sections already listed from Cover through Appendixes. These sections should be identified and numbered according to a set plan.

The pages within the sections of semi-formal and formal reports are usually given lowercase Roman numerals and Arabic numbers in the following manner:

Section	**Numbering**
Cover	No number
Title fly	No number
Title page	No number but counted as "i"
Letter of Transmittal	ii
Abstract or Executive Summary	iii
Table of Contents	iv
List of Figures	v
Introduction	1, 2, 3 . . .
Body	7, 8, 9, 10 . . .
Conclusions	12, 13 . . .
Recommendations	15, 16 . . .

Notes	18, 19 . . .
Bibliography or Works Cited	21, 22 . . .
Appendixes	A-1, A-2 . ,. . B-1, B-2 . . . C-1, C-2 . . .

Internal Organization of Formal Reports

Every report must also have an *internal structure* or organization. This is primarily needed for the body of the report, that is, the sections titled Introduction and Body. There are two principal ways to organize information:

- Sequential, in which all the items in a group have equal importance in relationship to one another. Examples of sequential order include chronological, alphabetical, and numeric order.
- Hierarchical, in which the items in a group are not of equal importance. This type of organization is needed when a writer is dealing with complex ideas and relationships. Hierarchical organization is very reader-based. This is because readers absorb such complex information much more quickly when it is arranged in a meaningful way, for example, by grouping the major ideas and their subdivisions in order of importance (descending or ascending).

The following list of methods for developing the central idea of a memo or letter was introduced in Chapter 8. The report writer can also choose the pattern from among these that would best convey the research, analysis, and conclusions drawn.

- *Chronological:* by time order
- *Spatial:* by a pattern of place or location
- *Logical:* by one of the following patterns:
  - Cause and effect
  - Comparison-contrast
  - Classification and division
  - Illustration
- *Problem–analysis–solution:* what the problem is and why it exists, and what can be done to change or solve it.
- *Order of importance:* either ascending, climactic order from the least to the most important, or descending from the most significant to the least. This method works well in tandem with the preceding problem–analysis–solution pattern.

The Relationship between Organization and Outline

Providing information on a subject or analyzing a problem was the goal the report writer accepted after the first of the meetings with management discussed in Chapter 16. The report, therefore, must be organized around this subject or problem not around the writer's own discovery process. Only when this goal is achieved in the writing process can it be shared with the various audiences of the report and its findings.

The subject of a report and the central idea of a report are inseparable. The thesis or central idea of a report is the reporter's *answer* to a question or *solution* to a problem. It is the findings of the report or what the report writer has learned about the problem or subject. With this as a starting point, the reporter can proceed to group or prioritize the report's ideas in outline form. This process includes separating the major and secondary topics and making sure the relationship between them is clear. If the organization of the outline is clear, the report itself should be equally clear.

How Graphic Highlighting and Writing Style Reinforce the Logic of the Report's Organization

When the logic of the organizational plan has been achieved in the outline, it should be visually reinforced in the report itself to make understanding quicker and more pleasurable for the report's audiences.

Headings are the primary means for readers to grasp the organization of a report. They provide a map to help the reader follow the flow of the major and secondary topics and the interrelationship between greater and lesser points.

Writing style is also an effective agent for underscoring the logic of the report's structure.

Guidelines for graphic and verbal reinforcement of a report's organization:

- Create appropriately titled headings and subheadings to divide the report into units that are immediately evident. Following is one way to do this. There are other ways, but whatever choice of headings has been made the most important thing is to be consistent.

    1. Titles of report, chapters, and major units: center heading and use ALL CAPS.
    2. Major topics: center heading and capitalize the first letters of all words except articles and prepositions.
    3. Subordinate units: justify left and capitalize the first letter of all words except articles and prepositions.
    4. Lesser subdivisions such as evidence and examples: the heading becomes the first words of a paragraph.

- Choose different fonts to parallel the headings and subheadings, for example, **BOLD** all caps, **Bold** upper- and lowercase, regular ALL CAPS. Stay with variations of the same or similar fonts. Too much variety of widely differing fonts will distract and confuse rather than assist the reader.
- Consider "talking" versus generic headings. Generic headings are very brief. They identify topics but give little direction to the reader. They are usually used in formal reports because they preserve a sense of distance and objectivity about the information. A "talking" heading is the equivalent of a good topic sentence that begins a paragraph. Both have a controlling idea and a key word or phrase that gives the reader a sense of direction for the paragraph or section to follow. *Employment* is too brief to be clear; it is a dead end for the reader. *Strict Adherence to Equal Opportunity Regulations* gives a clear sense of direction to the reader, especially with its key word *strict.*
- Observe parallelism by using the same part of speech or verbal construct to begin each heading:

  1. Participial phrases: *removing asbestos, training new employees, directing traffic.*
  2. Noun phrases: *reduction in staff, installation of equipment, change of direction.*
  3. Questions: *What reductions can be made? What innovations should be considered? Which programs need new management?*

- Use transition words to connect ideas under headings:

  1. For classifying the parts of a whole: *the first group, the second group, the third group.*
  2. For drawing comparisons or contrasts: *similarly, likewise, also*: or *on the other hand, in contrast, however.*
  3. For showing time order: *first, second, third; to begin, next, finally.*
  4. For clarifying concepts: *in other words, that is, for example.*
  5. For reinforcing ideas: *moreover, in addition, furthermore.*

DECIMAL REPORT OUTLINING STYLE

TITLE

Central idea: a summary of the subject and purpose of the report that follows

1.0 **INTRODUCTION OR FIRST MAJOR TOPIC**

1.1 **First Subordinate Unit**
1.1.1 Evidence, examples, reasons
1.1.2 Evidence, examples, reasons

1.2 **Second Subordinate Unit**
1.2.1 Evidence, examples, reasons
1.2.2 Evidence, examples, reasons

2.0 **SECOND MAJOR TOPIC**
2.1 **First Subordinate Unit**
2.1.1 Evidence, examples, reasons
2.1.2 Evidence, examples, reasons

2.2 **Second Subordinate Unit**
2.2.1 Evidence, examples, reasons
2.2.2 Evidence, examples, reasons

3.0 **THIRD MAJOR TOPIC**

(as needed)

20

Organizing and Writing a Formal Proposal

In the following section, we will go through the steps required to establish the subject and outline a formal proposal. The particular case involves a proposal to obtain government funding for a university program. There will be three steps:

1. The government notice inviting applications for the funding.
2. The decision on the subject of the report proposal.
3. The detailed outline needed to support the proposal.

The Department of Education sends out what amounts to Requests for Bids (RFB) or Requests for Proposals (RFP) when it sends out the following notice to universities that have applied for particular grants. The grant at issue is the Robert Watson Post-Baccalaureate Achievement Program.

DEPARTMENT OF EDUCATION
(CFDA NO: 84217)

Notice inviting applications for new awards for fiscal year (FY) 1999 – Robert Watson Post-Baccalaureate Achievement Program.

PURPOSE: The purpose of this program is to provide grants for higher education institutions to prepare low-income, first-generation college students, and students from groups underrepresented in graduate education, for doctoral study.

ELIGIBLE APPLICANTS: Institutions of higher education and combinations of those institutions.

DEADLINE FOR TRANSMITTAL OF APPLICATIONS: October 2, 1998.

DEADLINE FOR INTERGOVERNMENTAL REVIEW: December 31, 1998.

APPLICATIONS AVAILABLE: August 1, 1998.

SUPPLEMENTARY INFORMATION: The Department is publishing this notice at this time to give potential applicants adequate time to prepare their applications, even though the Congress has not yet reauthorized the Robert Watson Post-Baccalaureate Achievement Program or appropriated money to fund new awards under this program. In addition, the Department anticipates that funds will be appropriated to fund new awards. However, if legislative changes are made that materially affect the grant award process or the operation of grant projects, the Department will provide additional time for applicants to amend their applications to reflect these changes.

Currently, there are Robert Watson Post-Baccalaureate Achievement Program grants that expire in Fiscal Year 1999 and Fiscal Year 2000. However, to receive a new 4- or 5-year grant, applicants, including those that have 5-year grants that expire in Fiscal Year 2000, must submit an application under this funding competition.

Grantees whose grants expire in Fiscal Year 2000: If such a grantee is successful under this competition, its new award will begin when its existing grant expires, i.e., October 1, 2000.

AVAILABLE FUNDS: The estimated amount of funds available for this program is based in part on the President's 1999 budget.

ESTIMATED RANGE OF AWARDS: $190,000–$285,000 per year.

ESTIMATED AVERAGE SIZE OF AWARDS: $215,000 per year.

ESTIMATED NUMBER OF AWARDS: 109

NOTE: The Department is not bound by any of the estimates in this notice.

PROJECT PERIOD: Up to 60 months.

APPLICABLE REGULATIONS: (a) The Education Department General Administrative Regulations (EDGAR) in 34 CFR Part 74, 75, 77, 79, 82, 85, and 86; (b) The regulations governing the Robert Watson Post-Baccalaureate Achievement Program in 34 CFR Part 647.

FOR FURTHER INFORMATION CONTACT: Ellen K. Connery, Federal RIO Programs, U.S. Department of Education, 293 Independence Avenue SW, The Portals Building, Suite 100M, Washington, D.C. 20202-5134. Telephone number: (202) 608-6804 or by Internet to RIO@ ed.gov. Individuals who use a telecommunications device for the deaf (TDD) may call the Federal Information Relay Services (FIRS) at 1-800-778-3889 between 8:00 AM and 8:00 PM, Eastern time, Monday through Friday.

Individuals with disabilities may obtain this document in an alternate format (eg., Braille, large print, audiotape, or computer diskette) on request to the contact person listed in the preceding paragraph.

The report writer can find complete information about the Robert Watson program in the *Federal Register's* Rules and Regulations Vol. 59, No. 164, dated Thursday, August 25, 1994.

In these rules and regulations, the report writer can find such necessary information such as:

- What is the Robert Watson Post-Baccalaureate Achievement Program?
- Who is eligible for a grant?
- Who is eligible to participate in a Name project?
- What regulations apply?
- What definitions apply?

Perhaps the most pertinent information the report writer may find in seeking to narrow the focus and determine the precise subject of the proposal is found under the section heading "What Selection Criteria does the Secretary Use?"

"The secretary uses the following criteria to evaluate an application for a new grant:

(a) *Need* (16 points). The Secretary reviews each application to determine the extent to which the applicant can clearly and definitively demonstrate the need for a Watson project to serve the target population. In particular, the Secretary looks for information that clearly defines the target population; describes academic, financial, and other problems that prevent potentially eligible project participants in the target population from completing baccalaureate programs and continuing to post-baccalaureate programs; and demonstrates that the project's target population is underrepresented in graduate education, doctorate degrees conferred, and careers where a doctorate is a prerequisite.

(b) *Objectives* (9 points). The Secretary evaluates the quality of the applicant's proposed project objectives on the basis of the extent to which they—

1) include both process and outcome objectives relating to the purpose of the Watson program stated in 647.1;
2) address the needs of the target population; and
3) are measurable, ambitious, and attainable over the life of the project.

(c) *Plan of Operations* (44 points). The Secretary reviews each application to determine the quality of the applicant's plans of operation, including—

1) (4 points) the plan for identifying, recruiting, and selecting participants to be served by the project, including students enrolled in the Student Support Services program;
2) (4 points) the plan for assessing individual participant needs and for monitoring the academic growth of participants during the period in which the student is a Watson participant;
3) (5 points) the plan for providing high quality research and scholarly activities in which participants will be involved;
4) (5 points) the plan for involving faculty members in the design of research activities in which students will be involved;
5) (5 points) the plan for providing internships, seminars, and other educational activities designed to prepare undergraduate students for doctoral study;
6) (5 points) the plan for providing individual or group services designed to enhance a student's successful entry into post-baccalaureate education;
7) (3 points) the plan to inform the institutional community of the goals and objectives of the project;
8) (6 points) the plan to ensure proper and efficient administration of the project, including, but not limited to, matters such as financial management, student records management, personnel management, the organizational structure, and the plan for coordinating the Watson project with other programs for disadvantaged students; and
9) (5 points) the follow-up plan that will be used to track the academic and career accomplishments of participants after they are no longer participating in the Watson project.

(d) *Quality of Key Personnel* (9 points). The Secretary evaluates the quality of key personnel the applicant plans to use on the project on the basis of the following:

1) The job qualifications of the project director.
2) The job qualifications of each of the project's other key personnel.
3) The quality of the project's plan for employing highly qualified persons, including the procedures to be used to employ members of groups underrepresented in higher education, including blacks, Hispanics, Native Americans, Alaska Natives, Asian Americans, and Pacific Islanders (including Native Hawaiians).
4) In evaluating the qualifications of a person, the Secretary considers his or her experience and training in fields related to the objective of the work.

(e) *Adequacy of the Resources and Budget* (15 points). The Secretary evaluates the extent to which—
   1) the applicant's proposed allocation of resources in the budget is clearly related to he objectives of the project;
   2) project costs and resources, including facilities, equipment, and supplies, are reasonable in relation to the objectives and scope of the project; and
   3) the applicant's proposed commitment of institutional resources to the Watson participants, as, for example, the commitment of time from institutional research faculty and the waiver of tuition and fees for Watson participants engaged in summer research projects.

(f) *Evaluation Plan* (7 points). The Secretary evaluates the quality of the evaluation plan for the project on the basis of the extent to which the applicant's methods of evaluation—
   1) are appropriate for the project's objectives;
   2) provide for the applicant to determine, in specific and measurable ways, the success of the project in—
      (i) making progress toward achieving its objectives (a formative evaluation);
      (ii) achieving its objectives at the end of the project period (a summative evaluation); and
   3) provide for a description of other project outcomes, including the use of quantifiable measures, if appropriate.

HOW TO DETERMINE THE SUBJECT AND OUTLINE A FORMAL PROPOSAL

After studying this notice of application and the excerpts from the criteria for selection quoted, the report writer can clearly see the answers to two major questions:

1. *What is the subject of the report?* The notice of application provides the subject of the report under the heading of *PURPOSE*: "The purpose of this (Robert Watson) program is to provide grants for higher education institutions." The purpose of the program and the subject of the report become one. The subject is not the Watson program but answering the question "How do we *achieve* the purpose? Or how do we *obtain* the grant?"
2. *How should the report be organized and outlined?* The notice of application and the criteria for selection published in the *Federal Register* show the report writer where the money is and, therefore, how to base the proposal on it. In order for the report to achieve its purpose, the report writer will have to show how each of the six points in the selection process will be met. This must become the framework of the outline for the body of the proposal.

Following is how the report writer would incorporate these six points into an outline for the body of the proposal. The six points appear as part of the Table of Contents for the complete report proposal. When such a proposal is created and written we can expect that it will be granted. This really is communication for change. It persuades government agency personnel, it increases the funding of a university program, it improves the lives of groups of students, and it enriches our society as a whole for generations to come.

TABLE OF CONTENTS

ROBERT WATSON POST-BACCALAUREATE
ACHIEVEMENT PROGRAM APPLICATION

APPENDICES

Tables and Figures

Tables

Figures

Anselm University
Watson Project Abstract

The overarching goal of the Robert Watson Post-Baccalaureate Achievement Program proposed by Anselm University in this application is to prepare low-income, first-generation college students and students from groups underrepresented in graduate education for doctoral study. Anselm is particularly well-suited to implement a Watson program given its institutional mission, the makeup of its undergraduate population, and its location in one of the most multicultural urban centers in the United States. Our proposed Watson Scholars Program will provide services and experiences for project participants, which will enhance their chances of successfully completing college, attending graduate school, and earning a doctoral degree, despite the many educational, financial, and psychological barriers to success that they face.

Fifteen beginning juniors who meet project eligibility requirements will be selected each year of the project and will participate in a variety of project activities during their junior and senior years and in a summer research internship during the summer following their junior year. Three eligible juniors designated as alternates will also be selected each year. They will participate in all junior-year activities and will replace scholars in the event that any drop out of the program prior to the summer internship. Accordingly, except for Year 1, when 18 participants will be served by the project, the project will serve a minimum of 30 participants each year during Years 2 through 5.

All project participants will be guided throughout their years as Watson Scholars by volunteer faculty mentors, whose academic interests will be a close match with those of the project participants. Faculty mentors will seek to induct scholars and accompany them into the world of the university professor and researcher. Mentors will help scholars to design and implement research studies that scholars will conduct during their summer research internships; then, mentors will help scholars to prepare and disseminate results of that research. Scholars will have the option of completing their surnmer internship experience at Anselm University, at other doctoral-granting universities in New York City, or at doctoral-granting universities throughout the United States.

Proposed project activities during the junior year will include seminars and workshops designed to enhance scholars' knowledge about the benefits, requirements, and demands of doctoral study; and that will improve their library and information technology skills, their writing ability, their computer literacy, and their knowledge of research design. Proposed project activities during the senior year will provide opportunities for scholars to become knowledgeable about data analysis methods, research report writing, and research report presentations at scholarly meetings. In addition, throughout their junior and senior years, Watson Scholars will participate in field trips to doctoral-granting universities, to professional conferences, and to cultural events. Scholars will also be provided with the opportunity to enhance their chances for acceptance into doctoral programs through participation in seminars / workshops that focus on preparing for graduate entrance examinations and on completing applications for admissions into doctoral programs and for financial aid. Individual subject area tutoring, personal and career counseling, and individual assistance in library and information technology, writing, and computer literacy will be available to scholars throughout the project.

Moreover, Anselm's Watson Project will host an annual scholars' induction ceremony and orientation program for Scholar parents; an annual Watson Research Symposium to which scholars, mentors, parents, and alumni will be invited; and an annual Watson Teleconference in which Anselm's Watson Scholars and participants in up to four other Watson programs will participate.

Appendix A

A Governmental Agency Environmental Report with Tables

Yarmouth Water

Annual Drinking Water Quality Report for the year ending 1999

Massachusetts Public Water Supplier # 435 1000

We Want You to Know About Your Drinking Water

If you have questions about this report call the Water Superintendent at 771-7921

Your Water is Safe to Drink

Yarmouth Water is committed to providing Yarmouth residents and visitors with highest quality drinking water 24 hours a day 365 days a year. To ensure we deliver this quality product Yarmouth Water has made significant investments in water treatment facilities, water quality monitoring, water source protection, and distribution systems. We are pleased to be reporting the results of our 1999 water testing directly to you the consumer.

Water Quality Testing

Each year the Yarmouth Water conducts more than 1,000 water quality tests on samples taken throughout the Town of Yarmouth. These tests confirmed that your tap water meets all state and federal drinking water quality standards, and that your water is safe to drink. We will be mailing a report to you each year with information about the quality of your drinking water.

Your Drinking Water Source

Within the Town of Yarmouth there are 24 groundwater wells that draw water from 2 aquifers or lens. The Sagamore Lens which supplies most of the water Yarmouth, and the Monomoy Lens which supplies the remainder to a lesser extent. Your tap water may come from either of these sources depending up where you live and the time of year.

Protecting Source Waters

Even though Yarmouth Water uses basic treatment techniques along with so of the most advanced equipment available, it is still necessary to start with the highest quality water sources. That is why Yarmouth Water owns and protects over 963 acres of land surrounding well fields and aquifer recharge areas. Also inspect these areas regularly for any condition that could adversely a quality of the water. In addition our staff reviews and comments on local land development plans near our well fields that could impact water quality. A complete list of all the contaminants tested for is available at our offices, located at 99 Buck island Road W. Yarmouth, 8:30am-4:30pm.

In addition to water quality test results, this report will provide information about:

- Where your water comes from
- Vulnerable Population information
- Definitions You Need to Know
- Associations we use to help us safe guard your water
- Other issues that effect the water you drink

Water Quality Summary

The table below shows only the substances that were detected in the Yarmouth Water in 1999. Not all substances were detected at each of the 24 well fields and none of the samples collected at the 24 well fields exceeded the highest level (MCL) allowed for any one substance.

The "Level Found" column represents an average of sample result data collected during the Water Quality Parameters (WQP) calendar year beginning January 1st, 1999 through December 31st, 1999. The "Range of Detection" column represents a range of individual sample results, from the lowest to the highest that were detected during the WQP calendar year. If a date appears in the "Date of Sample" column, the State of Massachusetts DEP require monitoring for this contamination less than once a year because the concentrations found previously do not frequently change. If no date appears in column, monitoring for that contaminant was conducted during the annual WQP calendar year.

Microbial Contaminates

Yarnmouth Results see Definitions You Need to Know

Contaminant	MCLG	MCL	Level Found	Range of Detection	% of highest month	Violation	Date of Sample	Typical Source of Contaminant
Total Coliform Bacteria (% pos/mon)	0	>=5%	0.009	0-1	3.70 % for Aug	None		Naturally present in the environment.
Fecal Coliform bacteria and e. Coli	0	>=5%	0	0	0	None		Human and animal fecal waste.

Inorganic Contaminates

					# samples above AL			
Copper (ppm)	1.3	AL--1.3	0.221	<0.022 - 1.80	1 out of 135	None		Corrosion or electrical grounding problem household plumbing systems. Erosion of n deposits. Leaching from wood preservative.
Lead (ppm)*	0	AL=0.015	0.006**	<0.001 - 0.2	9 out of 135	None	6***	Corrosion of natural industrial deposits; plumbing solder, less expensive brass alloy faucets, electrical grounding problems of household plumbing systems.
Nitrate (ppm)	10	10	1.76	<. 10 - 5.60	l sample above 50% of EPA health standard	None		Runoff from fertilizer use. Leaching from septic systems, sewage, and erosion of natural deposits.
Nitrite (ppm)	1	1	<0.05	<0.05	0	None		Runoff from fertilizer use. Leaching from septic systems, sewage, and erosion of natural deposits.
Sodium (ppm)	N/A	N/A	18.28	16.9-20.0	0	Unregulated contaminant		Sodium can occur naturally and can also be attributed to road runoff.
Organic Contaminants								
Chloroform (ppb)	N/A	N/A	2.20	0-6.0	0	Unregulated contaminant		Occurs naturally here on Cape Cod. Future studies by D.E.P. are planned to determine why.
Cis-1,2 Dichl oroethylene (ppb)	70	70	0.375	0.0-0.9	0	None		Refrigerant
Methyl Tertiary Butyl Ether (ppb)	N/A	N/A	0.125	0.0-2.0	0	Unregulated contaminant		Methyl Tertiary Butyl Ether is an ether compound used in gasoline to help gasoline engines prod2ce less harmful emissions.
Radioactive contaminants								
Alpha emitters (P/C /1)*	0 1	15pCi/l	0.2(+- 1.6)	0-0.2(+-	None		7-17-951	Erosion of natural deposits

Lead sampling was from consumers systems which may be effected by plumbing solder, less expensive brass alloy faucets and or electrical grounding problems. ** 90th percentile action level, which the EPA defines as the equation: (number of samples) x (0.9) = the sample corresponding to the 90th percentile. *** Number of sites above action level. This report was prepared by Dan Mills Assistant Superintendent of the Yarmouth Water Department. For more information, call the Yarmouth Water at 508-771-7921 or visit our web site at www. yarmouth water. org.

The Safe Drinking Water Act (SDWA) was signed into law on December 16, 1974. The purpose of the law is to assure that the nation's water supply systems serving the public meet minimum national standards for the protection of public health.

As amended and re-authorized by the 1996 U.S. Congress the SDWA requires that all public water systems with piped water for human consumption with at least 15 service connections or a system that regularly serves at least 25 individuals, must provide such consumers with an "Annual Drinking Water Quality Report".

The SDWA directed the U.S. Environmental Protection Agency (EPA) to establish national drinking water standards. These standards limit the amount of certain contaminants provided by public water. The Food and Drug Administration (FDA) regulations establish limits for contaminants in bottled water. More information about contaminants and potential health effects can be obtained by calling the EPA Safe Drinking Water Hotline (800-426-4791).

The Substances Found in Your Tap Water

Drinking water, including bottled water, may be reasonably expected to contain at least some small amounts of certain substances that the EPA calls "contaminants". The presence of these substances does not necessarily indicate that the water poses a health risk. For example, naturally occurring dissolved minerals are commonly found in well water. More information about substances found in your tap water and their potential health effects can be obtained by calling the Environmental Protection Agency's Safe Drinking Water Hotline (800-426-4791

Vulnerable Population

Some people may be more vulnerable to contaminants in drinking water than the general population. Immuno-compromised persons such as persons with cancer undergoing chemotherapy, persons who have undergone organ transplants, people with HIV/AIDS or other immune system disorders, some elderly and infants can be particularly at risk from infections. These people should seek advice from their health care providers.

Consumer Educational Statements

Nitrate. Nitrate in drinking water at levels above 10 ppm is a health risk for infants of less than six months of age. High nitrate levels in drinking water can cause blue baby syndrome. Nitrate levels may rise quickly for short periods of time because of rainfall or agricultural activity. If you are caring for an infant, you should ask for advise from your health care provider.

Lead. Infants and young children are typically more vulnerable to lead in drinking water than the general population. It is possible that lead levels at your home may be higher than at other homes in the community as a result of materials used in your home's plumbing. If you are concerned about elevated lead your home's water, you may wish to have your water tested. Additionally, flushing your tap for 30 seconds to two minutes before using tap water to reduce lead content. Additional information is available from the Safe Drinking Water Hotline, 1-800-426-4791

Unregulated Contaminants

Unregulated contaminants are those for which the EPA has not established drinking water standards. The purpose of unregulated contaminants monitoring is to assist the EPA in determining the occurrence of unregulated contaminants in drinking water and whether future regulation is warranted.

Definitions You Need to Know

Microbial contarninants, such as viruses and bacteria, from sewage treatment plants, septic systems, agricultural livestock operations and wildlife.

Total Coliform Bacteria, Coliforms are bacteria that are naturally present in the environment and are used as an indicator that other, potentiafly-harmful bacteria may be present.

Fecal Coliform and e. Coli, Fecal coliforms and e. Coli are bacteria whose presence indicates that the water may be contaminated with human or animal waste. Microbes in these wastes can cause short-term effects, such as diarrhea, cramps, nausea, headaches, or other symptoms. They may pose a special risk for infants, young children, and people with severely-compromised immune systems.

Inorganic contan-dnants, such as salts and metals, which can be naturally - occurring or resulting from urban storm-water runoff, industrial or domestic water discharges, oil and gas production, mining or farming.

Organic Chemical contan-driants, include synthetic and volatile organic chemicals that are by-products of industrial processes and petroleum product can also come from gas stations, urban stormwater runoff, and septic systems.

Radioactive contaminants, can be naturally-occurring or be the result of oil and gas production, and mining activities.

pCi/l, picocuries per liter. A measure of radioactivity.

MCL, The "Maximum contaminant level" is the highest level of a contaminant that is allowed in drinking water. MCLs are set as close to the MCLGs as feasible using the best available treatment technology.

MCLG, "The Maximum contaminant level goal" is the level of a contaminant in drinking water below which there is no known or expected risk to health.

MCLGs allow for a margin of safety.

ppm, "Parts per Million" which is also the same as saying Milligrams per liter (mg/1). One part per million corresponds to a single penny in $10,000.
minute in a two year period.

ppb, "Parts per Billion" which is the same as saying Micrograms per liter. One part per billion corresponds to a single penny in $10.000,000.00 or one minute in a 2,000 year period.

AL, Action level, the concentration of a contaminant which if exceeded, triggers treatment or other requirements that a water system must follow.

Variances and Exceptions

Yarmouth Water was granted a renewal of waivers December 18,1998 by the Massachusetts Department of Environmental Protection, Division of Water Supply Office, not requiring our system to monitor for synthetic organic compounds (SOC's). Previous years of testing have indicated that these substances do not occur in our source water. Yarmouth Water however does test for these contaminants for our historical database and will continue sampling annually. A complete list of all the contaminants tested for, is available at our offices, located at 99 Buck Island Road W. Yarmouth, 8:30 am - 4:30pm. 771-7921

Water Related Informational / Educational Sites

Visit these web sites at your public library or-from your home for more information on all aspects of water. American Water Works Association - www.awwa.org - an international nonprofit scientific and educational society dedicated to the improvement of drinking water quality and supply. Water Environment Federation - www.wef.org - a not-for profit technical and educational organization. Its goal is to preserve and enhance the global water environment. Yarmouth Water - www.yarmouthwater.org - your local water provider with links to other water related sites and updated information on our department activities.

Yarmouth Water is proud to be a member of the following Associations. American Water Works Association (AWWA), Massachusetts Watt Works Association (MWWA), New England Water Works Association (NEWWA), Plymouth County Water Works Association (PCWWA) and the Barnstable County Water Utilities Association (BCWWA), North East Rural Water Association (NERWA), Barnstable County Public Works Association (BCPWA).

Appendix B

Some Sample Charts and Graphs

SIMPLE BAR CHART

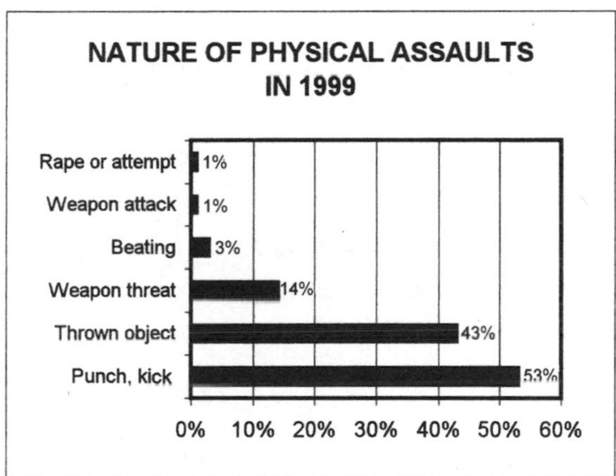

Source: National Center on Addiction and Substance Abuse at Columbia University

MULTIPLE BAR CHART

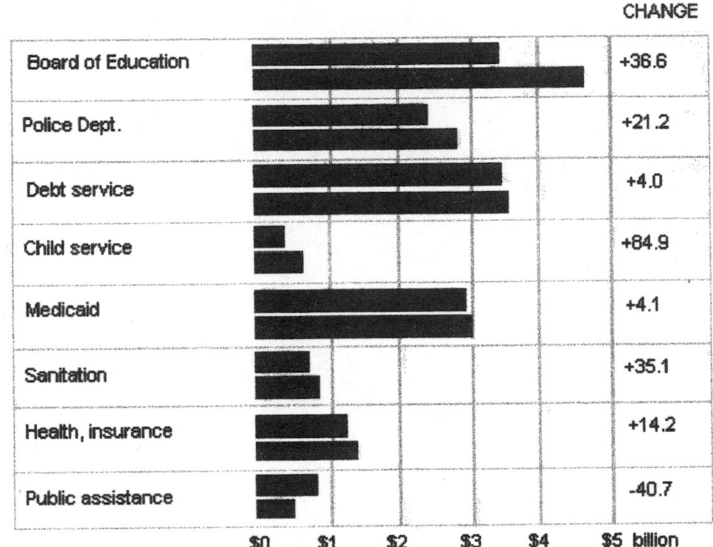

Source: Office of State Deputy Comptroller for the City of Ne York (overall spending); City Comptroller

SIMPLE LINE GRAPH

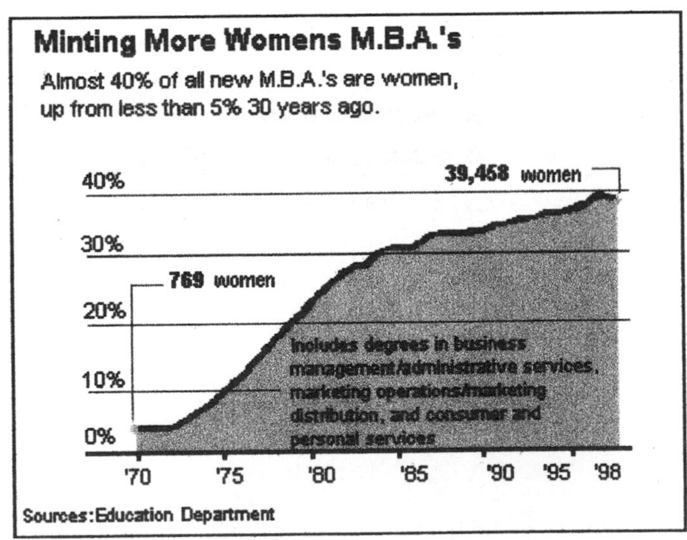

MAP CHART

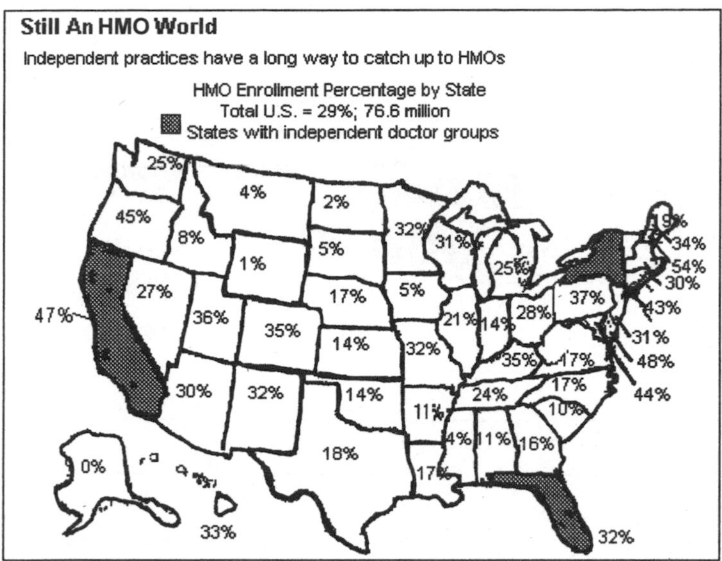

Estimated number of independent doctors: 2,000
Total number of U.S. physicians: 720,000

Source: U.S. Department of Health, Education, and Welfare

PIE CHARTS
ELDERLY BENEFITS' INCREASING BITE

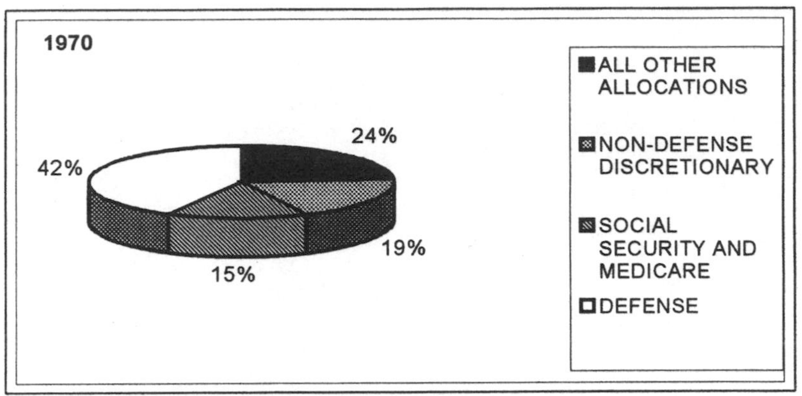

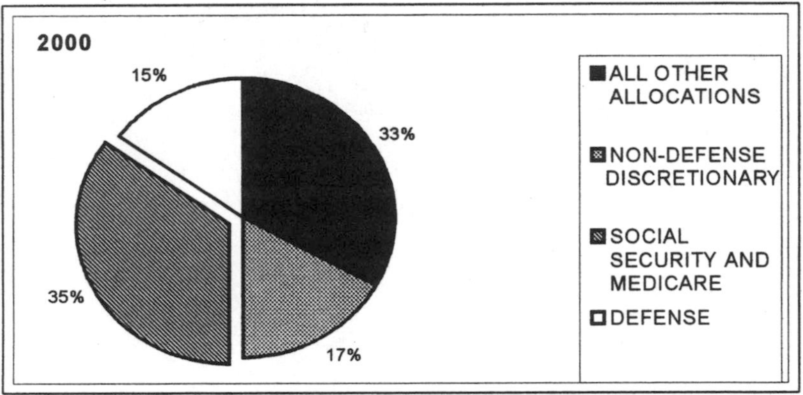

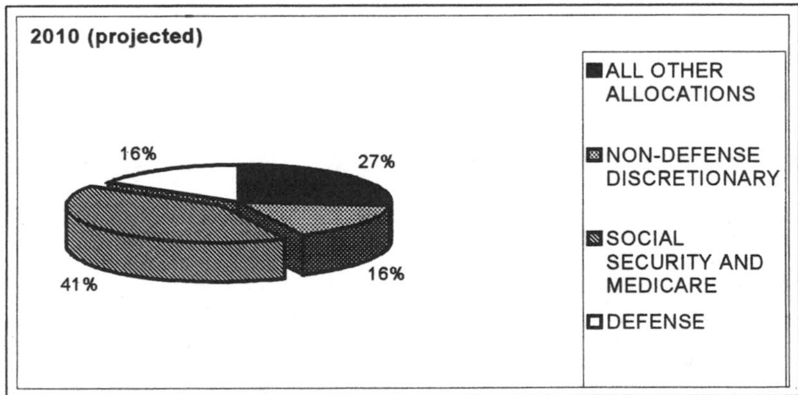

Source: Congressional Budget Office

FLOW CHART

CUSTOMER ORDERS RECEIPT THRU DELIVERY

ORGANIZATIONAL CHART

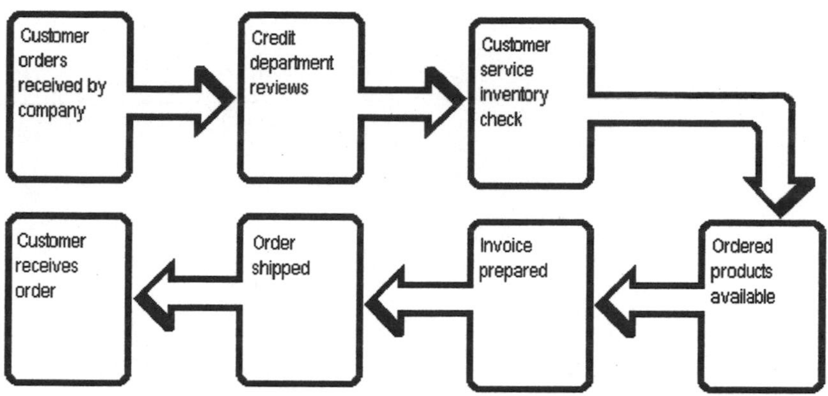

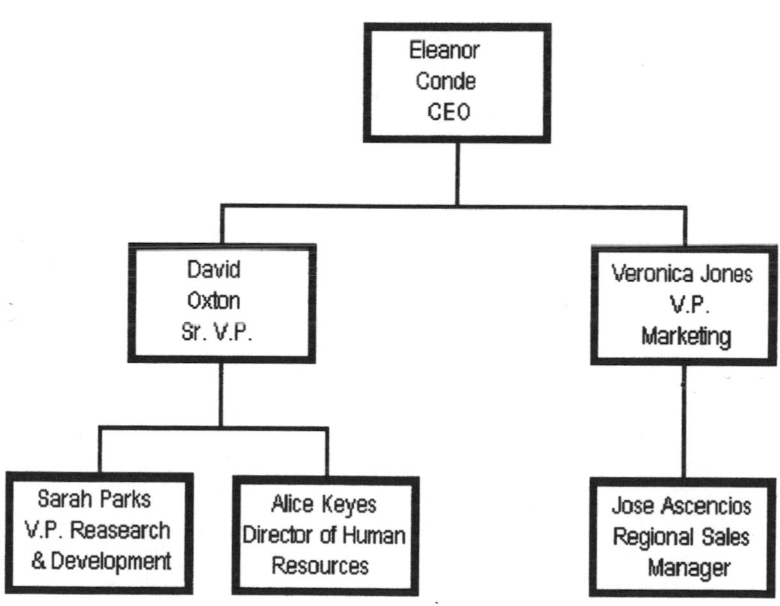

Notes

CHAPTER 1

1. Marshall McLuhan, *Understanding Media* (New York: McGraw Hill, 1964).
2. Andrew Kohut, "America the Connected," *The New York Times*, 23 June 2000: A25.
3. Stephanie Armour, "Failure to Communicate Costly for Companies," *USA TODAY*, 30 Sept. 1998: B1.
4. Armour, B1.
5. Armour, B1.
6. U.S. Census Bureau
7. "Julius Caesar," 1. 3. 139–140. This and all quotations from Shakespeare are from *The Yale Shakespeare*, ed. Wilbur L. Cross and Tucker Brooke (New York: Barnes and Noble, 1993).
8. "Coaching: The Ten Killer Myths," *Harvard Management Update* Vol. IV, Number 1 (Cambridge, MA: Harvard Business School, 1999).

CHAPTER 2

1. Albert Mehrabian, *Silent Messages* (Belmont: Wadsworth, 1971): 44.
2. Margaret M. Sloane, "Love, Marriage, Kids, Facelift," *The New York Post*, 24 Jan. 2000: 50.
3. James Bennett, "A Charm School for Used Car Salesmen," *The New York Times*, 24 Sept. 1998: D1.

CHAPTER 3

1. Doreen Carvajal, "Forsooth, Check This Consultant," *The New York Times*, 22 Dec. 1999: C1.
2. Carjaval, C1.
3. "Henry V," 4. 3. 43–46.
4. Robert Frost, *The Poetry of Robert Frost* (New York: Henry Holt, 1969): 33.

CHAPTER 4

1. Erica Goode, "How Culture Molds Habits of Thought," *The New York Times*, 8 Aug. 2000: F1.
2. William J. Lederer, *The Ugly American* (Westminster, MD: Ballantine Fawcett, 1968).
3. U.S. Census Bureau
4. Clifford Krauss, "Selling to Argentina (As Translated from the French)," *The New York Times*, 5 Dec. 1999: B7.
5. Howard W. French, " 'Japanese Only' Policy Takes Body Blow in Court," *The New York Times*, 15 Nov. 1999: A1.
6. Seth Schiesel, "Lucent Picks Boeing Executive as Finance Chief," *The New York Times*, 25 Apr. 2000: C1.
7. John Markoff, "Hewlett-Packard Picks Rising Star at Lucent as Its Chief Executive," *The New York Times*, 20 Jul. 1999: C1.
8. Stendahl (Marie Henri Beyle), *The Red and the Black* (New York: Oxford University Press, 1981): 259.
9. "The Merchant of Venice," 3. 1. 50–52.

CHAPTER 5

1. "King Lear," 4. 6. 167–168.

CHAPTER 6

1. Steve Lohr, "Medium for Main Street," *The New York Times*, 11 Jan. 2000: A1.
2. Carl Rogers, *Carl Rogers on Personal Power* (New York: Delacorte Press, 1977).

CHAPTER 7

1. Douglas Martin, "David Mellinkoff, Enemy of Legalese," *The New York Times*, 16 Dec. 2000: B37.
2. "Hamlet," 3. 4. 27.

Chapter 10

1. "Hamlet," 1. 1. 137–138.

2. FEMA (Federal Emergency Management Agency) spokesperson as recorded by the author from a newscast.
3. Franklin Delano Roosevelt, First Inaugural address, 1933.
4. Douglas Martin, "David Mellinkoff, Enemy of Legalese," *The New York Times,* 16 Dec. 2000: B37.

CHAPTER 11

1. Lisa Guernsey, "You've Got Inappropriate Mail," *The New York Times,* 5 Apr. 2000: C1.
2. Edward Wong, "A Stinging Office Memo Boomerangs," *The New York Times,* 5 April 2000: C1.

CHAPTER 19

1. Joseph Gibaldi, *MLA Handbook for Writing Research Papers,* 5th ed. (New York: Modern Language Association of America, 1999).

Bibliography

Allen, Jo. *Writing in the Workplace* (Upper Saddle River, NJ: Prentice Hall, 1998).

Alred, Gerald. *The Business Writer's Handbook,* 6th ed. (New York: St. Martin's Press, 2000).

American Management Association. *The AMA Style Guide for Business Writing* (New York: AMACOM, 1996).

Bailey, Edward P. *The Plain English Approach to Business Writing* (Oxford, U.K.: Oxford University Press, 1997).

Bartell, Karen H. *American Business English* (Ann Arbor: University of Michigan Press, 1995).

Blake, Gary, and Robert W. Bly. *The Elements of Copywriting: The Essential Guide to Creating Copy That Gets the Results You Want* (New York: McGraw-Hill, 1998).

Bovee, Courtland L. L., and John V. Thill. *Business Communication Today* (Upper Saddle River, NJ: Prentice Hall, 1999).

Campbell, Nancy. *Writing Effective Policies and Procedures: A Step-by-Step Resource for Clear Communication* (New York: American Management Association, 1997).

Economist Staff. *The Economist Style Guide: A Concise Guide for All Your Business Communications* (London: John Wiley & Sons, 1998).

Flaherty, James. *Coaching: Evoking Excellence in Others* (Woburn, MA: Butterworth-Heinemann, 1998).

Foster, Bill, and Karen R. Seeker. *Coaching for Peak Employee Performance: A Practical Guide to Supporting Employee Development* (Irvine, CA: Richard Chang, 1997).

Geffner, Andrea B. *Business English* (New York: Barron's, 1998).

Hemphill, Phyllis Davis, Donald W. McCormick, and Robert Hemphill. *Business Communication with Writing* (Upper Saddle River, NJ: Prentice Hall, 2000).

Kliment, Stephen A., and Hugh S. Hardy. *Writing for Design Professionals: A Guide to Writing Successful Proposals, Letters, Brochures, Portfolios, Reports, Presentations, and Job Applications* (New York: W. W. Norton, 1998).

Munter, Mary. *Guide to Managerial Communication: Effective Business Writing and Speaking* (Upper Saddle River, NJ: Prentice Hall, 1999).

Pfeiffer, William S., Charles H. Keller, and Stephen Helba. *Proposal Writing: The Art of Friendly and Winning Persuasion* (Upper Saddle River, NJ: Prentice Hall, 1999).

Roman, Kenneth, and Joel Raphaelson. *Writing That Works: How to Improve Your Memos, Letters, Reports, Speeches, Resumes, Plans, and Other Business Papers* (New York: Harper, 1995).

Whitmore, John. *Coaching for Performance (People Skills for Professionals)* (London: Nicholas Brealey, 1996).

Index

ABOUT THE AUTHOR

RICHARD P. PICARDI is a communications consultant and Adjunct Associate Professor of English and Speech at St. John's University, New York. Throughout a career of more than 30 years he has served as a department chairperson and assistant principal, and has owned his own business. Currently, in addition to his position at St. John's, he teaches writing in the City University of New York system. He is the recipient of the 2001 Teaching Excellence Award at St. John's University.